GEORGE MÜLLER

ROGER STEER

GEORGE MÜLLER

1805–1898

Delighted in God

ROGER STEER

CHRISTIAN
FOCUS

Copyright © Roger Steer 1997

Paperback ISBN 978-1-84550-120-4
epub ISBN 978-1-78191-098-6
Mobi ISBN 978-1-78191-100-6

10 9 8

Previously published in 1997,
reprinted in 2001, 2004, 2006, 2008, 2012, 2015, 2018 and 2020
by
Christian Focus Publications, Ltd.
Geanies House, Fearn, Tain,
Ross-shire, IV20 1TW, Great Britain.

www.christianfocus.com

Cover Design by Alister MacInnes

Printed by Norhaven, Denmark

Contents

Introduction

George Müller has a special claim on your attention. It is not just that he believed in a God who answers prayer – even in today's rather secular world there are many people who believe that. What is unique about Müller is that he put his belief in the reality of God publicly to the test. Thousands of people in Müller's day, and in the years since his death, have grown convinced that – if I may say it reverently – God passed the test with honours.

I am an even greater fan of George Müller today than I was forty years ago when I wrote the first edition of this biography. I see him as a humble man who thought of himself as a sinner, but who is now rightly seen as a giant of church history who offers unique inspiration to a new generation of seekers after truth. I have no hesitation in agreeing with W. H. Harding who wrote in 1914 that the story of Müller's life presents 'one of the most striking testimonies to the faithfulness of God that the world has even seen'.

George Müller's efforts to demonstrate the truth of his assertion that God answers prayer brought him international fame during his lifetime. A letter from a doctor telling him that his life was 'the most wonderful and complete refutation of scepticism' he had ever come across was typical of many he received. But I suspect that in his modesty he would have regarded these verdicts on him as exaggerated and insisted that all the honour for anything he achieved should go to God.

In the early decades of the twenty-first century, prayer is back on the agenda. In September 1999, a group of young people at a church on the south coast of England had what seemed to many the crazy idea of trying to pray non-stop for a month. They reported that 'God turned up and we couldn't stop till Christmas!' From there the prayer meeting has spread into many countries, denominations and age-groups. Hundreds of non-stop prayer meetings now link up on the Internet to form a unique chain of prayer. 24-7 has become a worldwide, non-stop prayer movement with a network of people in prayer rooms across the world determined to pray as if it all depends on them, and live as if it all depends on God.

Today, someone somewhere is praying 24-7. The dream is to turn the tide of our culture back to Jesus in the knowledge that things change when God's people pray. 24-7 has captured the imagination. Young people today are as likely to turn up at a prayer meeting at 3 a.m. as at 7.30 p.m.! They dare to be alone with God for a whole hour even in the middle of the night. Very few of them 'pray and stop', the vast majority 'pray and go' – the 'going' involving a renewed vision for local mission, or social involvement in local communities or wider mission teams.

Imaginatively decorated prayer rooms have been opened in a barn in the English countryside; a skate park in Switzerland; a bus in the slums of Delhi; a police station in London; an office in Tulsa Oklahoma; the U.S. Naval Academy; a brewery in Missouri; in tents; in student basements; campus chaplaincies; and of course in church buildings. You can find out more about this exciting enterprise to move the hand of God by visiting www.24-7prayer. com or by emailing info@24-7prayer.com

In heaven, George Müller must be delighted by all this. The last person he spoke to at the end of his long life on earth was a young student teacher who was singing with happiness after a prayer meeting. Müller loved to quote the words of Jesus: 'Ask and it will be given to you, seek and you will find; knock and the door will be opened to you. For everyone who asks receives; he who seeks finds; and to him who knocks, the door will be opened' (Matt. 7:7-8). 'Do not be anxious about anything,' said the Apostle Paul, 'but in everything, by prayer and petition, with thanksgiving, present your requests to God' (Phil. 4:6).

There was nothing magical about Müller's answers to prayer. In the famous story from Arabian Nights, Aladdin discovered that when he rubbed the magician's lamp, a genie appeared who said, 'I am the slave of the lamp. Command me and I will obey.' The power through prayer which Müller discovered didn't work like that at all. For him, prayer was supernatural but not magical and his success was a consequence of a life-time's walk with God.

Like the organisers of today's 24-7 movement for non-stop prayer, George Müller believed he was putting into practice basic Biblical principles which are available to every Christian believer. The principles involved marvellous promises to be claimed and quite demanding conditions to be fulfilled. These promises and conditions are set out in the second half of chapter 20 below. If you believe the promises, study the principles and conscientiously resolve to put them into practice I believe that your life of prayer will be transformed. That's not to say that you will no longer find prayer perplexing at times, that you will suddenly know all the answers, or that prayer will cease to be a mystery.

For George Müller, putting Biblical prayer principles into practice resulted not only in spectacular answers, but also a growth in an attractive personal holiness. Those who knew him spoke of a 'smile which so habitually lit up his eyes and played over his features that it left its impress on the lines of his face'. And although he relished a joke which was wholesome and free from malice, nobody was inclined to engage in idle chatter in his presence. They sensed that he walked with God.

Müller knew his God. He enjoyed spending time in his presence. He believed God's promises. He approached his heavenly Father in the name of Jesus, his Saviour, friend and master. In obedient trust, he expected answers to his prayers – and, as the world knows, he got them.

Few sagas in the history of the Christian church can equal the excitement and drama of Müller's life which spanned nearly the whole of the nineteenth century. Few men or women have touched more hearts or inspired more commitment to Christ. In the years since Müller died, the work which he established has adapted to meet changing needs, diversifying into new areas, but the principle of never appealing for funds has not been broken. I am so grateful to Keith Hagon of the George Müller Foundation for bringing the story up-to-date by revising the final chapter. I am glad that this new edition of a book which has been continuously in print for nearly forty years will make the whole story known to a fresh audience.

One hundred and forty-two years have elapsed since George Müller opened the fifth of his large children's homes on Ashley Down in Bristol. He was now caring for two thousand children and employing a staff of over two hundred people. Much has changed since the year 1870, but Müller's God remains the living God. He is alive in the hearts of prayerful people all over the world. I pray that your knowledge and experience of him will grow as you read the remarkable tale which follows.

Roger Steer
Down St Mary, Devon, April 2012

1

PRUSSIAN PLAYBOY

Half a century earlier, Wolfenbuttel's medieval castle had been the favourite residence of a local noble family; by the early nineteenth century, although the royal visitors had departed, the little seventeenth-century town nestling in the hills of Lower Saxony had lost none of its charm. In one of the half-timbered buildings, clustered around the castle, a police officer looked up from his desk. Two soldiers stood guard over a handsome Prussian youth. The officer began his interrogation.

'What is your name?'

'George Müller.'

'Age?'

'Sixteen.'

'Place and date of birth?'

'Kroppenstedt, Prussia, September 27th 1805.'

'Is it true that you have been living in style at Wolfenbüttel, and that you are unable to pay the innkeeper?'

'Yes, it is, but....'

'Is it also true that you spent last week at another hotel near Brunswick, living in similar luxury, and that when asked for payment you were forced to leave clothes as a security?'

Müller could say little in his defence. He was penniless and in debt: after three hours of questioning, and with no indication as to when he could expect a trial, the two soldiers marched him away to prison.

December 18th 1821: George Müller looked at the tiny cell where he was to spend his first night in prison. A narrow window covered with stout iron bars provided the only light and thick wooden partitions divided it from adjacent cells. That evening, Müller received some meat to eat with his bread, but he loathed the smell of it and left it untouched. This must have offended the chef who laid on no more special favours. On the second day he was treated to the same menu as his fellow-prisoners: for lunch, water and coarse bread; for dinner, vegetables and cold meat – and, beginning to feel distinctly underfed, he ate a little.

The warder locked Müller in his cell day and night and gave him no work and no exercise.

'Could I have a Bible to read?' Müller enquired in order to help pass the time.

'No.'

On the third day he ate all his food, and after the fourth would always have been glad of more.

After some days, he discovered there was another prisoner in the cell next to him. He shouted through the partition and discovered that his neighbour had been imprisoned for stealing. Perhaps to keep the noise down, the governor decided to allow the prisoner to share Müller's cell and they spent their time describing their adventures. Warming to his task, Müller began to invent stories which impressed his friend immensely; then after about a week of this, the two prisoners disagreed and for day after day refused to speak to each other. In the silence, Müller began to reflect on his life.

His earliest memory went back to January in 1810 when, at the age of four, his family had moved from Kroppenstedt to Heimersleben where his father was appointed collector of taxes. Before his tenth birthday, he had begun to steal government money from his father; and he remembered the day when his father had scored a tactical victory. Suspecting his son, Herr

Müller had counted a small sum and placed it in the room where he was left. Left alone for a while, George had taken some of the money and hidden it in his shoe. His father returned and counted the money; George was searched and found out. He remembered being punished on this and other occasions, but recalled that his reaction to being found out was usually to consider how he might do the thing again more cleverly, so as not to be detected.

Herr Müller had hoped that George would become a clergyman: not that he might serve God, but in order that he should have a comfortable living. There in his cell, George reflected on his five years at the cathedral classical school at Halberstadt; and remembered – with some shame – a Saturday night, some two years previously, when, not knowing that his mother had been taken ill, Müller had played cards until two on the Sunday morning. Then, having quenched his thirst at a tavern, he had toured the streets, half drunk, with friends.

He remembered that on the following day he had attended the first of a series of confirmation classes. On returning to his rooms, he found his father waiting for him.

'Your mother is dead,' Herr Müller told him. 'Get yourself ready for her funeral!'

Three or four days before he was confirmed, he was guilty of what he described in his journal as 'gross immorality'; and the day before his confirmation, in a vestry to confess his sins, he defrauded a priest by handing over only one-twelfth of the fee his father had given him.

With nothing to disturb the routine of life in the cell, and with neither prisoner inclined to communicate, Müller continued to reflect on the past. He had taken his first communion in Halberstadt cathedral on the Sunday after Easter 1820. That afternoon and evening, in search of quiet, he had stayed at home while the young people who had been confirmed with him were out and about.

'I'll turn over a new leaf and spend more time studying,' he had resolved.

But he soon broke his resolution and his behaviour grew worse rather than better. In the twenty months following his confirmation, he spent some of his time studying, but a great deal more time playing the piano and guitar, reading novels, drinking in taverns, making resolutions to improve but breaking them almost as fast as they were made.

On January 12th 1822, the sound of the unbolting of his cell door interrupted Müller's recollections.

'You are wanted at the police office,' said the warder. 'Follow me.'

'Your father has sent the money you will need for travelling expenses, to pay your debt at the inn and for your maintenance here in prison,' the police commissioner told him. 'You are therefore free to leave at once.'

Herr Müller celebrated his reunion with his son by severely beating him; he took him home to Schoenebeck, near Magdeburg, where he had held another government appointment since the summer of 1821. George tried desperately hard to regain his father's favour and began to tutor pupils in Latin, French, German grammar and arithmetic. He made progress in his studies, became popular with everyone – including after a time, his father. But he later admitted that he was 'still in secret habitually guilty of great sins'.

When he was just seventeen, Müller entered the gymnasium (pre-university school) at Nordhausen, one of the oldest towns in Prussia. Despite his enthusiasm for study, and attempts to reform himself, Müller still found it almost impossible to make ends meet. On one occasion, after receiving an allowance from his father, he purposely showed the money to some friends. Then he deliberately damaged the locks of his guitar case. A few minutes later he ran into the director's room with his coat off.

'All the money my father sent me has been stolen!' he announced breathlessly.

Everyone was wonderfully sympathetic. Some of his friends clubbed together and managed to give him as much money as he had lost, while his creditors agreed to extend their loans. However, the director – older and wiser – was suspicious and never fully restored George to his confidence. And for his part, Müller never again felt at ease in the presence of the director's wife, who had acted like a mother to him during an illness.

Müller's great ambition was to enter Halle, the famous university founded in 1694 by Frederick III of Brandenburg who later became King of Prussia. Most important for Müller's later development, Halle was a seat of Pietist theology and practice. Pietism had breathed new life into the religious life of Germany in the seventeenth century; when the insights of Luther and the reformers had hardened into rigid formulas, the Pietist revival had emphasised the importance of the new birth, personal faith in Christ and the warmth of Christian experience as a spur to effective evangelicalism. Müller fulfilled his ambition in the Easter of 1825.

Halle is built on a sandy plain on the banks of the River Saale. The central market square in the inner town is overlooked by a fine medieval town hall, and the Gothic *Marienkirche* – where Handel learnt to play the organ. On arrival at the University, Müller resolved yet again to live a better life; and this time he really meant it. He knew that no parish would ever choose him as its pastor if he carried on in his current state. And even if he were accepted, he would need a good knowledge of divinity to obtain a comfortable living which in Prussia depended on the standard of a man's university degree.

But the freedom of university life offered too many temptations, and George Müller yet again found it impossible to manage money. Before long he had to pawn his watch and some clothes; he began again to borrow extensively. He felt utterly miserable: worn out by his constant unsuccessful attempts to improve himself.

In one of Halle's taverns (where he once drank ten pints of beer in a single afternoon), he thought he recognised a young man from his old school at Halberstadt. They hadn't been close friends, for Beta had been quiet and serious, but it occurred to Müller that if he struck up a close friendship, it might help him to lead a steadier life. He picked his way across the crowded *Bierkeller* and shook his old friend warmly by the hand.

'Beta! How are you? How nice to see you after so long!'

Beta welcomed his friendship because he thought it would enliven his social life.

Müller loved travel and made a suggestion to his friends.

'Why don't we make a trip to Switzerland?'

'But we have no money and no passports.'

'Leave that to me,' said Müller. 'This is my plan. Forge letters from your parents which entitle you to passports. Sell all you can, especially books which fetch a good price, so that we can raise enough funds to make the journey. Let me have the money and I will buy the necessary tickets.'

The party, which included Beta, left Halle on August 18th 1825. They travelled to Erfurt and then westward to Frankfurt and south via Heidelberg, Stuttgart and Zurich to the heart of Switzerland. There before them, set between steep limestone slopes and a rising mist, lay Lake Lucerne. They climbed to the top of the Rigi and the view took Müller's breath away. He looked at the mountains which thrust themselves into the lake: Burgenstock, Seelisburg and away to the south-west, Pilatus, all so irregular but magnificent.

'Now,' he thought, 'I have lived!'

They travelled home via Lake Constance and then east to Ulm and medieval Nuremberg in Bavaria arriving back in Halle at the end of September. None of Müller's friends discovered that the man they had trusted with their money had cleverly arranged things so that he himself paid far less towards the cost of the trip than any other member of the party.

2

'Constrained by the Love of Jesus'

'For some weeks I have been attending a meeting on Saturday evenings at the home of a Christian,' Beta told Müller in the middle of November 1825. He paused, wondering how George would react.

'And what happens at this meeting?'

'They read the Bible, they sing, they pray, and someone normally reads a sermon.'

'I should like to go with you this evening.'

'I'm not sure you will enjoy it.'

George had made up his mind: 'I am most anxious to go.'

'Then I will call for you this evening.'

Müller felt sure Herr Wagner, at whose home the meeting was held, wouldn't welcome him. On arrival, he apologised for coming. Herr Wagner smiled.

'Come as often as you please; house and heart are open to you! Now come and join the others.'

They sang a hymn and then Herr Kayser – later to become a missionary in Africa with the London Missionary Society – knelt down and asked God to bless the meeting. Müller had never before seen anyone on his knees; he'd never himself knelt to pray.

Herr Kayser read a chapter from the Bible and then a printed sermon. Prussian law at that time made the extempore exposition of Scripture an offence unless an ordained clergyman were present. At the end of the meeting, they sang a hymn and Herr Wagner closed the meeting with prayer. While he prayed, Müller thought, *I could not pray as well, though I am much more educated than this man.*

'All we saw on our journey to Switzerland, and all our former pleasures, are as nothing compared with this evening,' he said to Beta as they walked home.

It was the turning point of his life; and that night he lay peacefully and happily in his bed. The next day and on several days during the following week, Müller returned to Herr Wagner's house to study the Bible. Writing about this time later he wrote:

> It pleased God to teach me something of the meaning of that precious truth:
>
> 'God so loved the world, that He gave His only Son, that whosoever believeth in Him should not perish, but have everlasting life.' I understood something of the reason why the Lord Jesus died on the cross, and suffered such agonies in the Garden of Gethsemane: even that thus, bearing the punishment due to us, we might not bear it ourselves. And, therefore, apprehending in some measure the love of Jesus for my soul, I was constrained to love Him in return. What all the exhortations and precepts of my father and others could not effect; what all my own resolutions could not bring about, even to renounce a life of sin and profligacy: I was enabled to do, constrained by the love of Jesus. The individual who desires to have his sins forgiven, must seek it through the blood of Jesus. The individual who desires to get power over sin, must likewise seek it through the blood of Jesus.

In January 1826, six or seven weeks after becoming a Christian, and after much prayer, Müller made an important decision and went home to see his father.

'Father, I believe God wants me to become a missionary. I have come to seek your permission as is required by the German missionary societies.'

His father shouted his reply.

'I've spent large sums of money on your education. I hoped that I could spend my last days with you in a parsonage. And now you tell me that this prospect has come to nothing. I can no longer consider you as my son!'

Then Herr Müller began to cry.

'I beg you to reconsider' he pleaded.

But George had made up his mind and believed that God gave him the strength to stick to what he saw as His call.

Müller returned to Halle, and although he still had two years of study ahead, he made up his mind never to take any more money from his father. It seemed wrong to do this, now that his father could no longer look forward to seeing his son become what he had wished – a clergyman with a good living.

Müller was now faced with the problem of how to live without his father's support. Would he be able to honour his resolution? It soon became clear that he would. For a number of events followed – the first of many during his remarkable life – which demonstrated to Müller, and later to the world, that 'there is no want to them that fear Him' (Ps. 34:9).

It came about in this way. Shortly after he returned from visiting his father, several Americans arrived in Halle to study, three of whom were lecturers in American colleges. Their problem was that they didn't understand German. However, Halle now had a new Professor of Divinity, Dr Tholuck, a Pietist, who made a suggestion to his new colleagues.

'I have a student who would I believe make an excellent tutor in the German language.'

The Americans were delighted.

'The student's name is George Müller,' said Tholuck.

The Americans paid Müller so well for his tuition that, in the absence of his father's support, he had enough money to look after himself and some left over.

He now embarked on the task of proclaiming his new-found faith with the energetic dedication which was to become such a characteristic of his life. He circulated monthly about two hundred missionary papers in different parts of the country; he often stuffed his pockets full of tracts so that he could give them to people he met on his walks; he wrote letters to his former friends pleading with them to turn to Christ; and for thirteen weeks he visited a sick man who eventually became a Christian.

Not all his early efforts at evangelism were entirely successful. 'Once I met a beggar in the fields, and spoke to him about his soul. But when I perceived it made no impression on him, I spoke more loudly; and when he still remained unmoved, I quite bawled in talking to him; till at last I went away, seeing it was of no use.'

In August 1826 a schoolmaster who lived in a village near Halle approached Müller with a request.

'Would you be prepared to preach in my parish?'

'I have never once preached a sermon,' Müller replied, 'but I believe that if I could commit a sermon to memory I might be able to help you.'

It took him nearly a week to memorise the sermon and early in the morning of August 27th 1826, in a small chapel, he got through the sermon but didn't enjoy it. He repeated the same sermon word for word later in the morning in the parish church; in the afternoon he planned to use the same sermon a third time. But when he stood in the pulpit to face his congregation, something seemed to tell him to read from Matthew 5 and to make whatever comments came into his mind.

As he began to explain the meaning of the words 'Blessed are the poor in spirit', he felt that he was being helped to speak. And whereas in the morning his sermon had been too difficult for the people to understand, he noticed in the afternoon that the congregation listened with great attention. He seemed to be understood, and actually enjoyed the work.

From then, he preached frequently in the villages and towns surrounding Halle. On Saturday evenings he enjoyed going to the meetings in Herr Wagner's house. On Sunday evenings a group of students from the university met together, and from Easter 1827 these meetings were held in Müller's room.

In August 1827 the Continental Missionary Society in England decided to send a minister to Bucharest. They asked Professor Tholuck, at Halle, to keep his eye open for a suitable man. Müller thought and prayed about it, and found that his father didn't disapprove of the idea.

'I believe that this is the opportunity for service I have longed for,' Müller told Tholuck. 'I should like to go to Bucharest.'

As he waited to hear more details from London, he counted the cost of going to Bucharest and prayed earnestly about his future work. At the same time, oddly because it had nothing to do with the planned move to Bucharest, he developed a passionate interest in the Hebrew language and began to study it out of sheer enjoyment.

At the end of October 1827 an unexpected but welcome visitor turned up at one of the Sunday evening meetings in Müller's room. Hermann Ball was a missionary to Jews in Poland, whom Müller had first met in the Easter of 1826.

'Because of poor health at the moment,' he told Müller, 'I will have to give up my work among Jews.'

As he listened to Ball, Müller felt what he described as a 'peculiar desire to fill up his place', but he didn't think seriously about the matter in view of the Bucharest assignment.

In November, Müller called on Professor Tholuck.

'Have you ever wanted to be a missionary to the Jews?' Tholuck asked. 'I am an agent for a Missionary Society in London which works amongst them.'

Müller was startled and told Tholuck about Ball's visit.

'But it surely wouldn't be right for me to think any more about the matter as I am going to Bucharest,' he said.

Tholuck agreed.

Next morning, however, Müller felt that he had lost all his longing to go to Bucharest and thought this very self-indulgent.

'Dear God,' he prayed, 'please restore to me my former wish to work in Bucharest.'

His prayer was answered immediately, but his love for Hebrew continued.

Towards the end of November, the Continental Missionary Society wrote to Tholuck: 'Owing to the war between the Turks and the Russians, the committee has decided for the time being to abandon the idea of sending a minister to Bucharest.'

'Have you thought any more about becoming a missionary to the Jews?' Tholuck asked Müller.

In response Müller prayed; he reflected; he talked to his friends and invited them to probe his motives; and at last he gave Tholuck his reply.

'I cannot say for certain that it is God's will that I should be a missionary to the Jews. But I believe I should offer myself to the committee and leave it with the Lord to do with me what seems best to Him.'

Early in 1828 a new workhouse for men convicted of minor offences was established in Halle. Müller successfully applied to fill a temporary vacancy as chaplain to the inmates while he waited to hear from London. As well as preaching he counselled the men individually, explaining the Christian faith to them. 'I had at least some qualification for ministering there,' he wrote, 'for I knew the state of those poor sinners, having been myself formerly, in all probability, a great deal worse than most of them, and my simplicity and plainness of speech they would not have found in every minister.'

Despite his many extramural activities, Müller successfully completed his course at Easter 1828. A very different George Müller graduated from Halle compared to the wayward and unhappy fresher who had arrived in 1825. Now his life had purpose, peace and joy; and if, with the passage of time, memories of Halle became dimmed, he would surely remember vividly that Saturday evening in November 1825 when he had visited Herr Wagner's home and his life had been transformed.

In June 1828 Müller received a letter from the London Society for Promoting Christianity among the Jews (later to become the

Church Mission to the Jews). The committee had decided to take him as a missionary student for six months on probation, provided he would come to London.

Just one obstacle remained, however, before Müller could obtain a passport for England. Every male Prussian graduate was required to serve one year in the army provided he was healthy. Müller had been declared fit for service when he was twenty but at his own request had had his service postponed until his course had been completed. However, those who intended to become missionaries were often exempted. King Frederick William III, however, replied that the matter must be referred to the appropriate ministry and that no exception was to be made in Müller's case.

The solution to the problem was unexpected: Müller became quite seriously ill. An eminent doctor prescribed tonics and wine, and a well-to-do and rather worldly friend – one of the American professors – took Müller to the country near Berlin. 'As long as I was day after day in the open air, going from place to place, drinking wine and taking tonics I felt well; but as soon as I returned to Halle, the old symptoms returned.' The main symptoms seem to have been severe giddiness, weakness of the stomach, and a cold which Müller couldn't throw off.

Müller and his American friend went together to the famous Michaelmas fair at Leipzig, and then on to the opera, but Müller didn't enjoy it. After the first act he drank a glass of iced water; after the second act he fainted. He recovered sufficiently to return to their hotel where he spent a comfortable night.

'I'm not happy about the way we've been carrying on,' Müller said to his friend the next day.

'Neither am I,' replied his friend, who was a Christian whose love for Jesus had grown cold. 'When you fainted at the opera last night, it struck me that it was an awful place to die in!'

On their return to Halle, Müller suffered a haemorrhage in his stomach which he put down to the glass of iced water.

'Why don't you offer yourself for service in the army and hope that while you are so weak you'll be rejected?' a Christian major in the Prussian army suggested to Müller, adopting a rather doubtful ethical stance.

Müller was examined and found unfit; it was stated that he had a tendency to tuberculosis. One of the generals in the Prussian army, in the absence of his adjutant, wrote out the necessary papers himself which gave Müller a complete exemption for life from all military engagements.

'May I particularly advise you to draw the attention of Jews to the eleventh chapter of Paul's epistle to the Romans?' said the General, a devout Christian himself.

Müller's health continued to be poor until, acting on the advice of a medical professor, he gave up all medicine and his condition began to improve.

In February, Müller left Berlin for London, visiting on the way his father at the house in Heimersleben where he had spent his boyhood. At Rotterdam the ice had only just broken on the river and no steamer dared venture out. After nearly a month's delay, Müller boarded a ship which was bound for England; and on March 19th 1829 he arrived in London.

3

ENGLAND, 1829

You could smell the spring in London in 1829. The City had hardly begun to invade the country north of Hyde Park Corner. John Nash had recently made over four hundred acres of rough heathland north of Oxford Street into a beautiful park for the Prince Regent: they called it Regent's Park. Leading south from the Park to the Mall, where the Prince lived, Nash had designed and built Regent Street. As one of the street's prominent features he had built a fine church with a circular Ionic portico: All Souls, Langham Place, just five years old when Müller arrived in London.

By 1829 Nash was busy with the rebuilding of Buckingham Palace for George IV, but the King died the following year before the work was done. William IV preferred to live at St James's Palace and the young Princess Victoria, now living at Kensington, would not move into the Palace until after her Coronation in 1837. Müller was no doubt intrigued by the modern gas lamps which lit Pall Mall: a sign to all that London was the most advanced city in the world.

Müller eventually found some inexpensive lodgings – not in the fashionable west end – but in Hackney, said at that time to be a haunt of highwaymen. He longed to become fluent in English as quickly as possible, but most of his fellow students being German, opportunities to further this ambition were limited. In the country beyond Hackney he spoke English for the first time 'to a little boy ... about his soul thinking that he would bear with my broken English'.

'Anthony Norris Groves,' one of Müller's colleagues told him, 'worked as a dentist in Exeter but has given up his fifteen-hundred-pound-a-year practice and plans to go as a missionary to Persia with his wife and children. He'll have no salary but simply depend on God alone to supply his needs.'

This news delighted Müller so much that he made a note of it in his journal and wrote to his friends in Germany about it.

Characteristically, Müller worked hard in London: for about twelve hours a day, mainly at Hebrew, Chaldee and the Rabbinic alphabet. 'I looked up to the Lord even whilst turning over the leaves of my Hebrew dictionary, asking His help, that I might quickly find the words.'

In May 1829 Müller, then aged twenty-three, fell ill. He'd been far from well when he left Germany, and the long hours of study in London took their toll. He felt sure he was dying; introspection set in but an inner happiness prevailed. 'It was as if every sin of which I had been guilty was brought to my remembrance; but, at the same time, I could realise that all my sins were completely forgiven – that I was washed and made clean, completely clean, in the blood of Jesus. The result of this was great peace. I longed exceedingly to depart and be with Christ.' But this departure was not to be just yet.

'You are getting better,' his doctor told him.

'This instead of giving me great joy,' he wrote, 'bowed me down, so great was my desire to be with the Lord; though almost immediately afterwards grace was given me to submit myself to the will of God.'

'You should go to the country for a change of air,' his friends advised. 'What about south Devon?'

And so it was that in Teignmouth, in the summer of 1829, Müller struck up a friendship that would last thirty-six years and change the course of his life.

Henry Craik was a Scotsman, who, like Müller, was nearly twenty-four and who, also like Müller, had been converted while at university. After graduating with some distinction at St Andrews, he had moved to Exeter in 1826 to become a private tutor in the home of Anthony Norris Groves – the dentist about whom Müller had been told in London. Groves had greatly influenced Craik's thinking.

'For years I was a high churchman,' Groves had told Craik. 'In 1822, I began an intensive study of the Bible and I came to regard the Scriptures alone as a sufficient source of spiritual growth.'

Groves let Craik have a copy of a tract he had written in 1825 entitled *Christian Devotedness* in which he set out the reasons why he thought Christ was speaking *literal* truth, and meant to be understood as such, when he said things like 'Sell your possessions and give to the poor' (Matt. 19:21). He argued for a return to the spirit and practice of the early church whose members 'sold their possessions and goods and gave to anyone as he had need' (Acts 2:45).

'This,' Groves told Craik, 'is as consonant with reason as it is with revelation.'

Groves had proceeded to practise what he preached: he and his wife had given up first a tenth and then a quarter of their income and distributed it among the poor. Then they abandoned any idea of saving money or putting it aside for their children and, reducing their expenses by simplifying their living, they gave away all the rest.

In preparation for missionary service, Groves had enrolled as an external student of Trinity College, Dublin, intending to take a degree in theology before ordination in the Church of England. In Dublin he had met the group of men who are now regarded as the founders of the 'Plymouth Brethren' (due to the location some time later of their first large church). They had no idea they were founding a movement: indeed the last thing any of them would have wished to do would have been to add another denomination to what they saw as a sadly divided Christendom.

Groves' decision to go to Persia as a missionary had forced Craik to seek another job; and in the summer of 1828 he'd taken up a position in Teignmouth as tutor to a member of a family which was also linked to the circle which Groves had met in Dublin. What really attracted Müller to Craik was 'his warmth of heart towards the Lord'; both were fascinated by the study of Hebrew. Müller received a full account from Craik of developments in Dublin. Moreover Craik's and Müller's case were to become particularly close.

A few days after his arrival in Teignmouth, Müller attended the reopening of Ebenezer Chapel and was greatly impressed by one of the preachers. He recorded, 'Though I did not like all he said, yet I saw a gravity and solemnity in him different from the rest'. After the service Müller made enquiries to find out more about this preacher and was invited to Exmouth, where he was staying, to spend ten days with him in the same house. Müller readily accepted the invitation and recorded that 'through the instrumentality of this brother the Lord bestowed a great blessing upon me, for which I shall have cause to thank Him throughout eternity'. Unfortunately we don't know who 'this brother' was; what is clear however is that the development of Müller's thought during and immediately following his stay in Exmouth reflects the influence of his contacts with the early Brethren movement.

Müller felt that God was teaching him a 'higher standard of devotedness' than he had known before. His comments on this in his journal suggest that he had carefully studied Groves' tract *Christian Devotedness*: 'It ill becomes the servant,' he wrote, 'to seek to be rich, and great, and honoured in that world, where his Lord was poor, and mean, and despised.'

He described the change which he experienced during his stay in Devon as being 'like a second conversion'. In a letter written many years later, Müller wrote of this time as follows:

I became a believer in the Lord Jesus in the beginning of November 1825.... For the first four years afterwards, it was for a good part in great weakness; but in July 1829 ... it came with me to an entire and full surrender of heart. I gave myself fully to the Lord. Honour, pleasure, money, my physical powers, my mental powers, all was laid down at the feet of Jesus, and I became a great lover of the Word of God. I found my all in God....

Müller returned to London in September, determined to share his new insights and enthusiasms with his colleagues. He organised a meeting every morning for prayers and Bible reading, at which each man present explained what God had shown him from the Bible portion he had read. One of his fellow students in particular shared Müller's enthusiasm for spiritual things. On several evenings, when Müller enjoyed especially good times of communion with God, he went to his friend's room after midnight and found him in a similar state. The two of them continued in prayer together until one or two in the morning. Müller would then return to his room, but a few times he felt so full of joy that he hardly slept until six when it was time for him to meet his colleagues again for prayer and fellowship.

Müller believed that God had called him to preach the gospel, and was not prepared to wait until he became a fully qualified missionary before he began to work amongst London's Jews. He wrote his name and address on hundreds of tracts, and, as he gave them out, invited the recipients to come and talk to him about the Christian faith. He preached at favourite Jewish meeting points and regularly read the Bible to about fifty Jewish boys: he became a teacher in a Sunday school.

Towards the end of November 1829, Müller began to wonder whether he should continue to be associated with the London Society for Promoting Christianity among the Jews. He was coming to the view that as a servant of Jesus Christ he ought to be guided by the Holy Spirit in his missionary work and not by men. One of the requirements of the committee would be that he should spend the greater part of his time working amongst the Jews. It now seemed to him that the Biblical approach for him, on arrival in an area, would be to seek out and work especially among the Jews, but to preach to Gentiles as well.

By December he had more or less made up his mind to write to the committee of the Society to make his views known to them. But, typically, he decided to wait another month to consider the matter; before making his final decision, he travelled again to Devon, intending to spend a short holiday there. As things turned out, however, he never returned to London as a student.

He planned to spend a fortnight in Exmouth and determined not to idle away his time. On the second day, a devout Devonian approached him.

'I have been praying for this month past that the Lord would do something for Lympstone, a large parish where there is little spiritual light. There is a Wesleyan chapel, and I don't doubt that you would be allowed to preach there.'

Müller gladly took up the suggestion, and the next day, a Sunday, found him at Lympstone enjoying the rich smells of the mud-flats on the Exe estuary. He had no difficulty in getting permission to preach twice a day at the Wesleyan chapel in the village. On most days in the following week he held a meeting 'in a room with several ladies, for reading the Scriptures with them'.

In view of these growing commitments he decided to write straight away to the Society committee in London so that while they were making up their minds about him he could continue to preach. His letter set out what his views on missionary service had been before he had joined the Society and how they had changed since. He said that he owed them a lot for their part in bringing him to England; and that he would be happy in future to serve them without salary if they would allow him to go from place to place throughout England, as the Lord directed him, and to preach to nominal Christians as well as Jews. He would like to obtain his supplies of Hebrew Scriptures and tracts for Jews from the Society.

In reply he received a friendly personal letter from one of the secretaries plus an official letter which pointed out politely that the Society couldn't employ anyone who was unwilling to submit to its guidance, and that it could not therefore continue to consider him a missionary student. If more mature reflection caused him to change his mind, the Society would gladly reconsider the matter.

Thus ended Müller's studentship with the Society he had come to England to serve. He didn't attach any blame to the Society, and always appreciated the help it had been to him; but, at the same time, never regretted the break he had made. He was now free to put into practice his belief 'A servant of Christ has but one Master' and to work whenever and wherever his Master directed him.

After three weeks in Exmouth, Müller left for Teignmouth intending to spend ten days with the friends he had made there during his convalescence the previous summer. The journey from Exmouth lies just east of the estuary where the Exe meets the sea, and Teignmouth lies on the other side a few miles to the south-west. But for those, like Müller, unable to fly, the journey involves either a detour of twenty miles to the lowest bridging point of the Exe at Countess Wear, or the use of a tiresome ferry from Exmouth to Starcross. However, the compensation for the weary traveller is the magnificent scenery. There is the fine view across the estuary to Powderham and the woods of Mamhead. And beyond, on the Haldon Hills, Belvedere Tower already stood out, in 1830 as it does today, a landmark over much of Devon. This was the country which was to become familiar to Müller – not as he thought for ten days or so, but for the next two and a half years. Who would have expected that the young Prussian who had so recently been rejected by the army on grounds of health, and who spoke such broken English, would now make the West Country his home until his death at the close of the century? He travelled to Teignmouth with little more than five pounds in his pocket, no income and no employment. But in those two and a half years George Müller began to learn the lessons which would fit him for the work which lay ahead.

4

Training by the Teign

Teignmouth already had a long history as a small seaport, fishing and market town when, in the late eighteenth and early nineteenth century, it became a fashionable seaside resort. Both Keats and Fanny Burney stayed there, among other notables. In 1827, a bridge was opened which linked the town to Shaldon, the charming village on the opposite bank of the Teign estuary where Henry Craik lived.

'Would you consider becoming Minister of Ebenezer Chapel?' a member of the congregation asked Müller very soon after he arrived in Teignmouth.

'I don't intend to put down roots in any one place, but to travel around preaching as and where God directs me,' Müller replied.

'Will you preach for me at the Baptist Chapel in Shaldon?' Henry Craik asked.

Müller accepted Craik's invitation. In the congregation when he preached were three ministers: none of them liked his sermon. But a young lady who had been servant to one of them was converted after the service; Müller couldn't help reflecting that she had heard her master preach many times.

Müller preached every night that first week either at Shaldon or Teignmouth. Some of those who listened, who had been friendly to him in the summer, now turned hostile.

'The Lord intended to work through me at Teignmouth,' Müller concluded, 'and therefore Satan, fearing this, sought to raise opposition against me.' Nevertheless there were a number who responded to the gospel and became Christians in that first week.

Despite some opposition, the pressure from a section of the congregation at Ebenezer Chapel for Müller to become their minister increased until, after twelve weeks, the whole congregation unanimously invited him to become their pastor.

'I am happy to accept your kind invitation,' replied Müller after a great deal of prayer, 'but I must make it clear that I can only stay as your pastor as long as I am sure that this is God's will.'

He had not given up his intention to go from place to place as God directed him. The congregation offered him fifty-five pounds a year, a sum which they later increased as the size of the congregation grew. Still later, this method of support was abandoned as Müller's views developed. He began to preach regularly at Exeter, Topsham, Shaldon, Exmouth, Lympstone, Bishopsteignton, Chudleigh, Cullompton and Newton Abbot.

At about the beginning of April (1830) Müller went to preach at the select little town of Sidmouth and got embroiled in an argument with three equally select ladies who knew their own minds.

'What are your opinions on the merits of infant and believers' baptism, Mr Müller?'

Müller had often spoken against believers' baptism.

'I don't think I need to be baptised again,' he replied.

'Have you ever read the Scriptures and prayed with reference to this subject?' asked one of the select ladies who had herself been baptised as an adult.

'No.'

'Then I entreat you never to speak any more about it till you have done so.'

Thus chastened, Müller made up his mind to examine the subject. Characteristically he read the New Testament from the beginning looking particularly at references to the disputed matter. He decided that believers only were the proper subjects for baptism, and that total immersion was the scriptural patter.

He was especially struck by Acts 8:36-38 and Romans 6:3-5; some time later he was baptised by Henry Craik, and almost all of his friends followed suit.

Devon is big – about seventy-five miles from north to south and with many more miles of road than any other English county – but news of the able young Prussian who had settled at Teignmouth was spreading rapidly. In the north at Barnstaple, a lawyer, Thomas Puglsey, had built a chapel and invited Müller to preach at the opening in June (1830). Müller accepted the invitation and two locals were converted. In fact almost every time Müller now preached there was a response.

In that summer of 1830 Müller decided that Ebenezer Chapel should follow what he took to be the example of the Apostles in Acts 20:7 and observe the Lord's Supper every Sunday, although he admitted there is no specific commandment to do so either from Christ or in the epistles.

'I believe also,' he told his congregation, 'that it is Scriptural, according to Ephesians 4, and Romans 12 in particular, that we should give room for the Holy Ghost to work though any brother in Christ whom He pleases to use. What I mean is that one member may benefit the other with the gift which the Lord has bestowed upon him. At certain meetings any of the brethren will have an opportunity to exhort or teach the rest, if they consider they have something to say which may be beneficial to the hearers.'

Thus Ebenezer Chapel, with Müller as pastor, adopted a distinctively Brethren-style observance of the Lord's supper.

Throughout that summer of 1830, Müller never refused an opportunity to visit Exeter. It wasn't only the beauty of the journey along the coast from Teignmouth to Starcross and then up the road by the Exe estuary to the county town that he enjoyed. The attraction lay at the end of the journey: Müller had fallen in love. He had never confined his admiration of the Groves family to Anthony, but extended it to his sister who had been left behind in 1829. Mary Groves kept house for Mrs Hake, an invalid who ran a boarding school in Northernhay House. Müller felt sure that it was better for him to be married, and prayed much about the choice of a life's partner. Miss Groves could hardly have been a more ideal answer to his prayers. She shared her brother's earnest devotion to her Lord, and fully supported him in his decision to trust God for material supplies. According to Müller, she played the piano nicely and painted beautifully; and as for providing him with intellectual companionship, she had studied English grammar, geography, history, French, Latin and Hebrew – and she could teach George a thing or two about astronomy. On August 15th he wrote asking her to be his wife; four days later he happened to be in Exeter, and called at Northernhay House. Mary accepted his proposal and they fell to their knees asking God to bless their marriage.

They found another housekeeper for Mrs Hake, and the couple were married on October 7th. They walked to St David's Church for a simple service which was conducted by the Rev. John Abbot. They then returned with friends to Northernhay House for a celebration of the Lord's Supper. Off then in a stagecoach to Teignmouth; and the next day began their work together for the Lord. Whoever heard of a honeymoon?

Soon after returning to Teignmouth, the newly married couple decided that it was wrong for George to receive a set salary. This had been made up by pew-rents, and, as the better seats were more expensive, they now took the view that the system encouraged social discrimination and was contrary to the spirit of James 2:1-6. Therefore Müller abandoned pew-rents and made all seats free; at the end of October he made this announcement.

'I intend to give up my salary from the church.'

He gave his reasons and read from Philippians 4; he placed a box in the chapel with a notice saying that anyone who wanted to support Mr and Mrs Müller might put their offerings therein.

Müller also decided that from that time onward he would ask no one, not even his fellow Christians in Ebenezer Chapel, to help him financially in any way. There would be no more 'going to man, instead of going to the Lord'. Müller admitted that this decision 'required more grace than to give up my salary'. But it was this decision, probably more than anything else, which makes the story of his life from this time so exciting. At this time also George and Mary decided to take literally Luke 12:33: 'Sell your possessions and give to the poor'.

Throughout their married life the Müllers never disagreed about the principle of practice of these momentous decisions made at the beginning of their life together. Looking back on this period later Müller wrote, 'this has been the means of letting us see the tender love and care of our God over His children, even in the most minute things, in a way which we never experimentally knew before; and it has, in particular, made the Lord known to us more fully than we knew Him before, as a prayer hearing God'.

Bishopsteignton is an attractive village on a hill overlooking the Teign estuary with magnificent views over the river and Dartmoor beyond. Some of the congregation at Ebenezer Chapel lived in the village. From the Norman conquest it had belonged to the bishops of Exeter and traditionally was one of their richest manors. But two visitors to the village in November 1830 weren't rich: nearly three weeks after giving up their salary the Müllers were reduced to about eight shillings. (For most of the nineteenth century, which was remarkably free from inflation, a farm labourer typically earned about ten shillings (50p) a week.) That morning they had asked God to give them some money.

During a conversation with a lady member of their congregation who lived in the village, their hostess asked Müller:

'Do you need any money?'

'I told the brethren, dear sister, when I gave up my salary that I would for the future tell the Lord only about my wants.'

'But He has told me to give you some money,' she replied. 'About a fortnight ago I asked Him what I should do for Him and He told me to give you some money: and last Saturday it came again powerfully to my mind, and has not left me since, and I felt it so forcibly last night that I couldn't help speaking of it to brother P.'

Still thinking it better not to mention their circumstances, Müller changed the subject to other matters. When they left, the lady gave him two guineas.

The following week at Exmouth, when they were reduced to about nine shillings, Müller prayed again for money and within thirty hours they were given £7 10s from three different sources.

'Admire the gentleness of the Lord,' Müller commented on the first weeks following their decision to ask God alone for funds, 'that He did not try our faith much at the commencement, but gave us first encouragement and allowed us to see His willingness to help us, before He pleased to try it more fully.'

What some would call Müller's fanatical principles on the reception of gifts sometimes led to amusing incidents. In March 1831, while staying at Axminster to preach, he was invited to spend a Sunday at Chard in Somerset. On that sort of occasion, anxious to avoid giving the impression that he preached for money, he was reluctant to accept gifts. After one service a member of the congregation tried to give him some money wrapped in paper, but Müller refused to accept it. However, Somerset people are not easily discouraged: this determined saint forced the paper into Müller's pocket and ran away. Another gentleman from Chard forced him to accept a sovereign, but only after a tussle.

At Barnstaple, they developed some ingenious solutions to the problem of Müller's reluctance to accept gifts while preaching away from Teignmouth. While Mr and Mrs Müller were there in April 1831 they found a sovereign in Mary's handbag which had been put there anonymously. On their return to Teignmouth, when they opened their case, an envelope fell out on to the floor. It contained two sovereigns and threepence. The threepence had obviously been put in to make a noise when the case was emptied.

When Müller gave up his salary he asked the responsible brethren at Teignmouth to open the box in Ebenezer Chapel once a week. However, as these gentlemen either forgot to take it out weekly or were ashamed to bring it to Müller in very small sums, it was usually emptied once in three to five weeks. Although this created difficulties for the Müllers, George decided to say nothing on principle; but for a while the practice led to some narrow financial scrapes. On a Saturday in June 1831, Müller and Henry Craik returned from a preaching visit to Torquay. The Müllers had ninepence left.

'Dear Father,' Müller prayed, 'please impress it on Brother Y that we want money so that he will open the box.'

Next morning at breakfast the Müllers had just enough butter for a friend and a relative who were staying with them. They made no mention of their circumstances, of course, lest their visitors should feel uncomfortable. After the morning meeting, 'Brother Y' quite unexpectedly opened the box and gave Müller the contents - £1 18s and 10 ½d, the equivalent of rather more than two weeks' wages. Poor Brother Y had evidently learnt his lesson the hard the way.

'My wife and I couldn't sleep last night worrying that you and Mrs Müller might be in need!'

Müller found it hard to conceal a smile.

Henry Craik's way of living was the same as Müller's and this deepened their friendship. On June 18th he called on the Müllers.

'I have only 1½d left,' he mentioned in the course of conversation. He later returned to their home having been given a sum of money and gave them ten shillings. They had only three shillings left themselves.

In July a shoulder of mutton and a loaf of bread were sent to the Müllers anonymously. They later discovered that a false rumour had been circulating that they were starving and that an anxious friend had sent these provisions. The truth was that although in the early days they were often brought so low they hadn't even a penny left, or not enough money to buy bread when the last of the loaf was on the table, they never sat down to a meal without nourishing food on the table. Müller conceded, however, that God sometimes used these false rumours to remind people of their needs.

On September 10th Müller was given £6 and recorded in his diary that in the previous month he had received £40 plus all sorts of gifts in kind. On November 16th, the Müllers were forced to pray for dinner as they had no money to buy any. After praying, they opened a parcel which had arrived from Exmouth. Among other things it contained a ham which was ample both for them and a friend who was staying with them.

Müller hadn't yet fully recovered from the illness which had brought him to Devon in the first place. On February 18th 1832 he suffered a haemorrhage in his stomach and lost a good deal of blood. A doctor who, at my request, has studied Müller's diary entries for this period believes that the various symptoms described suggest a type of bleeding which is often fatal – though it is impossible to be certain precisely what his condition was. Whatever it was, Müller doesn't appear to have been unduly alarmed. Next day, on the Sunday morning, two members of Ebenezer who had heard about the incident called at Müller's house.

'What are the arrangements for today's preaching?' they asked. 'We are both due to preach away from Teignmouth today, but assume that one of us will have to stay at Ebenezer to substitute for you while you are ill.'

'Please call again in an hour and I will give you an answer,' Müller replied.

After they had gone, Müller prayed and felt that God gave him the faith to get up. He made up his mind to go to the morning service. Even walking the short distance to the chapel tired him out, but he was able to preach. At lunch time a medical friend called to see him.

'I beg you not to preach in the afternoon. If you do, it may seriously injure you.'

'In normal circumstances,' Müller replied, 'I agree that it would be foolish to preach after what has happened. But God has given me the faith to carry on.'

He preached again in the afternoon, after which his medical friend called again.

'I implore you not to preach again today. If you do, you will be taking a great risk.'

The doctor was no match for the faith of the stubborn Prussian; he preached yet again in the evening. After the service, he returned home and went straight to bed; the time had come when even he knew when enough was enough.

Next morning he rose early and spent a normally busy day. On the Wednesday, after attending a meeting in the morning, he walked six miles with two friends to Newton Abbot and then rode to Plymouth. Strangely, this odd form of convalescence worked, for on the Thursday he felt as well as he had before the haemorrhage.

'I could not say,' he wrote, 'that, if such a thing should happen again, I would act in the same way; for when I have been not nearly so weak as when I had broken the blood vessel, having no faith, I did not preach; yet if it were to please the Lord to give me faith, I might be able to do the same, though even still weaker than at the time just spoken of.'

At this time, Müller frequently prayed with sick believers until they recovered. He would ask God, unconditionally, for the blessing of health; later in his life, he gave up the practice of asking unconditionally for this blessing. Nearly always his prayers were answered, but on some occasions they were not – or were answered with a 'No'. Müller drew a distinction between the 'gift' and the 'grace' of faith. He believed that at this time of his life he was given in some cases the 'gift' of faith so that unconditionally he could ask and expect the answer. With the 'gift' of faith, Müller believed that he was able to do something which if he hadn't done, or hadn't believed, wouldn't have been sinful. But with the 'grace' of faith, Müller believed a man could do something or believe something, respecting which he had the word of God to rest upon, and which if he hadn't done, or believed, would have been sinful. For instance, it would need the 'gift' of faith to believe that a seriously ill person would be restored, for there is no promise that he should be; but it simply needs the 'grace' of faith to believe that God will give us the necessities of life if we seek first the Kingdom of God and his righteousness, for this is promised in Matthew 6.

'I have again felt much this day,' Müller wrote in his diary on April 8th 1832, 'that Teignmouth is no longer my place, and that I shall leave it.'

Since the previous August he had begun to feel that his work at Teignmouth was done and that he should move. He found that wherever he went he seemed to preach with more power and enjoyment than at Teignmouth, which was the opposite of his experience in his early days in the town.

On April 13th Henry Craik, on a working visit to Bristol (attracting large crowds to Gideon Chapel to hear him), wrote to Müller inviting him to come and help him. He replied that he would come if he clearly saw it to be God's will. After preaching at Ebenezer Chapel on the evening of April 15th Müller made a painful announcement to his flock.

'...I have to tell you that I may soon be leaving you. You will remember that when I became your pastor I warned you that I would stay only as long as I felt it was God's will to do so.'

There was a lot of weeping; but Müller was by this time sure he knew God's will. On April 19th, Müller preached the last of his regular weekly sermons at Torquay, and the following day left Teignmouth to join Craik at Bristol. Müller and Craik spent ten days together in Bristol, preaching mainly in Gideon and Pithay Chapels. Their visit was judged a success and there were many striking conversions; they felt sure God was indicating His will for them to work in Bristol. On the evening of April 29th they held a meeting in Gideon Chapel, the last service of their visit, and Henry Craik preached. The aisles, pulpit stairs and vestry were packed while hundreds were turned away when no further square inches could be found. They left Bristol the following day: dozens of people pressed them to return.

'I will rent Bethesda Chapel for you at my own expense,' one man promised.

May 2nd found them back at Teignmouth.

On May 18th, while Müller was praying about Bristol, a message arrived for him to visit Henry Craik.

'A member of the congregation of Gideon Chapel, Bristol,' Craik told Müller, 'has written accepting the offer we made to work amongst them under the conditions we laid down.'

The conditions the two men had insisted on were: that they would preach and work amongst the Gideon congregation not according to a fixed pastoral relationship governed by any rules, but as they themselves interpreted God's will; that pew-rents should be abolished; and that they would continue the practice they had established at Teignmouth with regard to their financial support.

On May 21st, Müller began to call in turn on each member of his congregation at Ebenezer to say his farewells. He found it a trying day with a lot more weeping.

'Were I not so fully persuaded,' he wrote in his diary that night, 'we should go to Bristol, I should have been hardly able to bear it.'

On May 23rd, Müller left Teignmouth for Exeter with his wife and father-in-law. Henry Craik followed the next day. They arrived in Bristol on the evening of May 25th 1832. Just before they left Teignmouth they had been given fifteen pounds without which they couldn't have afforded to make the journey.

Müller had spent two years and five months at Teignmouth. When he arrived, the congregation at Ebenezer Chapel had numbered eighteen; when he left it numbered at fifty-one. Both men had gained invaluable pastoral experience which would be stretched to the full as they worked amongst far larger congregations in Bristol; and both of them, too, had learned to depend on God alone for their needs. Müller was still only twenty-six when he arrived in Bristol and his early maturity is perhaps one of the most striking features of the story so far; but he would need sterling character indeed to carry out the work God planned for him.

5

THE BELL TOLLS

High above the Avon Gorge, where Bristolians enjoy fresh channel breezes, Lady Elton had laid a new foundation stone eleven months before the Müllers came to Bristol. But soon after the ceremony in June 1831 funds ran low and work on Brunel's daring suspension bridge came to a temporary halt. In fact the bridge wasn't completed until after the designer's death in 1859, carrying a new road nearly two hundred and fifty feet above the Avon to link with Clifton with the suburbs at Leigh Woods and Failand.

Magnificent as they were, the high cliffs of the gorge had the awkward habit of depriving a ship of wind; add to this the hazards of Avon's steep mudbanks and a Bristol fog and you begin to understand why already by the turn of the century the city had begun to lose its place as England's second port to Liverpool with its miles of easily accessible estuary. And then, in 1833, a year after Müller's arrival, the emancipation of the West Indian slaves dealt Bristol a blow which hastened the decline of the city in the early Victorian era. Isambard Kingdom Brunel, however, did much to maintain the prestige of the city by his completion of the Great Western Railway and his construction in Bristol of the steamships *Great Western and Great Britain.*

After their arrival, Müller and Craik spent nearly a fortnight looking for lodgings. They paid eighteen shillings a week for two sitting-rooms, three bedrooms, 'coals and attendance'. Craik lived with the Müllers at this time.

By the end of June the way had opened for Müller and Craik to work in the heart of Bristol at Bethesda Chapel in Great George Street; this was in addition to their prior arrangement to work at Gideon Chapel in Newfoundland Street. Large and modern, Bethesda had been built a few years earlier by a group led by a seceding clergyman named Cowan. The congregation, however, had broken up following a theological dispute. The offer for Müller and Craik to take the empty building gave them the opportunity to build up a work on their own lines, as they interpreted Scripture. A local supporter provided the first year's rent, and they began to preach at Bethesda on July 6th 1832.

'They preached alternately,' recalled W. Elfe Tayler; 'one Lord's day Mr Craik preached in the morning, and Mr Müller in the evening; the next Lord's day the order was reversed. From the first they attracted great attention; the chapel, especially at night, was crowded to excess. No doubt this was owing, in some degree, to certain peculiarities connected with their ministry. They were neither of them Englishmen – one being a Scotsman, the other a German, with a strong accent and pronunciation.' Müller saw the funny side of this bonus attraction of his sermons; after one Bristolian was converted, he recorded that she came to hear him preach 'merely out of curiosity to hear my foreign accent, some words having been mentioned to her which I did not pronounce properly. Scarcely had she entered the chapel, when she was led to see herself a sinner.'

During July 1832 Müller and Craik began the practice, which they never abandoned, of setting aside evenings when people could come to the vestry to talk with them individually. On the first of these evenings, so many enquirers came that the two pastors were kept busy for well over four hours.

July 1832 was also the month that cholera broke out in Bristol. By mid-August, the outbreak had reached horrifying proportions and between two and three hundred people met at 6 a.m. in Gideon Chapel to pray for relief from the suffering.

On August 24th Henry Craik wrote in his diary: 'Our neighbour, Mrs Williams, a few yards from us, was attacked about three this morning, and died about three in the afternoon. Her husband was also attacked and is not expected to recover. The bell is incessantly tolling; it is an awful time.' The same evening Müller recorded: 'just now, ten in the evening, the funeral bell is ringing, and has been ringing the greater part of this evening. It rings almost all day.... If this night I should be taken in the cholera, my only hope of trust is in the blood of Jesus Christ, shed for the remission of all my many sins.'

Both men displayed courage throughout and carried on their pastoral work undaunted, visiting many cholera victims day and night; throughout September the epidemic showed no signs of abating.

In the midst of all this danger, Mary Müller was due to have a baby. As labour began, she became very ill, though her illness was not cholera. Müller spent a whole night in prayer; next day Mary gave birth to a daughter. Despite everything, mother and child did well. They called the little girl Lydia and she was their only child to survive infancy.

A week later Müller and Craik were called out of bed to a woman suffering intensely with cholera. They had never seen such a distressing case. They could hardly say anything to her because she screamed so loudly. Müller felt as if he himself had caught the disease.

At home later, the two men commended themselves into God's hands. The poor woman died the next day.

By the beginning of October, the epidemic had passed its peak and Müller and Craik set aside a day for thanksgiving. Miraculously, only one member of the two chapels had died.

Craik's first wife had died young early in 1832 at Teignmouth. In October he remarried. For this reason, and as a result of the birth of Lydia, their first lodgings became too small. When the tenant occupying a house belonging to Gideon Chapel unexpectedly gave it up, the church offered it to Müller and Craik.

'We shall be delighted to furnish it for you,' the church elders said.

The two men objected fearing this would be a financial burden – but their objections were overruled. The house was duly furnished, and Müller recorded that 'the love of the brethren had done it more expensively than we wished it'.

In May 1833, the two churches at Gideon and Bethesda met together for tea. It was the first of many such occasions and Müller loved them – not least because, as he said, 'they gave us a sweet foretaste of our meeting together at the marriage supper of the Lamb'. The two congregations prayed together and sang and then, characteristically, Müller made it clear that 'any brother has an opportunity to speak what may tend to the edification of the rest'.

It was just twelve months since he had arrived in Bristol, and as he looked at the crowd gathered in the hall, Müller thought about the year that had passed. Bethesda already had sixty members; and nearly fifty new members had joined the congregation at Gideon. He knew of sixty-five people who had been converted under the preaching of Craik and himself. Many 'backsliders' had regained their first love for Christ and a number of Christians had been strengthened in their faith. Surely, Müller thought, this was proof enough that it had been God's will for them to come to Bristol.

All this time Müller lived in the way to which he had become accustomed at Teignmouth – depending on God for his needs and those of his family. During his second summer in Bristol (1833), he carefully recorded his gifts both large and small.

June 22. A brother sent a hat to brother Craik, and one to me, as a token of his love and gratitude, like a thank-offering, as he says. This is now the fourth hat which the Lord has kindly sent me successively, whenever, or even before, I needed one. Between August 19th and 27th was sent to us, by several individuals, a considerable quantity of fruit. How very kind of the Lord, not merely to send us the necessities of life, but even such things as, on account of the weakness of our bodies, or the want of appetite, we might have desired! Thus the Lord has sent us wine or porter (beer) when we required it; or, when there was want of appetite, and, on account of the poverty of our brethren, we should not have considered it right to spend money on such things, He has kindly sent fowls, game, etc., to suit our appetite. We have indeed not served a hard Master.

By the end of December 1833 over three years had passed since Müller's decision never to ask anybody for anything he needed, but to rely on God alone. In the first of those three years he had received just over £150, in the second nearly £200 and in 1833: £267 15s 8 ¼d – Müller's accounts never lacked precision!

In 1834 Müller and Craik founded the 'Scriptural Knowledge Institution for Home and Abroad', which still flourishes today despite its unimaginative title. The three aims of the Institution were first, to assist and establish Day Schools, Sunday Schools and Adult Schools in which scriptural teaching was given; second, to distribute Bibles; and third, to aid missionary work. In the financial year ending in 1989, the Institution sent nearly seventy thousand pounds abroad to help missionaries.

In its first seven months after Müller and Craik established it, the Institution provided for about one hundred and twenty children to be taught in Sunday Schools, forty adults in an Adult School and over two hundred children to be taught in two Day Schools. One thousand Bibles and New Testaments were circulated and fifty-seven pounds was sent abroad to missionaries.

On March 19th, Mary Müller gave birth to a son whom they called Elijah – 'My God is Jehovah'. For this reason, after living for nearly two years with the Craiks, George and Mary decided that they and the two children should live in a house of their own. Thus on May 15th they moved into No. 21 Paul Street, an end of terrace house in High Kingsdown. Solid but not beautiful, nine steps led up above a basement to the front door on the first floor of the four storey house. At the back was a small garden which Müller was to use for prayer and meditation. In the eighteenth century Kingsdown had been a much sought after suburb of the city, popular with merchants made wealthy by the slave trade. But by Müller's day it had become less desirable and a little scruffy. The Müllers received several substantial sums to help with furnishing the new house and some carpeting.

Two diary entries in the autumn of 1834 show that Müller's personal needs were still well provided for: 'September 18. A brother, a tailor, was sent to measure me for new clothes. My clothes are again getting old, and it is very kind of the Lord to provide thus. September 25. A brother sent me a new hat today.'

At the end of 1834 Müller recorded that his income had been nearly £230 and that he had received gifts in kind worth about £60. Bethesda Chapel now numbered one hundred and twenty-five and Gideon, one hundred and thirty-two. Of these, over one hundred souls had been converted under Müller's and Craik's preaching.

Müller spent a few months in Germany early in 1835 staying mostly at Heimersleben with his father and brother.

'Tell me about political and social conditions in England,' pleaded his father. 'You scarcely mention them in your letters. Does the English Government forbid the sending abroad of letters dealing with such matters?'

Müller obliged as best he could. By the middle of April he was back in Bristol to find Henry Craik suffering from a throat infection and unable to preach. In May Craik travelled to Devon for a change of air.

June 1835 was a sad month for the Müllers – especially for Mary. On the 22nd she lost her father, and a few days later their son Elijah, now fifteen months old, was taken ill with pneumonia.

'Dear Father, be pleased to support my wife under this trial,' Müller prayed. 'If it is Your will for the little one to die, please take him soon to Yourself and spare him from suffering.'

'I did not pray for the child's recovery,' he recorded. Two hours after Müller's prayer, the child died. 'The eldest and the youngest the Lord has thus removed from our family in the same week. My dear Mary feels her loss much, yet is greatly supported.'

Why didn't Müller pray for Elijah's recovery? According to his distinction between the 'gift' and 'grace' of faith, this was the sort of situation where, early in his Christian life, he sometimes received the 'gift' of faith – that is he felt able to ask God unconditionally for the blessing of health. It appears that on this occasion he didn't feel able to do so. On the day before Elijah died Müller simply recorded in his journal, 'The Lord's holy will be done concerning the dear little one.' And several years later, he wrote: 'When the Lord took from me a beloved infant, my soul was at peace, perfectly at peace; I could only weep tears of joy when I did weep. And why? Because my soul laid hold in faith on that word: "Of such is the Kingdom of Heaven." Matthew 19:14. Believing, therefore, as I did, upon the ground of this word, my soul rejoiced, instead of mourning, that my beloved infant was far happier with the Lord, than with me.'

Financial worries followed these losses. Early in June, the Müllers' taxes were due, and for the first time they had no money to pay them having spent the money they had put aside for the taxes on various outgoings arising from the family deaths.

'Dear Lord, please send us the funds we need to pay our taxes,' Müller prayed.

Two days later he recorded: 'I was enabled today, by the free-will offerings through the boxes, and by what I had left, to pay the taxes before they were called for. How kind of the Lord to answer my prayer so soon.'

Craik returned from Devon in mid-August but was still unable to speak very much, though feeling much better in himself. Müller was suffering from a stomach disorder and considered leaving Bristol for a while. He'd had an invitation from a lady to spend a week with her in the country, but couldn't afford to make the journey. Then £5 was sent him 'for the express purpose of using for a change of air'; and then another £10 came in for the same purpose.

At the beginning of September he travelled with Mary, Lydia and one servant whom they now employed, to Portishead where he settled down to read Foxe's *Book of Martyrs*, feeling too weak for talking, walking or writing. The book inspired him; and as his strength returned he took to horse riding in the country. However, he soon began to feel depressed and bored with 'having for my chief employment eating and drinking, walking, bathing and taking horse exercise ... I would rather be again in the midst of the work in Bristol, if my Lord will condescend to use His most unworthy servant'.

The family travelled next to the Isle of Wight and before retiring to bed on September 29th Müller felt able to pray for the first time during his illness that God would restore his health. 'I now long to go back to Bristol,' he wrote in his diary, 'yet without impatience, and feel assured that the Lord will strengthen me to return to it.' On October 15th (1835), the Müllers returned from the Isle of Wight to Bristol; Müller was fit again and about to embark on the adventure of faith which would make him famous.

6

A Visible Proof

What an excellent example of the power of dress young Oliver Twist was! Wrapped in the blanket which had hitherto formed his only covering, he might have been the child of a nobleman or a beggar, it would have been hard for the haughtiest stranger to have fixed his station in society. But now that he was enveloped in the old calico robes, which had grown yellow in the same service, he was badged and ticketed, and fell into his place at once – a parish child; the orphan of a work-house; the humble half-starved drudge; to be cuffed and buffeted through the world – despised by all, and pitied by none.

Oliver cried lustily. If he could have known that he was an orphan, left to the tender mercies of churchwardens and overseers, perhaps he would have cried the louder.

Thus, in *Oliver Twist* (1837), Charles Dickens drew the British public's attention to the desperate plight of orphans. The book levelled a series of charges against the Poor Law Amendment Act of 1834, which *The Times* attacked as 'that appalling machine ... for wringing the hearts of forlorn widowhood, for refusing crust to famished age, for imprisoning the orphan in workhouse dungeons and for driving to prostitution the friendless and unprotected girl!' The main aim of the new Act was to stop the benevolent Allowance

Systems – under which labourers' wages were supplemented to subsistence level by contribution to the Poor rate – by abolishing relief to the able-bodied outside the workhouses. No able-bodied man would receive assistance unless he entered a workhouse; the workhouses themselves were intended to be kept deliberately uninviting places of 'wholesome restraint'. In fact conditions in the workhouses became a national disgrace; and the children imprisoned within their walls became quickly demoralised by the inadequate and handicapped adults who also lived there.

Leah and Harriet Culliford lived in Bristol in 1835: Leah was five and Harriet nine. The girls' parents were poor and – like so many of their contemporaries – had fallen victim to tuberculosis. Medical science was powerless to help: the future for poor Leah and Harriet looked grim. If they could expect little from the State to compensate them for the loss of both their parents, the attitude of the public was, in general, equally unsympathetic.

In 1835 orphanages supported by private charity were rare. Dr Barnardo founded his first home in 1866 and Spurgeon followed in 1867; the National Children's Home was founded in 1869 and Mr Fegan began his work in 1870. The Church of England Children's Society (then 'Waifs and Strays') began in 1881. But in 1835 private orphan homes were regarded as revolutionary experiments.

In the whole of England and Wales it is possible to trace a dozen orphanages which date back to the 1830s or earlier. They were all small and there was none in Bristol. Eight of the orphanages were in London and the other four in the Home Counties. But even if the Cullifords had lived in this area they would still have been ineligible for nearly all the homes. They would have been barred in the first place on grounds of cost, most homes stipulating that admission was by election by subscribers or by the purchase of annual or life subscription. The cost of a life subscription ranged from about £100 to £250. Secondly, the Cullifords would have been barred from most of the homes on grounds of class: typical prospectuses made it clear that they were for 'children of middle-class parents ... who in their life-time were in a position to provide a liberal education for their children' or 'children who are respectably descended'; one prospectus boasted that 'of the children on the foundation many are the orphans of clergymen, officers and professional men ... no candidate is admitted whose parents have not filled respectable positions in society and, *ceteris paribus*, its eligibility is proportionate to the former respectability of its family'. Another orphanage stated that 'children of domestic or agricultural servants and of journeymen tradesmen are ineligible.'

Fortunately, provision for orphan children, now one of Britain's major social problems, began in the closing months of 1835 increasingly to occupy the thoughts of one citizen of Bristol. While a student at Halle in 1826, Müller had lodged for two months in one of the great orphan houses built in the late seventeenth century by the German Pietist, August Herman Francke, Professor of Hebrew at the University of Leipzig. He never forgot the experience; and late in 1835 he was particularly reminded of Francke's work. Müller's diary contains the following entries:

> November 20. This evening I took tea at a sister's house, where I found Francke's life. I have frequently, for a long time, thought of labouring in a similar way, though it might be on a much smaller scale; not to imitate Francke, but in reliance upon the Lord. May God make it plain!
>
> November 21. Today I have had it very much impressed on my heart, no longer merely to think about the establishment of an Orphan-House, but actually to set about it, and I have been very much in prayer respecting it, in order to ascertain the Lord's mind....
>
> November 23. Today I had £10 sent from Ireland for our Institution. Thus the Lord, in answer to prayer, has given me, in a few days, about £50. I had asked for only £40. This has been a great encouragement to me, and has still more stirred me up to think and pray about the establishment of an Orphan-House....

November 25. I have been again much in prayer yesterday and today about the Orphan-House, and am more and more convinced that it is of God. May He in mercy guide me!

Müller spent many hours praying about his proposed orphanage. He examined his motives asking himself whether the whole idea didn't originate in a desire to win glory for himself. He called on Henry Craik so that his friend could have the opportunity of probing his heart.

'I can find nothing in your motives which I believe to be unworthy,' Craik told him. 'I want to encourage you to go ahead with the project.'

Müller's concern over the plight of orphans in nineteenth century England began rather more than a year before Dickens popularised the situation in Oliver Twist. There can be little doubt either about the tragic proportions of the problem or that Müller's concern was genuine. When he first arrived in Bristol he had been deeply moved by the sight of children begging in the streets; and when they knocked on his own door he longed to do something positive to help. In October 1834, he had recorded in his journal his distress on hearing an 'account of a poor little orphan boy, who for some time attended one of our schools, and who seems there, as far as we can judge, to have been brought to a real concern about his soul ... and who some time ago was taken to the poorhouse some miles out of Bristol' The entry concludes, 'May this, if it be the Lord's will, lead me to do something also for the temporal wants of poor children, the pressure of which has occasioned this poor boy to be taken away from our school!'

But there was another equally important reason why Müller contemplated founding an orphanage: *he wanted to demonstrate to the world that there is reality in the things of God.* As he visited members of his two congregations in Bristol he discovered repeatedly that people needed to have their faith strengthened. On one occasion he visited a man who was in the habit of working at his trade for nearly sixteen hours every day. His health was suffering and his Christian faith meant little to him.

'If you worked less,' Müller suggested, 'your health would improve and you would have more time to read your Bible and pray. You would then know more joy spiritually.'

'But if I work less,' the man replied, 'I don't earn enough to support my family. Even now, while I work such long hours, I scarcely have enough. The wages are so low, that I have to work hard to obtain what we need.'

'This is not trust in God,' Müller thought. 'This is not belief in the words of Christ, "Seek ye first the Kingdom of God, and His righteousness: and all these things shall be added unto you."'

'My dear brother,' he replied, 'it is not your work which supports your family, but the Lord; and He who has fed you and your family when you couldn't work at all, on account of illness, would surely provide for you and yours, if, for the sake of obtaining food for your inner man, you were to work only for so many hours a day as would allow you proper time for recreation. And isn't it the case now that you begin the work of the day after having had only a few hurried moments for prayer, and when you leave off your work in the evening, and mean to read a little of the word of God, aren't you much too worn out in body and mind to enjoy it? And don't you often fall asleep while reading the Scriptures, or while you're on your knees in prayer?'

As he waited for the reply, Müller looked at this friend's expression. He could see that the man agreed that the advice was sound; but yet there was doubt. He wasn't fully prepared to take God at His word.

'How should I get on? How should I get on if I carried out your advice?'

Müller wasn't annoyed. He was sad. He thought, 'How I long that I had something to which I could point this brother! Something that would act as a visible proof that our God and Father is the same faithful God as ever He was; as willing as ever to prove Himself to be the Living God, in our day as formerly, to all who put their trust in Him.'

Sometimes Müller met businessmen who were conducting their affairs in a way which was less than honest. As a result they suffered from guilty consciences; some excused their behaviour by pointing to the fierceness of competition or the depressed state of trade and maintained that if they carried on their businesses according to the Bible, they would never prosper. Only rarely was a stand made for God; only rarely did Müller come across a determination to trust God for everything. In these cases, too, Müller longed to demonstrate that God had not changed: that He would reward those who didn't regard iniquity in their hearts' (Ps. 66:18). Müller had proved God in his own life; he was anxious that others should enjoy the same experience.

'I judged myself bound,' he wrote, 'to be the servant of the Church of Christ, in the particular point on which I had obtained mercy: namely in being able to take God at His word and to rely upon it.'

He felt that God had used his encounters with Christians who lacked assurance and conviction in their lives 'to awaken in my heart the desire of setting before the church at large, and before the world, a proof that He had not in the least changed; and this seemed to me best done by the establishing of an Orphan-House. It needed to be something which could be seen, even by the natural eye.'

Müller had decided to embark on an adventure far more daring and exciting even than the construction by Brunel of his mighty bridge at Clifton. He put the challenge which faced him like this.

Now, if I, a poor man, simply by prayer and faith, obtained, *without asking any individual* (Müller's italics) the means for establishing and carrying on an Orphan-House: might be instrumental in strengthening the faith of the children of God, besides being a testimony to the consciences of the unconverted of the reality of the things of God.

Was the most important consideration which led Müller to found a Children's Home a desire to ease the orphan's plight, or an attempt to demonstrate God's reality?

I certainly did from my heart desire to be used by God to benefit the bodies of poor children, bereaved of both parents, and seek, in other respects, with the help of God, to do them good for this life – I also particularly longed to be used by God in getting the dear orphans trained up in the fear of God – but still, the first and primary object of the work was that God might be magnified by the fact that the orphans under my care are provided with all they need, only by *prayer and faith*, without anyone being asked by me or my fellow-labourers, whereby it may be seen that God is faithful still and hears prayer still.

One evening that December (1835), Müller was struck by the words in Psalm 81:10, 'Open wide your mouth and I will fill it'. Until that evening, although he had prayed much about the pros and cons of establishing a Children's Home, he had not prayed specifically that God would provide the means to do so. But on reading this Psalm he decided to apply the Scripture to the needs of the Orphan-House.

'Dear God,' he prayed, 'will you please provide the premises, one thousand pounds and suitable staff to look after the children?'

Müller had learnt to rely on God alone for the needs of his own family. Now he looked to Him to house, feed and clothe an altogether larger and needier family; he dared to ask God to give further proof of His reality and love.

7

'Whose is the Gold and the Silver'

'December 7. Today I received the first shilling for the Orphan-House. Afterwards I received another shilling from a German brother. December 9. This afternoon the first piece of furniture was given – a large wardrobe.'

On the evening of the 9th, Müller addressed a meeting in which he outlined his proposals for the Children's Home.

'The home will only be established,' he said, 'if God provides the means and suitable staff to run it. But I have been led more and more to think that the matter may be of Him. Now, if so, He can influence His people in any part of the world. I don't look to Bristol, nor even to England, but the living God, whose is the gold and the silver. He will entrust me and brother Corser, whom the Lord has made willing to help me in this work with the means (John Corser was an Anglican Clergyman who had resigned his living to work as a city missionary in Bristol and to help Müller.)

'Under no circumstances,' Müller continued, 'will any individual ever be asked for money or materials. There will be no charge for admission and no restriction on entry on grounds of class or creed. All who wish to be engaged as masters, matrons, and assistants will have to be both true believers and appropriately qualified for the work. Only children bereaved of both parents will be received. Girls will be brought up for service, boys for trade; they will be employed according to their ability and bodily strength in useful occupations and thus help to maintain themselves. The Institution will be for truly destitute children and any orphan whose relatives are able and willing to pay for their maintenance will be ineligible. The children will receive a plain education. The chief and special end of the Institution will be to seek, with God's blessing, to bring the dear children to the knowledge of Jesus Christ by instructing them in the Scriptures.'

When Müller had finished speaking no collection was taken; however someone gave him ten shillings. A woman offered to help in the work and Müller went home happy and full of confidence that he would be able to go ahead with the project.

Next day it began to look as if this confidence would be rewarded. Müller received a letter from a husband and wife.

We propose to offer ourselves for the service of the intended Orphan-House if you think us qualified for it; also to give up the furniture etc. which the Lord has given us, for its use; and to do this without any salary whatever; believing that if it be the will of the Lord to employ us, He will supply all our need.

In the evening a friend arrived at the Müller's home with three dishes, twenty-eight plates, three basins, one jug, four mugs, three salt-stands, one grater, four knives, and five forks – all carefully and precisely recorded in Müller's journal.

'Dear God, please give me further evidence of Your favour towards the Orphan-House,' Müller prayed the next day. While he was on his knees someone delivered three dishes, twelve plates, one basin and a blanket.

'Thank you, Father,' said Müller. 'Please give me yet more encouragement today!'

A little later he was given £50 from an unexpected source.

'Dear Father, I dare to ask for even more evidence of your favour this very day.'

In the evening, twenty-nine yards of material were sent and a woman offered herself for the work. And so it went on.

December 13. A brother was influenced this day to give four shillings per week, or £10 8s yearly, as long as the Lord gives the means; eight shillings was given by him as two weeks' subscriptions. Today a brother and sister offered themselves, with all their furniture, and all the provisions which they have in the house if they can be usefully employed in the concerns of the Orphan-House.

December 14. Today a sister offered her services for the work. In the evening another sister offered herself to the Institution.

December 15. A sister brought from several friends ten basins, eight mugs, one plate, five dessert spoons, six tea spoons, one skimmer, one toasting fork, one flour dredge, three knives and forks, one sheet, one pillow case, one table cloth; also one pound. In the afternoon were sent fifty-five yards of sheeting, and twelve yards of calico.

December 16. I took out of the box in my room one shilling.

December 17. I was rather cast down last evening and this morning about the matter, questioning whether I ought to be engaged in this way and was led to ask the Lord to give me some further encouragement. Soon after were sent by a brother two pieces of print, the one seven and the other twenty-three and three-quarter yards of calico, four pieces of lining, about four yards long altogether, a sheet and a yard measure. This evening another brother brought a clothes horse, three frocks, four blankets, two pewter salt cellars, six tin cups, and six metal tea spoons he also brought 3s 6d given to him by three different individuals. At the same time he told me that it had been put into the heart of an individual to send tomorrow one hundred pounds.

December 18. This afternoon the same brother brought from a sister a counterpane, a flat iron stand, eight cups and saucers, a sugar basin, a milk jug, a tea cup, sixteen thimbles, five knives and forks, six dessert spoons, twelve tea spoons, four combs, and two little graters; from another friend a flat iron and a cup and saucer. At the same time he brought the one hundred pounds above referred to.

When he heard who had sent the £100, Müller was reluctant to accept it. He knew that the donor earned about 3s 6d a week by needlework and decided to visit her.

'While I am most grateful for your generous gift,' he said, 'I want to make quite sure that you thought carefully about what you are doing.'

'I have been left £480 on the death of my father,' she told Müller. 'I have parted with a large sum to pay off some outstanding family debts and I have given my mother £100. I then sent the £100 towards the Orphan-House.'

Müller spoke at length trying to persuade her to reconsider.

'The Lord Jesus has given His last drop of blood for me,' she replied, 'should I not give all the money I have? Rather than the Orphan-House should not be established, I will give all the money I have. Here is another £5 for the poorer members of Gideon and Bethesda Chapels.'

Gifts for the orphanage had, by the end of the year, become so encouraging that Müller was able to talk in terms of opening a small home at the beginning of the following April. At first, he would confine admission to girls between the ages of seven and twelve and allow them to stay until they were ready to go into domestic service. Children would be accepted from any part of the United Kingdom.

Gifts continued to arrive in the new year. On the evening of January 5th, Müller's house-bell rang. A servant opened the door, not to a visitor but to – a kitchen fender and dish, left, no doubt, by a donor with strong views on anonymous giving.

Müller prayed about every detail of his plans and requirements for the proposed home; but until this time he had never asked God to send children. He had taken it for granted that there would be plenty of applications. However by the beginning of February, although he had publicised his willingness to receive applications, not one had been received. He therefore spent the whole evening praying for applications; next day the first was received.

'A large terraced house, No. 6 Wilson Street, is available at a low rental,' someone told Müller.

The situation of the house, close to Gideon chapel, was ideal and he went to inspect it. The property was three storeys high and solidly built. After prayer he decided to rent it for a year and began to furnish it for thirty children. Gifts continued to arrive, eminently suited to the needs of the moment: 'April 2 ... six blankets, two counterpanes, four sheets, eight bonnets, five frocks, six pinafores....

'April 6. One dozen washing basins and one jug ... a set of fire irons, a tea kettle, a coal box, a tin saucepan, a tripod, a tea pot, three cups and saucers, a wash-hand basin, three small basins, and two plates ... 222 Hymn Books.' Müller and his assistants finished fitting out and furnishing No. 6 by early April.

April 11th 1836: the first children arrived, looking pale and nervous. One of them was named Harriet – Harriet Culliford. Some of their temporary guardians, who might have expected Mr Müller to be elderly and bearded, were surprised to find a young man – still only thirty; the children, although they could detect a 'no-nonsense' look about their new father, responded to the air of kindness and calm in his expression. Müller introduced them to the smiling matron and governess whom he had engaged: no one could ever give these little girls back their parents, but here were folk who were determined to do everything they could to make up the loss.

The task ahead was immense: every day, three times a day, for seven days a week there would be thirty hungry children to feed, besides the staff. Thirty pairs of feet would wear out thirty pairs of shoes; clothes would grow too worn or too small and need replacement. Müller knew that if ever the children went hungry or badly clothed, his God would be discredited. But he wasn't alarmed; instead he would repeat to this family and helpers Christ's words in Matthew 6:31 and 33.

'So do not worry, saying, "What shall we eat?" or "What shall we drink?" or "What shall we wear?" But seek first His Kingdom and His righteousness, and all these things will be given you as well.'

By early May, nearly thirty girls lived in No. 6, and money and provision were still arriving steadily, 'twenty pounds of bacon and ten pounds of cheese ... six straw bonnets ... six night caps and two petticoats ... a basket of apples, and three pounds of sugar'. The friends from Teignmouth had evidently not forgotten their former pastor, for in June, a considerable sum of money arrived from Teignmouth plus a gown, a boy's pinafore, a pair of socks, coloured cotton for three children's frocks, two babies' bed gowns, and five babies' night caps.

At the end of September a Bristol doctor offered to attend the orphans, and supply them with medicine free of charge. Müller gladly accepted the offer. In October he recorded the arrival of four and a half gallons of beer, but sadly doesn't tell us whether the children were allowed to indulge.

While Müller made it a firm rule that neither he nor his assistants ever asked any individual for anything 'that the hand of the Lord may be clearly seen', he didn't hesitate on occasions to ask God to 'incline the heart' of certain individuals to give towards the work. In December 1835 he had noted in his diary a prayer that a particular person known to him should give £100. Some months later the gentleman in question had sent him £50. Unusually for Müller, it was some days before he remembered his prayer of the previous December. In his delight, he called on the donor and showed him the diary entry for December 12th 1835, so that they could rejoice together over the precision of this answer to prayer.

Soon after the opening of the Home in No. 6 for girls aged from seven upwards, Müller realised that there was a need for a Home catering for children under the age of seven. In October (1836) he managed to obtain the use of No. 1 Wilson Street for an Infant Orphan-House, together with a piece of land for a playground. He engaged a suitably qualified matron and governess; furnished the house and took in the first children – boys and girls – at the end of November. Some of the eldest girls at No. 6 helped at No. 1 as Müller felt that this training in nursery work would be useful for them when they went into service – Leah Culliford was one of the early occupants of No. 1.

As Christmas 1836 drew near Müller recorded the arrival in Wilson Street of a number of ducks and turkeys – and a hundredweight of treacle. He was pleased, too, that Christmas when a pound arrived attached to a note recalling that occasion when Jesus took a child in his arms and said, 'Whoever welcomes one of these little children in my name welcomes me; and whoever welcomes me does not welcome me but the one who sent me' (Mark 9:37).

In the closing minutes of 1836 – the year it all began – Müller led a meeting to praise God for the blessings of the past year, and to pray for continued favours in the year ahead.

By April, sixty children lived in the two Orphan-Houses, thirty infants at No. 1 and thirty girls at No. 6. Typhus fever raged in Bristol that spring, but mercifully only two children caught the disease and both recovered.

In the early summer of 1837 Müller planned to publish the first volume of his *Narratives of some of the Lord's dealings with George Müller*. He had finally decided to write this only after many months of consideration and examination of his motives. On the one hand he wasn't keen to add to the number of religious books on the market; but on the other hand, his experience of visiting homes in Bristol convinced him that many of the trials which Christians went through arose either from a lack of trust in God, or from carrying on their business in an unscriptural way.

By May 1837, the manuscript was nearly ready to be sent to the publishers. But before he did this, Müller wanted to be able to record an answer to one prayer in particular: on December 5th 1835, he had asked God for £1,000 towards the orphan work. Since then he had repeated the prayer almost every day, and in eighteen months he had received over £900. On May 21st he devoted himself especially to praying that God would send the outstanding amount. On June 15th a gift of £5 made up the whole sum and Müller was delighted. Every shilling of this money, and all the articles of clothing and furniture which he had received, had been given to him without, in his words, 'one single individual having been asked by me for anything'.

8

A Change of Air

In London, the King's health had been breaking and early in the morning of Tuesday, June 20th 1837, King William IV died at Windsor Castle in the arms of Queen Adelaide. While Bristol and the rest of England slept, London saw a flurry of activity. The Archbishop of Canterbury, who had performed the last rites, took leave of Queen Adelaide and drove with the Lord Chamberlain in the darkness through country lanes to Kensington. At five in the morning they arrived at Kensington Palace but found great difficulty in getting in. The porter at first refused either to grant them entry or to rouse the young princess. Eventually the porter allowed the two men in and sent for the Baroness Lehzen; she reluctantly agreed to inform the princess of their presence. Princess Victoria entered the room, a shawl thrown over her dressing gown, her feet in slippers, and her hair falling down her back. The Lord Chamberlain knelt on one knee and saluted her as Queen.

Victoria was eighteen at her accession and her reign was to be the longest in history. Müller was thirty-one but would live to preach a lengthy sermon on the occasion of the Queen's diamond jubilee.

Later that day, news of the King's death reached Bristol and flags were lowered to half mast on ships, churches and public buildings. But Saturday June 24th was a day of rejoicing: the flags were raised again and the church bells rang out their finest peals.

At ten o'clock a procession 'for proclaiming her most gracious majesty Queen Victoria in the Borough of Bristol' wended its way from the top of the High Street over the bridge to Temple Cross through the Mansion House into Queen Square and finally to the Council House.

The Victorian era had begun; and for Müller and Craik the responsibility of caring for two large congregations at Gideon and Bethesda continued. The Bible was the final authority to which they looked in their handling of the two churches. A minor crisis in the summer of 1837, together with the events preceding it, illustrates that they combined their supreme respect for Scripture with an intelligent flexibility of approach – particularly when they were themselves uncertain what was 'the mind of God'. From the earliest days of their work in Bristol they were never quite sure whether only those who had been baptised after becoming Christians should be received into the fellowship at Bethesda or whether all who believed in Christ should be received irrespective of baptism. After a long period of controversy within the church and discussions with Robert Chapman, Müller and Craik decided that they ought to 'receive all whom Christ has received' (Rom. 15:7) irrespective of their views on baptism. Chapman, well-known in the history of the Brethren and a life-long friend of Müller, had given up a highly promising solicitor's practice in London to serve God in Barnstaple.

In June 1837 Müller decided to open a third home, for about forty boys aged seven years and above, first because the need for one was so obvious in Bristol and secondly because without one he had nowhere to send the infant boys when they reached seven. By September enough money had been provided and suitable staff had offered themselves; all that remained was to find a suitable house. Müller was offered another of the houses in Wilson Street – No.3 – which he gladly accepted.

Early in November, Müller's health again began to deteriorate. He woke in the night with a feeling of weakness in his head. After some time, he got off to sleep by tying a handkerchief around his head which seemed to ease the weakness. By November 7th he was unable to work, and although the Boys' Orphan-house was about to be opened and there were problems at Bethesda, he decided to leave Bristol for rest and quiet. An anonymous letter arrived enclosing five pounds for his personal expenses, and he took this as a sign that it was right for him to leave.

He left home with no idea where he would go. The first available coach was travelling to Bath, so Müller climbed aboard. He decided that he would not stay with Christians, because this would mean that he would have to talk which he didn't feel like doing. He booked into a hotel in Bath but found it so 'worldly' that he was forced to visit a Christian friend he knew in the city. This gentleman and his aunts persuaded Müller to stay with them which he did for about a week. The symptoms in his head were now so alarming that he thought he was going out of his mind. The effort required to make conversation proved too much and after a week he returned to Bristol. On receiving another £5 for personal expenses, he travelled with Mary, their daughter Lydia and their servant to Weston-Super-Mare where they took lodgings. Many times, at Weston, Müller was afraid that the trouble in his head indicated the approach of insanity. While there, he received news that one of the girls at Wilson Street had died – but that she had trusted Christ before her death. After ten days at Weston the Müller family returned to Bristol where Müller saw a doctor who assured him that, although his nerves were disordered, he had no reason to fear insanity.

Still he remained ill; he took comfort in the kindness of friends who sent him gifts including pickled tongue, poultry, cakes and grapes. He wrote to his father thinking it might be the last letter he would write. In December, doctors diagnosed the problem as an inactive liver; he now found that going to any sort of meetings at Bethesda made him feel worse, and that any form of mental exertion exhausted him.

The work continued to grow and funds were ample: seventy-five children now lived in the three homes and more arrived daily. On December 12th, a hundred pairs of top quality blankets arrived at Müller's house for distribution to the poor. It was known that Müller was anxious to ease a number of cases of hardship which had come to his notice in the area, and, despite his illness, he arranged for this to be done.

By the end of 1837, eighty-one children and nine full time staff sat down to meals at the three homes. There were enough applications to fill another home with girls aged seven and above, and many more applications for infants than they were able to accommodate. Three hundred and fifty children were taught in the Day Schools run by the Scriptural Knowledge Institution, and three hundred and twenty children attended the Sunday School.

Continued illness and growing responsibilities were getting Müller down. He wrote in his journal: 'This morning I greatly dishonoured the Lord by irritability, manifested toward my dear wife, and that almost immediately after I had been on my knees before God, praising Him for having given me such a wife.'

Eighteen thirty-eight didn't get off to an encouraging start. On the night of January 1st thieves, apparently with an odd sense of humour, broke into Müller's house: they were prevented from access to much of the building by a second strong door and took nothing but some cold meat. They then proceeded to the school room at Gideon Chapel, broke open several boxes but took nothing. Next day some bones, less the meat, were found – some in the boxes at the Gideon schoolroom and one in a tree in Müller's garden.

Müller's doctor now advised a further change of air. Müller didn't want to leave Bristol; but when fifteen pounds 'for the express purpose of change of air' arrived from a lady who lived fifty miles from Bristol, and who had no way of knowing the doctor's advice, he took this as an indication of God's will. He travelled with Mary and Lydia to the home of some Christian friends in Trowbridge, where he settled down to read Philip's *Life of George Whitefield*. He was struck by the prayerfulness of the man and his habit of reading the Bible on his knees. On the Sunday, besides spending several hours in prayer, he spent two hours on his knees reading and 'praying over' Psalm 63. He wrote in his journal:

God has my soul much today....My soul is now brought into a state, that I delight myself in the will of God, as it regards my health. Yea, I can now say, from my heart, I would not have this disease removed till God, through it, has bestowed the blessing for which it was sent ... what hinders God to make of one, so vile as I am, another Whitefield? Surely, God could bestow as much grace upon me, as He did upon him. O, my Lord, draw me closer and closer to Thyself, that I may run after Thee! – I desire, if God should restore me again for the ministry of the Word (and this I believe He will do soon, judging from the state in which He has now brought my soul, though I have been worse in health the last eight days than for several weeks previously), that my preaching may be more than ever the result of earnest prayer and such meditation, and that I may so walk with God, that 'out of my belly may flow rivers of living water'.

The following day, he spent three hours on his knees praying over Psalms 64 and 65. While meditating on Psalm 65:2, 'O thou that hearest prayer', he noted down eight specific prayer requests. At the bottom of the list he wrote, 'I believe He has heard me'. Three years later he recorded that five of the requests had been answered in full and the other three in part.

Despite continued discomfort, Müller's mood lifted as, reading on in his Bible, he came across the fifth verse of Psalm 68 where God is described as 'A Father of the fatherless'. He wrote:

By the help of God this shall be my argument before Him, respecting the orphans, in the hour of need. He is their Father, and therefore has pledged Himself, as it were, to provide for them, and to care for them; and I have only to remind Him of the need of these poor children, in order to have it supplied.... The word 'a Father of the fatherless' contains enough encouragement to cast thousands of orphans, with all their need, upon the loving heart of God.

The Müllers stayed at Trowbridge for another fortnight. On the whole, the improvement in George's spirits lasted the stay – although once or twice he felt ashamed after spending time on his knees reading Whitefield's *Life* instead of his Bible! On February 2nd, although his physical health had not improved, he gave up his medicine and left on his own for Oxford where he arrived at the home of friends.

At Oxford Müller decided on a spell of horse riding. He managed to hire a well-behaved horse with a placid temperament, which, he thought, would suit his troubled nerves. For a while this excellent therapy worked well, and Müller followed Wesley's footsteps – although it's not known whether, like Wesley, he read his Bible as he rode. But –alas – after three days with Müller on his back, the horse himself was taken ill! Müller returned to his Bible study and prayer until the owner told him that the horse was well enough to resume its duties. And so to the stables again, but Müller hadn't long been seated in the saddle when he discovered, to his dismay, that this formerly good-natured animal had become self-willed and obdurate. He tried desperately to control the beast, but it was no use; the creature would not be tamed. Müller's equestrian diversion was thus abruptly and sadly halted.

A friend strongly advised Müller to try the waters at Leamington Spa, and offered to pay his expenses if he would stay there. Having consulted his doctor and receiving a favourable reply he decided to accept the offer. At the Spa he found excellent lodgings for ten shillings a week and was able to write up his journal by his own fireside. 'How very kind of the Lord!' he wrote – it was a typical Müllerism – and retired to bed.

Müller found that the Leamington waters seemed to help his condition, but after ten days inner tensions and temptations disturbed him, the nature of which we can only guess from this entry in his journal: 'Grace fought against evil suggestions of one kind and another, and prevailed, but it was a very trying season.... Today I earnestly prayed to God to send my wife to me, as I feel that by being alone, and afflicted as I am in my head, and thus fit for little mental employment, Satan gets an advantage over me.

Next day, the postman delivered a letter a day late announcing that Mary was on her way; and shortly afterwards, the good lady arrived in person to Müller's great delight. The couple spent some days taking long walks in the Warwickshire countryside and Müller's head began to feel better than it had for several months, although he was still far from well.

Müller was toying with the idea of making a short visit to Germany, partly so that he could offer advice and assistance to some contacts in Berlin who were keen to become missionaries, partly to witness to Christ before his father and brother, and partly also because he thought – rather optimistically perhaps – that his native air would do his health good. He wrote to Henry Craik and his doctor seeking their advice; Craik's reply was to go ahead, but the doctor's orders were to wait a month or two lest the trip should prove too exhausting. So Müller spent March at Leamington with Mary until in early April his doctor, on a visit to the area, pronounced him fit enough to make the trip. George and Mary read Psalm 121 together, 'The Lord will watch over your coming and going both now and for evermore', before going their separate ways – Mrs Müller back to Bristol and Mr Müller to the land of his childhood.

Müller arrived in Hamburg on April 9th, having suffered badly from sea-sickness on the voyage. He spent ten days in Berlin meeting a number of men who planned to become missionaries, and then travelled to Heimersleben to stay with his father. Herr Müller had aged markedly and apparently didn't have long to live. Müller doubted whether he would survive another winter. Relations between father and son were now good and the strain caused by George's conversion had been forgotten. Müller found that his brother was living in 'open sin' and took the opportunity to speak to both men about his faith in Christ. When the day came for Müller to leave, his father went with him some of the way to Magdeburg; as they parted both felt they would never meet again: as it happened they were wrong.

In May, Müller arrived back in Bristol. Since November 6th 1837, he had been unable to take part in any meeting at Gideon and Bethesda. But on 8th May 1838, the congregation at Gideon Chapel listened to the familiar voice reading Psalm 103.

'Praise the Lord, O my soul, and forget not all his benefits – who forgives all your sins and heals all your diseases....'

During the following months, as his strength increased, Müller found that he preached with more enjoyment, more earnestness and more prayerfulness than before he was taken ill. He felt more 'the solemnity of the work'.

Müller was approaching his thirty-third birthday. In the years immediately following he had two or three bouts of less severe illness, but during his long life was never again as seriously ill as he had been in 1829 and 1837-8. And the man whom the army had rejected, claimed many years later that he felt fitter in his seventies than he had in his thirties.

9

'A BANK WHICH CANNOT BREAK'

From the outset of Müller's orphan work in April 1836 to the end of June 1838, finances gave no cause for anxiety: there was always an excess of funds. But as the summer of 1838 drew towards its close, Müller's journal indicated that times were becoming difficult.

August 18, 1838. I have not a penny in hand for the orphans. In a day or two many pounds will be needed. My eyes are up to the Lord.

Evening. Before this day is over, I have received from a sister £5. She had some time since put away her trinkets to be sold for the benefit of the orphans. This morning, whilst in prayer, it came to her mind, I have this £5, and owe no man anything, therefore it would be better to give this money at once, as it may be some time before I can dispose of the trinkets. She therefore brought it, little knowing that there was not a penny in hand, and that I had been able to advance only £4 15s 5d for house-keeping in the Boys' Orphan-House, instead of the usual £10.

August 20. The £5 which I had received on the 18th had been given for house-keeping, so that today I was again penniless. But my eyes were up to the Lord. I gave myself to prayer this morning, knowing that I should want again this week at least £13, if not above £20. Today I received £12 in answer to prayer from a lady who is staying at Clifton whom I had never seen before.

August 23. Today I was again without one single penny, when £3 was sent from Clapham, with a box of new clothes for the orphans.

Müller was later to look back on the period from September 1838 to the end of 1846 as the time when he experienced the greatest trials of faith in the orphan work. They were not years of continuous difficulty: rather there tended to be a pattern of a few months of trial followed by some months of comparative plenty. During the whole period, according to Müller, the children knew nothing of the trial. In the middle of one of the darkest periods, he recorded, 'these dear little ones know nothing about it, because their tables are as well supplied as when there was £800 in the bank, and they have lack of nothing'. At another time he wrote, 'the orphans have never lacked anything. Had I thousands of pounds in hand, they would have fared no better than they have; for they have always had good nourishing food, the necessary articles of clothing, etc'. In other words the periods of trial were so in the sense that there was no excess of funds: God supplied the need by the day, even by the hour. Enough was sent, but no more than enough.

Müller's journal often hints at, but rarely attempts to analyse, why it was that God allowed this period of trial. The clue to his understanding of the situation is best expressed in an entry, in the autumn of 1838, commenting on a gift of money from Teignmouth. 'It is a most seasonable help, to defray the expenses of this day, and a fresh proof that not in anger, but only for the trial of our faith, our gracious Lord delays as yet to send larger sums.' Müller saw a purpose in the trial similar to that in the Old Testament story where God tested Abraham by telling him to offer Isaac as a burnt offering on the mountain of Moriah. In one sense the period was a test of Müller's obedience, and a time when his character was moulded – prepared, in fact, for his life's work.

In the evening of Thursday, September 6th, Müller listened to Henry Craik preach from Genesis 12.

'Everything went well for Abraham,' said Craik, 'as long as he acted in faith, and walked according to the will of God. But when he distrusted God, everything failed.'

As Müller listened to his colleague, he began to apply the lesson to his own difficult situation. That morning, he recalled, the order-books had been brought to him from the Infant Orphan-House, and shortly afterwards the matron had sent him a message.

'Please tell me when I should collect the books.'

Müller well knew that this was the matron's polite way of asking when she could expect the money she would need for the next few days' provisions. He had sent a message.

'Tomorrow.'

But he hadn't a penny in hand. As he listened to Craik, he made up his mind that, despite the seeming impossibility of the situation, he would never try to work out his own solution by means of his own considerable ingenuity. For instance, he thought about a sum of about £220 he had in the bank which had been given to him for other areas of Christian work. It would have been easy for him to write to the one who had given this and say that in the difficult situation he had taken twenty or even one hundred pounds for the orphans. For he could remember the donor saying several times that if he needed money he was to let him know. But Müller decided that this would have been 'a deliverance of my own, not God's deliverance'. In any case it would have been 'no small barrier to the exercise of faith, in the next hour of trial'. In the event he was sent just enough money to meet the immediate need at the Infant Home.

On the Saturday and Sunday no money came in at all so that by Monday morning, September 10th, Müller – with a rare touch of drama – described the situation as a 'solemn crisis'. He decided upon an unprecedented step. Until that day he had never taken any of his assistants into his confidence as to the state of the funds, with the exception of an obviously close helper, referred to in his journal only as 'Brother T'. On this occasion, however, he broke with tradition and went to each of the Orphan-Houses in turn. He called the staff of each house together, he frankly stated the financial situation and enquired how much money they needed for immediate needs. After he had established the exact proportions of the problem he said:

'I still believe that God will help. Although you must not buy anything more than we have the means to pay for, the children are not to lack anything in the way of nourishing food and necessary clothes. I would rather send the children away than see them lack anything.'

Müller ordered an investigation to see whether in any of the homes they possessed needless articles which could be sold; he led his staff in prayer.

At half-past nine in the morning, sixpence came in which had been put in the box at Gideon Chapel. Müller interpreted this as an earnest of greater things to come.

Müller left the Homes and visited Henry Craik to whom he unburdened his heart, putting him fully in the picture. The two men knelt together in prayer.

Soon after ten, Müller returned to his home. While he was praying in his room, a lady called and gave Mary two sovereigns (a farm worker's monthly salary) for the children.

'I felt stirred up to come and have already delayed too long,' she said to Mary.

A few minutes later, Müller entered the room where the lady was and she gave him two more sovereigns without having any idea of the current crisis. A little later a messenger arrived from the Infant Orphan-House: Müller gave him two sovereigns and sent some other money to the Boys' and Girls' houses.

That day, Craik left Bristol to stay with a friend in the country. Müller had intended to accompany his friend, but owing to the critical state of affairs at Wilson Street he cancelled his trip.

Later that week, after meeting with his staff for prayer, one of them approached him with sixteen shillings.

'It wouldn't be upright for me to pray if I didn't give what I had.'

Müller accepted the gift. It wasn't unusual in these years of trial for members of staff to give money to the work, and even to sell unnecessary personal articles to help out at difficult periods. Müller denied that this practice represented a failure of the principles on which he ran the homes. On the contrary he argued that under no circumstances could prayer for material things be expected to prevail unless there were a willingness to part with money or unnecessary personal belongings. 'An Institution,' he wrote, 'like the one under my care, could not be carried on by any rich believer on the principles on which we by grace are enabled to act, except it be that he were made willing himself to give of his own property, as long as he has anything, whenever the Institution is in real need.'

Early the following Tuesday, Müller took stock of the situation at Wilson Street. 'Brother T' had twenty-five shillings in hand; he himself had five shillings. He would, that day as any other day, be responsible for the well-being of about one hundred people, including staff, in the three homes.

The £1 10s enabled them to buy meat and bread which was needed, a little for tea for one of the houses, and milk for all three homes. No more was needed for that day and there was bread in hand for two days. But how would they get through the rest of the week? The funds were exhausted: all members of the staff had given as much as they were able. They met as usual for prayer, but as they rose and went about the duties of the day nothing came in. Everyone ate a good lunch in all three homes after which Müller returned to prayer. Still nothing came in. How could he face the children tomorrow and announce there was no breakfast? Müller became 'tried in spirit'. Seven years later he was to look back on this day as the only occasion when he felt this way. 'For the first time,' he wrote, 'the Lord seemed not to regard our prayer.'

At about the middle of the afternoon, Müller's house-bell rang. A lady introduced herself to him.

'I arrived four or five days ago from London. I am staying next door to the Boys' Orphan-House. My daughter gave me this money for your children's work.'

The envelope contained £3 2s 6d, enough at that time to provide comfortably for all the next day's needs. As soon as the woman had left Müller permitted himself a rare exclamation of excitement.

I burst out into loud praises and thanks the first moment I was alone, after I had received the money. I met with my fellow-labourers again this evening for prayer and praise; their hearts were not a little cheered. That the money had been so near the Orphan-Houses for several days without being given is a plain proof that it was in the beginning in the heart of God to help us; but because he delights in the prayers of His children, he had allowed us to pray so long; also to try our faith, and to make the answer so much the sweeter.

As autumn gave way to winter in 1838 the needs continued to be met almost by the day. On November 21st, after the children had eaten a good lunch in all three Homes, it became clear that no funds were left in any Home. By sharing the supplies of bread between the Homes, however, it looked as if they would get through another day. But there was no money to take in any more bread.

'We must wait for help and see how the Lord will deliver us this time,' Müller said.

As he climbed the hill after lunch towards Kingsdown he began to feel bitterly cold and decided that, to warm up, he would walk home a longer way via Clarence Place. About twenty yards from his house in Paul Street he met a friend who walked back with him. After a short talk, the friend handed him twenty pounds. Müller gave ten pounds to the deacons at Bethesda to help provide poorer members of the church with coal for the winter; he gave five pounds to the work of the Scriptural Knowledge Institution; and five pounds went to the Homes in Wilson Street.

A week later things looked difficult again. At twelve o'clock, November 28th, Müller met with his staff for prayer. Someone had cleaned the clock in No. 1 free of charge and had offered to keep all the clocks in the homes in good repair. But the Infant and Boys' Homes didn't have enough bread or milk for tea. As they prayed, there was a knock at the door and one of the ladies left the room. The rest continued silently in prayer and then rose from their knees.

'God will surely lend help,' said Müller as he stood up.

As he spoke he noticed a note on the table which had been brought in while they prayed. The note was from Mary and enclosed another letter with ten pounds for the children. The previous evening someone had asked Müller:

'Will the balance in hand be as great this time when the account are made up as last time?'

'They will be as great as the Lord pleases,' Müller had replied.

It was this man who had sent the ten pounds.

Next day, eighty pounds arrived from Suffolk and in December a single donation of one hundred pounds arrived besides many smaller gifts.

Thursday, February 7th 1839, the funds were again exhausted. Brother T called on Müller.

'About £1 2s will be needed to buy bread for the three homes and to meet other expenses. But we only have 2s 9d. I have to go to Clifton now to make arrangements to receive three new children.'

'Please be so good as to call on your way back to see whether the Lord might have sent any money in the meantime,' Müller said.

There was enough in the three homes that day for lunch. After lunch a lady from Thonbury came and bought one of Müller's *Narratives* and a copy of the latest Annual Report and left three shillings in addition. Five minutes later the baker called at the Boys' Home. When she saw him arrive the matron of the Girls' Home went immediately with over six shillings she had just received to prevent him being sent away; she knew there was no money in the Boys' Home. With this, plus some money in hand, she bought enough bread for all three homes. At four Brother T returned to Müller's house from Clifton.

'The Lord has sent nothing,' said Müller.

A member of staff gave five shillings of his own money. Müller had been asking God to show him a passage from the Bible to speak on that evening at Bethesda and seemed to be directed to Matthew 6:19-34.

Perhaps the congregation at Bethesda detected a specially fervent note in the voice of their young pastor as that evening he read the chosen portion in his strong Prussian accent.

'So do not worry, saying, "What shall we eat?"… your heavenly Father knows that you need them. But seek first his Kingdom and His righteousness, and all these things will be given to you as well. Therefore do not worry about tomorrow, for tomorrow will worry about itself. Each day has enough trouble of its own.'

After the Bethesda meeting he went to No. 6 for a time of prayer. When he arrived he found that a box had come from Barnstaple. He opened it to find that it contained £8 for the children and £2 for the Bible Fund and a separate donation of £3. Also there was some merino wool, three pairs of new shoes, two pairs of new socks, six books intended for sale, a gold pencil-case, two gold rings, two gold earrings, a necklace and a silver pencil-case.

'We have now to look to the Lord for further supplies,' Müller said to Brother T the following Wednesday afternoon, having just given him the lasts of the money they had in hand.

That afternoon a lady and gentleman visited the homes in Wilson Street. At the Boys' Home they met two ladies who were also on a visit.

'Of course, you cannot carry on these Institutions without a good stock of funds,' said one of the lady visitors.

'Have you a good stock?' the gentleman said, turning to the matron.

'Our funds are deposited in a bank which cannot break,' replied the matron, avoiding breaking the rule never to reveal the state of the funds.

On leaving, the gentleman left five pounds at the Boys' Home.

In March Müller received a letter from Brother T, spending a few days in Devon, which showed that his visit would benefit the children. He had given an Annual Report of the work of the homes to an obviously artful man, who, having read it, devoted himself wholeheartedly to asking the Lord to lead his sister to give some of her valuable jewellery to support the children. Before long his prayer was answered and Brother T returned from Devon with a heavy gold chain, a ring set with ten diamonds, a pair of gold bracelets and a sum of two pounds. Müller took the valuable ring, before parting with it, and neatly scratched the words *Jehovah Jireh* ('the Lord will provide') on a pane of glass in his room. Many times afterwards, until he left Paul Street, his heart was cheered as he looked at the words on the glass and remembered the remarkable way in which he acquired the ring.

Throughout the summer and autumn of 1839 supplies came in daily: rarely more than enough for a day or two at a time, but never too little. The events of one Monday in November illustrated how it often happened that just enough but no more than enough would arrive. Müller began the day with ten shillings left over from the weekend. On the Monday morning he was given a further £1 10s; shortly afterwards a note arrived from Wilson Street which said that three pounds would be needed that day. While he was reading the note another note arrived from Devon – enclosing a sovereign.

Public meetings to speak about God's provision for the children during the previous year had been fixed for December (1839). Müller and his staff now began to pray that when the time for the meetings came, they would be able to report that ample funds were in hand. They always tried to avoid giving the impression at the public meetings – the only time that the state of the funds was mentioned – that they were simply an opportunity to beg for money. On December 4th God answered their prayers: one hundred pounds arrived for the children from the East Indies. Everyone rejoiced that at the public meetings they'd be able to tell of God's rich supply after a time of trial.

At the end of the year, Müller recorded that his health and mental powers were better than they'd been for years. He put this down to God blessing his practice of early rising and plunging his head into cold water on getting up.

They held the usual end-of-year prayer meeting which went on until half past midnight. At about one in the morning, after the meeting, Müller was given a sealed envelope enclosing some money for the children. He knew that the woman who gave it was in debt and that she had repeatedly been asked by her creditors for payment. He therefore returned the envelope unopened believing that no one has a right to give while in debt. He did this knowing that there wasn't enough money in hand to meet the expenses of New Year's Day. However during the morning he received over ten pounds which more than met current needs.

Throughout January 1840, large sums arrived at the Homes and, at the beginning of February, Müller left Bristol for a trip to Germany. He spent ten days in Berlin before travelling to his father's home at Heimersleben. He found his father very weak, but throughout his visit Herr Müller was very affectionate to his son and George noticed that he read prayers and the Bible. Müller left Heimersleben at the end of February and said goodbye to his father for the last time. He died the following month.

Early in March Müller boarded at Hamburg one of the earliest channel steamers bound for London. On deck, he got into conversation with two Russian Jews, who listened politely to what he said, although he didn't tell them plainly that he believed Jesus to be the Messiah. After he left them he watched the two men talking to each other and surmised that they took him to be either a baptised Jew or a missionary to the Jews. After a while one of them came over and spoke to Müller.

'Tell me, what do you really think of that Jesus?'

'I believe that He is the Messiah, Lord and God.'

The Jew became offensive and from that time kept well away from Müller.

At dinner that evening at the captain's table, one of the passengers who had seen Müller's long conversation asked him about the two Jews.

'How remarkable it is,' Müller replied, 'that the Jews in all parts of the world can be recognised as such and aren't confused with other nations.'

'This can only be explained by the Scriptures,' the captain intervened, 'and shows the Bible to be true.'

'I agree,' said Müller and for the rest of the voyage to London had long conversations with the captain whom he described as a 'true brother in the Lord'.

10

LOOKING TO HIS RICHES

When Müller and Craik had arrived in Bristol in 1832, they had found less than seventy regular attenders at Gideon Chapel; they had taken over Bethesda as an empty building. During 1840 they gave up Gideon Chapel, and Bethesda now had well over five hundred members. Of these, over a hundred were added during 1840 of whom nearly fifty were converted under their preaching. In the next thirty years the numbers would again double so that by the 1870s there were over one thousand members. In May 1840, five orphans were baptised and received into the fellowship at Bethesda bringing the number of older children from Wilson Street in fellowship to fourteen.

In 1840 Mrs Anne Evans arrived in Bristol from London where she had attended a fashionable Baptist church. On arrival in Bristol she went to Bethesda with a friend to hear a sermon on the second coming. She has left us a memorable picture of Bethesda at that time and of the atmosphere at Wilson Street in the early 1840s.

> His (Henry Craik's) exposition of Scripture was quite a new feature of worship to me, and it was indeed 'marrow and fatness'. The meaning of the passage was brought out as I never heard it before, and I found myself truly in green pastures. Dr Maclaren of Manchester is the only man I know to compare with Mr Craik. His knowledge of the original language was beyond that of most men of learning, and his

insight into the meaning of Scripture also. It was a great privilege to hear such a man. 'I shall come again,' I said, and I did go again and again, and never went anywhere else while in Bristol. To me it was like a new conversion. Now I heard a clear gospel that I could understand. The Bible became a new book to me. The brotherly love shown was such as I had never seen before. The godly and simple lives of even wealthy people, who had moved in the highest society, was such as to carry one back to the days of the Apostles, and I felt this was indeed Christianity of a high type....

The day after I was twenty-one I took up my abode in No. 6 (Wilson Street) Orphan-House. There followed five years of happy service among the orphans, during which time I was behind the scenes and saw much of the private life of the Brethren, and can therefore testify to the truly spiritual lives they led; their devotion to the service of the Lord, and the unworldliness of their daily private surroundings. Here I saw men and women giving up all and following Jesus in one capacity or another.

The American Bible teacher and author, Dr A. T. Pierson, later described Bethesda as one of two truly apostolic churches he knew.

Towards the end of June 1840 Mr and Mrs Müller left Bristol for Liverpool with eight men and women who proposed to sail for the mission field. Müller accompanied the missionaries to their ship, and before they went on board one of the men gave Müller £6 10s for the orphans.

'The money we have in the common stock,' he said, as he handed Müller the money, 'is enough for us. (They had about £20 between eight of them.) For some months, while we are on board, we need no money at all, whilst you may lay it out; and when we need more, the Lord will again supply our need. The other brethren and sisters have no money of their own, and I desire likewise to have none. The Lord has laid the orphans particularly on my heart, and therefore you must not refuse to accept it.'

On Saturday, August 15th 1840, a crisis seemed to be looming at Wilson Street. All the stores were low, and the income during the past week had been small. On Saturday, too, needs were nearly double those of other days in order to buy in enough for the Sunday. At least three pounds was needed to see the homes through the day; but they were penniless.

At about half-past twelve two ladies called on Müller with £2 7s 6d; Müller took this to the Boys' Orphan-House at once and found the children sitting down to lunch. Brother B handed Müller a note which he was just about to send:

Dear Brother, With potatoes from the children's garden, and with apples from the tree in the playground (which apples were used for apple dumplings), and 4s 6d the price of some articles given by one of the labourers, we have a dinner. There is much needed. But the Lord has provided and will provide.

Also that day there came in from the sale of Reports one shilling; from the box in No. 6, one shilling; from children's needlework, 6s 6d; from a donation of one of the sisters in the Orphan-House, six shillings.

In December they held the usual public meetings to review progress during 1840. Müller felt that the first meeting went well; he was particularly glad that he felt happy that evening, so that no one present could have detected from the expression on his face that he had nothing at all in hand towards the supply of the following day's needs. After the meeting two and a half pence was left at his house.

Next morning, although funds totalled precisely two and a half pence, Müller looked to the living God. At no time had there been less bread in the homes and after breakfast all the bread in the Boys' Home and Infant-House had been cut up for use. Mercifully, at about eleven in the morning, Müller received from Barnstaple a £5 note and half a sovereign; the second public meeting was held that evening.

Müller reflected at this time on the first five years of the Home's existence.

> The chief end for which the Institution was established (he recalled) is that the Church of Christ at large might be benefited by seeing manifestly the hand of God stretched out on our behalf in the hour of need, in answer to prayer. Our desire, therefore, is not that we might be without trials of faith, but that the Lord graciously would be pleased to support us in the trial, that we might not dishonour Him by distrust.

This way of living brings the Lord remarkably near. He is, as it were, morning by morning inspecting our stores, that accordingly He may send help. Greater and more manifest nearness of the Lord's presence I have never had, than when after breakfast there was no means for dinner, and then the Lord provided the dinner for more than one hundred persons; or when after dinner, there were no means for the tea, and yet the Lord provided the tea; and all this without one single human being having been informed about our need....

It has been more than once observed, that such a way of living must lead the mind continually to think whence food, clothes, etc, are to come, and so unfit for spiritual exercises. Now, in the first place, I answer that our minds are very little tried about the necessities of life, just because the care respecting them is laid upon our Father, who, because we are His children, not only allows us to do so, but will have us to do so. Secondly, it must be remembered that, even if our minds were much tried about the supplies for the children, and the means for the other work, yet, because we look to the Lord alone for these things, we should only be brought by our sense of need into the presence of our Father for the supply of it; and that is a blessing and no injury to the soul. Thirdly, our souls realise that for the glory of God and for the benefit of the church at large, it is that we have these trials of faith, and that leads again to God, to ask Him for fresh supplies of grace, to be enabled to be faithful in this service.

During the 1840s, apart from the children's work, Müller's Scriptural Knowledge Institution entirely supported six Day Schools catering for over three hundred poor children besides supporting other schools in Bristol. Müller established an evening class for adults who could neither read nor write. Since the establishment of SKI in 1834 over six thousand Bibles had been circulated and after 1840 other books besides Bibles were also distributed – some sold and some given away. This aspect of the work of the Müller Foundation still flourishes today. During 1840, also, one hundred and twenty pounds was sent abroad to missionaries by SKI.

By the spring of 1841, although not seriously ill, Müller felt in need of a change of air. When he was sent a gift of five pounds for his own expenses he interpreted this as a sign that he should leave Bristol for a while. So he travelled to Nailsworth in Gloucestershire and stayed with friends.

At Nailsworth that spring he began a practice that he never abandoned during the rest of his life. Up until this time he had been in the habit, after he had dressed in the morning, of getting straight down to prayer. But while in Nailsworth he came to adopt the view that the most important thing was to concentrate on first reading the Bible, meditating on the chosen portion:

> that thus my heart might be comforted, encouraged, warned, reproved, instructed; and that thus, by means of the Word of God, whilst meditating upon it, my heart might be brought into experimental communion with the Lord.... The first thing I did (early in the morning), after having asked in a few words the Lord's blessing upon His precious word, was, to begin to meditate on the Word of God, searching, as it were, into every verse to get blessing out of it; not for the sake of preaching on what I had meditated upon; but for the sake of obtaining food for my soul. The result I have found to be almost invariably this, that after a very few minutes my soul has been led to confession, or to thanksgiving, or to intercession, or to supplication; so that, though I did not, as it were, give myself to prayer, but to meditation, yet it

turned almost immediately more or less into prayer.... With this mode I have likewise combined the being out in the open air for an hour, an hour and a half, or two hours before breakfast, walking about in the fields, and in the summer sitting for a little on the stiles, if I find it too much to walk all the time. I find it very beneficial to my health to walk thus for meditation before breakfast, and am now so in the habit of using up the time for that purpose, that when I get in the open air, I generally take out a New Testament of good-sized type, which I carry with me for that purpose, besides my Bible: and I find that I can profitably spend my time in the open air, which formerly was not the case for want of habit.... The difference, then, between my former practice and my present one is this. Formerly, when I rose, I began to pray as soon as possible, and generally spent all my time till breakfast in prayer, or almost all the time.... But what was the result? I often spent a quarter of an hour, or half an hour, or even an hour on my knees, before being conscious to myself of having derived comfort, encouragement, humbling of soul, etc; and often, after having suffered much from wandering of mind for the first ten minutes, or a quarter of an hour, or even half an hour, I only then really began to pray. I scarcely ever suffer now in this way. For my heart being nourished by the truth, being brought into experimental fellowship with God, I speak to my Father, and to my Friend (vile though I am, and unworthy of it!) about the things that He has brought before me in His precious Word. It often now astonishes me that I did not sooner see this point.

The summer months in 1841 were for the Homes a period of continuous prosperity, or as Müller put it: 'one continual even running of the river of God's bounty'. At no period for more than three years had there been so much wealth at Wilson Street. But it didn't last. For six months from September 1841, Müller reported, 'it pleased the Lord ... to try our faith more severely than during any time since the work first commenced'. A long, hard winter lay ahead.

Indeed, so sharp were the trials of our faith for more than six months after (September 1841); so long the seasons when, day after day, only daily supplies were granted to us, and when even from meal to meal we had to look up to the Lord; so long had we to continue in prayer, and yet help seemed to fail; that it can only be ascribed to the especial mercy of God, that the faith of those who were engaged in the work did not altogether fail, and that they did not entirely grow weary of this way of carrying on the Lord's work, and go, in despair of help from God, back again to the habits and maxims of this evil world.... In the midst of the trial I was fully assured that the Lord would lighten His hand in His own good time, and that, whilst it lasted, it was only in order that in a small measure, for the benefit of the Church of Christ generally, that word might be fulfilled in us – 'Whether we be afflicted it is for your consolation'.

After the period of comparative plenty which ended in September, the situation didn't suddenly deteriorate; it's true that by the morning of October 1st Müller had again to record that he hadn't a penny in hand. But help was on the way. In the middle of the morning ten shillings arrived with a note which read: 'Your Heavenly Father knoweth that you have need of these things. Trust in the Lord.' About five minutes later Müller received ten pounds from a lady in Ireland. At the same time he heard from Tetbury that three boxes full of articles to be sold for the children were on the way. Two hours later, fourteen small donations, amounting to nearly thirty shillings, were given to him.

A month later, however, it was rare for donations as large as ten pounds to arrive.

November 23. Yesterday came in five shillings for stockings, which provided today the means for the breakfast in the Boys' Orphan-House. A sister sent also a gammon and some peas. Now we are very poor indeed. One of the labourers (meaning a member of staff) was able to provide a dinner in the Girls' Orphan-House out of his own means. In this our great need came in 17s 6d by sale of Reports, which money had been expected for some months past, but which the Lord sent just now most seasonably. Besides this, 2s 6d was also received for the children's needlework. Thus we are provided for this day also. In the afternoon the Lord gave us a still further proof of the continuance of His loving care over us, now that we are so poor, for a box arrived from Plymouth containing clothes, trinkets etc.

Early next morning one of the articles in the box from Plymouth was sold for a sum sufficient to see them through the day. Müller now held prayer meetings daily at Wilson Street because of the urgency of the situation. When he arrived at this particular morning's prayer meeting, Müller heard that as the infants had taken a walk with their teacher that morning, a poor woman had approached her with two pence.

'It's but a trifle,' she had said, 'but I must give it to you.'

By the time Müller arrived at the prayer meeting one of these two pence had already been needed to make up the sum which was required for the bread.

December was the usual month when the public meetings were held to give an account of the work. But at the end of 1841, times being so unusually difficult, Müller decided to delay the meetings lest there should be criticism that they had been arranged in order to expose the need; the publication of the Annual Report was delayed for the same reason. Müller wrote:

What better proof, therefore, could we give of our dependence on the living God alone, and not upon public meetings or printed Reports, than that, in the midst of our deepest poverty, instead of being glad for the time to have come when we could make known our circumstances, we still went quietly on for some time longer, 'I will now see whether you truly lean upon me, and whether you truly look to me.'

This step of faith was not instantly rewarded. On the contrary, Müller wrote a few years later that:

> Of all the seasons that I had ever passed through since I had been living in this way, up to that time, I never knew any period in which my faith was tried so sharply as during the four months from December 12th 1841 to April 12th 1842.

Throughout this period it remained true that the children neither knew of the difficulties nor lacked good food, clothes or warmth. But there were some narrow scrapes. At midday on Tuesday, February 8th 1842, there was enough food in all the houses for that day's meals, but no money to buy the usual stock of bread (for future use) or milk for the following morning; two Houses needed coal. Müller thought that they had never been poorer and wrote that if God sent nothing before nine the next morning, 'His name would be dishonoured'. Late in the afternoon nine plum cakes arrived, baked by order of a kindly lady. Encouraging – and no doubt tasty – as these were, the situation was still grim as Müller retired to bed that night. He finished that day's journal entry with the words: 'Truly we are poorer than ever; but, through grace, my eyes look not at the empty stores and the empty purse, but to the riches of the Lord only.'

Next morning, Müller walked early to Wilson Street to discover how God would meet the need, only to find on arrival between seven and eight that it had already been met. A Christian businessman had walked about half a mile to his place of work when the thought occurred to him that Müller's children might be in need. He decided, however, not to retrace his steps then, but to take something to the homes that evening. But, as he later told Müller:

'I could not go any further and felt constrained to go back.'

He delivered three sovereigns to the Boys' Home. This gift, together with some other smaller sums, met the needs for two days.

By April 1842 Müller and his helpers had lived through six months of severe testing when week after week, with only short periods of relief, the funds had been no more than sufficient. Again and again money or supplies had arrived with only minutes to spare before the children sat down at table. Müller never wavered in his determination that neither he nor any member of his staff should ever appeal for funds. But his faith had at no time been more tried. How much longer would it last?

On Tuesday, April 12th, the need had never been greater: since the previous Saturday less than fourteen shillings had been received at Wilson Street. Early in the morning, Müller knelt in prayer.

'Lord pity us! You know we desperately need some oatmeal, some new pairs of shoes, money for the repair of old shoes and to replenish our stores, and some money for new clothes for the children as well as a little money which is needed for some of the lady helpers. Please send us some larger sums.'

Later that morning an envelope arrived from the East Indies: it contained one hundred pounds. 'It is impossible,' Müller wrote, 'to describe the real joy in God it gave me.... I was not in the least surprised or excited when this donation came, for I took it as that which came in answer to prayer, and had been long looked for.'

By May, Müller thought it right to publish another Report of the activities of the Scriptural Knowledge Institution including, of course, the Homes. The Report had been delayed for five months on account of the period of trial.

During the previous seventeen months SKI had financed, besides one hundred children in the Homes, a whole number of other activities including Sunday Schools, Adult Schools, Day Schools for children, the circulation of Bibles and Christian books and the support of missionaries abroad. During the seventeen months there had been very little sickness in Wilson Street and no children had died. Total expenditure at the Homes had been just over £1,337 and total income just over £1,339. Mr Micawber's happiness would have been complete.

11

A Just Complaint

Müller spent six months in Stuttgart, with Mary, from August 1843 to February 1844, attempting to sort out doctrinal wrangles which had arisen in a small Baptist church. At no time during this period was there the slightest financial difficulty at Wilson Street. While he was away the first children began to move into a fourth Wilson Street home.

Through most of the summer of 1844, too, there was little difficulty, but as summer gave way to autumn so the funds grew lower.

On the morning of Wednesday, September 4th, the funds at Wilson Street totalled one farthing; nearly one hundred and forty people – children and staff – had to be provided for. But as Müller set about his morning activities, he wasn't worried: he often said, 'Our need is my comfort'. Today, as on so many other days, he would be fascinated to see how God would send help. A little after nine he received at Paul Street a sovereign from an anonymous donor. Between ten and eleven a note arrived from Wilson Street to say that £1 2s would be required for the day. As Müller finished reading the note a hackney-carriage stopped outside his house and a gentleman from Manchester was announced.

'I am a believer in the Lord Jesus and am in Bristol on business,' he told Müller. 'I have heard about your Homes and have been surprised that without any regular system of collection, and without personal application to anyone, you receive more than two thousand pounds a year for your work.'

They talked for a while and the businessman gave Müller two pounds. Also that morning ten shillings came in, being profit from the sale of ladies' bags. More small quantities arrived during the day and a box of articles to be sold.

As winter approached Müller began to pray hard about some specific needs.

'Dear God, please supply me with the means to buy a large quantity of new clothes for the children. The Boys' Home needs painting and the staff could do with some extra money to spend on themselves.'

On the first evening in October his prayer was answered: he received a cheque for seventy pounds. The donor had asked Müller to let him know 'if anything in particular should be connected with the donation.' But Müller wrote in his journal 'though the donation comes in so seasonably, I cannot write to the kind donor thus, lest he should be induced to give more, by my exposing our circumstances, and lest also the hand of God should not be manifest, in providing me with the means for the work as otherwise it would'. The Boys' Home was, however, duly painted and the staff received their bonuses.

Everyone at Wilson Street enjoyed a prosperous Christmas in 1844: Müller described it as a 'season of rich abundance'. In a bitterly cold winter the children's appetites increased to fight the cold. Whenever possible the staff ordered food in large quantities, for instance, on a Saturday in February eight hundredweight of rice and eight bushels of peas were brought. February 12th was the coldest morning of the whole winter: on his morning walk for prayer and meditation Müller prayed:

'Dear loving Father, thank you that I am so well supplied with coal, good food and warm clothes. It may be that some of your children in Bristol are in need. Please grant me the means so that I may be able to be of more help to those in need.'

Three hours later he received a gift of ten pounds for his own needs. There can be no doubt what he did with the gift, although his journal is silent. It is known that during his long life he gave away over £80,000 out of money given for his own use. Apart from this, many donors were aware of Müller's concern for the poor in general and sometimes earmarked portions of their gifts for this purpose.

Lydia was now twelve and receiving what Müller described as a 'very good education' at a private school. After she had attended the school for six months, Müller asked for the account, only to be told by the headmistress, 'I have the pleasure in educating her gratuitously'. He pressed the matter, however, and eventually obtained an account which he paid. However, the exact sum was returned to him anonymously by the headmistress (as he later discovered). Lydia remained at the school until she was eighteen, but despite several attempts Müller was never again successful in procuring an account. 'I was able,' he recorded, 'and well able to pay for her education, and most willing to do so: but the Lord gave it gratuitously; thus also showing how ready He is abundantly to help me and to supply my wants.'

On Thursday morning, October 30th 1845, Müller received what he described as a 'polite and friendly' letter from a resident of Wilson Street'. The letter left it to Müller to decide what action to take.

Not until the following Monday did Müller find time to set aside some hours to pray and think about this new problem. Having asked God to guide him to a right decision he wrote down the reasons for and against moving the children from Wilson Street.

In the first place he accepted that the neighbour's complaint was 'neither without foundation nor unjust'. It was true that – particularly during play-time – the children were noisy 'even though', Müller maintained, 'the noise was only of that kind that one could not at all find fault with the dear children on account of it'. He thought, 'I should myself feel it trying to my head to live next door to the Orphan-Houses ... I therefore ought to do to others, as I should wish to be done by'. Second, with between one hundred and forty and one hundred and fifty people living in the four Homes in Wilson Street, there had been occasions when the drains had been unable to cope and had even affected the water supply.

There were other reasons for moving. The single playground at Wilson Street was only large enough for the children at one Home at a time; Müller wanted the children to have more room to play. Also he wanted to be within easy reach of land which could be turned into gardens where the older boys could work. Another advantage of larger premises would be that all the laundry could be done at the Homes.

Müller was also concerned that the air at Wilson Street wasn't as bracing as it might have been and, bearing in mind that many of the children were unhealthy on arrival at the Homes, he was anxious that they should be situated in as invigorating a position as possible. The teachers and staff, too, he thought, would be glad of somewhere where they could relax in a garden or walk in the fields after hours.

For some years Müller had been looking for property in Bristol which offered these advantages but had found none. Ordinary large houses, built for private families were, he felt, generally unsuitable for use as Homes, being inadequately ventilated.

The more Müller thought and prayed about the matter, the more he began to feel that it was God's will for him to embark on his boldest ever venture of faith: to build a brand new purpose-built Home.

I began to see that the Lord would lead me to build, and that His intentions were not only the benefit of the Orphans, and the better ordering of the whole work, but also the bearing of still further testimony that He could and would provide large sums for those who need them and trust in Him for them; and besides, that He would enlarge the work so that, if I once did build a house, it might be large enough to accommodate three hundred Orphans, with their teachers and other overseers and servants needful for the work.

During no period since the beginning of the work in 1836 had there been so many applications for admission – particularly boys – and Müller found it painful having to refuse so many children a home.

He asked his fellow-workers at Bethesda their opinion and all eight judged that he ought to leave Wilson Street and could see no objection to building new premises. George and Mary began to meet every morning to pray over the matter, and, as soon as they were sure that it was the Lord's will, they started to ask Him for the necessary funds. Müller estimated that he would need at least £10,000.

In November Robert Chapman arrived to work for a while in Bristol. Müller was glad to have the opportunity to consult his friend about the building project.

'I think you are right to contemplate this development,' said Chapman. 'You must ask help from God to show you the plan, so that all may be according to the mind of God.'

The last seven years hadn't been easy: for long periods there had been no excess of funds. Most men would have been content to continue the substantial and worthwhile work at Wilson Street, judging that expansion was neither feasible nor essential. Müller, however, wasn't content merely to consolidate the work; he was now quite sure that it was God's will for him to expand and build. His God, he often said, was a rich God without limit to His resources: 'The silver and the gold are His, the cattle upon a thousand hills.'

On December 10th 1845, Müller received the first donation towards the new building – a gift of one thousand pounds, the largest single donation he had ever received. 'When I received it,' he wrote, 'I was as calm, as quiet, as if I had only received one shilling. For my heart was looking out for answers to my prayers.'

Mary's sister returned from a visit to London.

'I met a Christian architect,' she told her brother-in-law, 'who has recently read your *Narratives* with great interest. He was anxious to hear more about the work. When I told him about your plans to build a new Home, he offered to draw up plans and superintend the building free of charge.'

Müller was delighted. He saw this offer plus the one thousand pounds as an earnest of great things to come.

He looked out for a piece of land of six or seven acres somewhere on the outskirts of Bristol. At that time there was a great deal of speculative building development over the whole area and suitable land was fetching high prices. Müller deliberately issued no circular giving details of his plans 'in order that the hand of God may be the more manifest'. But he spoke to people about his plans if conversation led to the subject. At the end of December he received two further gifts towards the new building – one of a thousand pounds and one of fifty pounds. Thrilled as he was by these gifts he was no less pleased to make the following entries in his journal early in the New Year:

> January 3. One of the Orphans gave sixpence.
> January 10. One of the Orphans having received half a crown from a cousin, gave 1s 6d of it towards the Orphan-House; a sister in the Lord also gave me three shillings, a ring, a pair of gold ear-rings, and a gold brooch.

During January Müller looked into the possibilities of a number of sites, but none proved either suitable or cheap enough. However next month, these two entries appeared in his journal:

> February 2. Today I heard of suitable and cheap land on Ashley Down.
> February 3. Saw the land. It is the most desirable of all I have seen.

Ashley Down certainly offered enormous possibilities: high up in a bracing position on the north side of Bristol with long views eastward towards Stapleton and north to Horfield. And yet it was within easy reach of the centre of Bristol and not too far from Bethesda.

The following evening Müller called at the home of the owner of the land.

'He is at his place of work,' Müller was told.

'May I ask where that is please?' said Müller.

Armed with the information he called at the landowner's office.

'He has just left,' he was told, 'but he is expected to return to his home at eight this evening.'

Müller decided it wasn't God's will for them to meet that evening and returned to Kingsdown.

Next morning Müller once again range the front door bell of the fine house where the owner of the Ashley Down site lived. A servant answered.

'He is at home and is anxious to see you as soon as possible.'

The servant led Müller to the gentleman's room. He looked tired.

'Your enquiry was passed to me yesterday evening,' the gentleman began, 'about the possibility of acquiring land for building an Orphan-House. This morning I awoke at three o'clock and couldn't sleep again until five. Finally I made up my mind that if you applied for it, I would let you have the Ashley Down site at £120 an acre instead of £200 which I was previously asking.'

'How good is the Lord!' thought Müller and signed an agreement to buy nearly seven acres.

Müller received a reply to a letter he had written to the London architect about his offer to help with the plans of the building.

My dear Sir,

It will afford me gratification, beyond what I can communicate by letter, to lend you a helping hand in the labour of love you are engaged in, and I shall esteem it a very great privilege being allowed to exercise my abilities as an architect and surveyor in the erection of the building you propose to erect for the orphans. I really do mean what I say, and, if all is well, by the blessing of God, I will gratuitously furnish you with plans, elevations, and sections; with specification of the work, so that the cost may be accurately estimated. I will also make you an estimate and superintend the works for you gratuitously....'

The following week the architect travelled to Bristol from London, and Müller and he visited the Ashley Down site together.

'This site is most suitable,' the architect told Müller, 'on grounds of situation, drainage and water supply.'

Money for the building was coming in steadily and in mid-February Müller received a promise that five hundred pounds would be paid to him.

The architect finished his plans by the end April: the new building would provide a home for three hundred children, one hundred and forty girls and eighty boys from eight upwards, and eighty infant boys and girls aged up to seven, as well as having proper quarters for staff and teachers. Work wouldn't begin until all necessary funds had been received. The land and building would be vested in the hands of trustees.

In July, Müller received the largest donation he had so far received for his work: £2,050 of which £2,000 was intended for the building fund. He wrote:

It is impossible to describe my joy in God when I received this donation. I was neither excited nor surprised; for I look out for answers to my prayers. I believe that God hears me. Yet my heart was so full of joy, that I could only sit before God, and admire Him, like David in 2 Samuel 7. At last I cast myself flat down upon my face, and burst forth in thanksgiving to God, and in surrendering my heart afresh to Him for His blessed service.

On November 19th Müller rose at five to pray.

'Dear Father in Heaven, You know that publicity has recently been given to the fact that a number of residents of Wilson Street are complaining of inconvenience caused by the Orphan-Houses. Please provide us with the funds so that we can begin building. You know, Lord, that applications for admission are now in excess of places in the Homes and I hate to turn children away. In Your mercy, hear my prayer.'

Müller opened his Bible and read the words of Jesus at Mark 11:24, 'Therefore I tell you, whatever you ask for in prayer, believe that you have received it, and it will be yours.'

'Lord,' he prayed, 'I believe that You will give me all I need for the work. I am sure that I shall have all, because I believe that I receive in answer to prayer.'

After breakfast he had another time of prayer and about five minutes after he had risen from his knees he was handed a registered letter. It enclosed a cheque for three hundred pounds of which £250 was for the building fund. This brought the building fund to over £6,000.

In December he received another gift of £1,000 and in January, 1847, another donation of £2,000 brought the total to well over £9,000.

The winter of 1846-7 hadn't been an easy time for meeting day-to-day needs in Wilson Street. The year 1846 saw catastrophic crop failure of both wheat and potatoes. The American cotton crop, too, was well below expectation, sending prices soaring. The British economy suffered a crisis of confidence with the soundness of the many railway companies being called into question, leading to financial panic. In May 1847 Müller recorded: 'Never were provisions nearly so dear since the commencement of the work, as they are now. The bread is almost twice as much as eighteen months ago, the oatmeal nearly three times as much as formerly, the rice more than double the usual prices and no potatoes can be used, on account of their exceeding high price. But,' he continued, 'the children have lacked nothing ... my heart is at peace, in great peace.'

In June he received another one thousand pounds for the building fund and now estimated that, including fittings and furniture, the whole project would not cost less than £14,500. However these extra expenses – mainly for heating, gas fittings, furnishing, three large playgrounds and a small road – wouldn't be required until some time after the beginning of the building work. He therefore decided to go ahead, and the first workmen arrived on Ashley Down on July 5th. On August 19th the foundation stone of the new building was laid.

A gift of one hundred pounds in February 1848 enabled Müller to buy a new suit of clothes for every boy in Wilson Street, something for which he had been praying for some weeks.

Throughout the winter, when the weather was fair, work proceeded on the new building and by May much of it was already at roof level. But before the first children moved up to Ashley Down, Müller had to deal with the final explosion of a sad affair within the Brethren movement which had been simmering for some years, and would have tragic and far-reaching consequences.

12

STRONGER THROUGH TURMOIL

Way back in October 1832, John Nelson Darby had preached at
Bethesda and Gideon Chapels in Bristol and commented on the
'marked work' which 'dear brothers Müller and Craik' were doing.
Darby was one of the most influential figures among the early
Brethren. Godson of the famous Admiral from whom he received
his second name, he was educated at Westminster School and
Trinity College, Dublin, where he graduated as a Classical Gold
Medallist.

Darby's was a complex personality. On the one hand, when
engaged in one of the many bitter controversies of his life, he
could be obstinate, harsh and rude. On the other, he would
show himself to be deeply sympathetic and warm-hearted.
When travelling, he often preferred to stay with poor families
rather than the affluent, and Brethren history, both written
and passed down orally, abounds with anecdotes which show
that he was especially fond of children – and in turn adored by
them.

His natural ability was matched by enormous energy: by his
death he had founded and guided some fifteen hundred churches
in many countries. His writings fill over forty volumes including
commentaries on most books in the Bible. He translated the Bible
into three languages and wrote many profound and sometimes
beautiful hymns.

Darby said that what led him out of the established church was 'the unity of the body: where it was not owned and acted on I could not go'. And his early years in the new movement were marked by impeccable non-sectarian principles. 'This is the true secret of a church well ordered,' he wrote, 'perfect largeness of heart, as large as Christ's ... keep infinitely far from sectarianism ... You are nothing, nobody, but Christians.'

Although in the early 1830s he had been impressed by Müller and Craik's work at Bethesda he had gone on to comment, 'I should wish a little more principle of largeness of communion'. This was an odd comment, considering that Craik frequently preached for non-conformist ministers and enjoyed friendly relations with ministers and scholars of the established church including Dean Alford, Archbishop Trench and Dean Ellicott. Furthermore, Müller and Craik sometimes invited well-known churchmen outside the Brethren movement to preach at Bethesda.

As early as 1835, however, Darby's early largeness of heart was being eroded by another false principle. In that year, Anthony Norris Groves (Müller's brother-in-law, home for a while from India) visited Plymouth and detected signs that the Brethren under Darby's influence there were becoming exclusive and sectarian. Instead of being knit together by the truth in Jesus, they were tending to enjoy maintaining a united testimony against all who differed from them.

In view of Darby's growing influence over so many newly established Brethren assemblies, Groves had written to him, referring to Darby's 'enlarged and generous purposes that once so won and riveted' him (Groves), but frankly told Darby 'you have departed from these principles ... and are in principle returning to the city from whence you departed'.

By the middle 1830s the early Brethren movement already embraced divergent tendencies within it. On the one hand, those like Groves, Müller, Craik and Chapman strove to maintain the original non-sectarian principle of receiving all 'whom Christ has received'; on the other, Darby and the growing number of churches under his influence envisaged the establishment of a corporate worldwide witness to the unity of the body of Christ and emphasised separation from evil as God's principle of unity.

Other tensions emerged. In 1839, after a fortnight's retreat to consider some matters of church order which had arisen at Bethesda, Müller and Craik had adopted the firm view that there was a need for a recognised eldership and for ordered government within the church. Darby, on the other hand, disapproved of any formal recognition of the gifts of preaching and teaching, fearing that this might lead to the emergence of a select group of ministers. He regarded the recognition of elders as a restriction upon the free movement of the Holy Spirit, drawing a false distinction between the arranged and formal (which was 'of man') and the spontaneous and informal (which was 'of the Spirit').

In the early 1840s, another figure enters the story. Benjamin Wills Newton had taken a 'first' at Oxford and had become a Fellow of Exeter College. He became, for a while, extremely influential at one of the first Brethren assemblies in England – Ebrington Street, Plymouth – the assembly which gave the movement its popular though misleading title. Between twelve hundred and fourteen hundred people regularly used to attend from different churches in the area to hear him preach.

Newton began to raise the alarm against what he considered to be Darby's strange system of dispensational doctrines which he had developed in order to defend a new doctrine of the timing of the second coming. According to this doctrine, known as the 'Secret Rapture', the second coming of Christ will take place in two stages: first there will be the 'rapture of the saints' when Christ will return to take all true Christians from the earth. Only then will the Antichrist arise and usher in the period of 'tribulation'. The rule of the Anti-christ will be brought to an end by the second stage of the coming – the public 'appearing' of Christ in glory. Newton, however – and he wasn't alone – objected. If the Church was to be removed before the tribulation began, he asked, who were the faithful ones who, according to the Book of Revelation, would suffer during that period? Newton didn't see the differences between him and Darby as trivial because he thought that Darby's theory conflicted with a central doctrine of faith. To Newton, the Church comprised all who were redeemed by Christ; the suffering 'faithful remnant' therefore must have been redeemed by an act of God other than Christ's redemption if they were to be separated from the Church at the first rapture.

Darby asserted that considerable sections of the New Testament applied not to the Church but only to a future dispensation of the restored Jewish remnant.

'In making that distinction,' Newton told him, 'you virtually give up Christianity.'

However, the influence of Darby's personality meant that his view of the second coming 'at any moment' gained a wide acceptance not only within the Brethren movement. Over the years it has been adopted by many evangelical Anglicans and large numbers of fundamentalists in Britain and America; the process has been forwarded by the adoption of the theory, and its elaborate dispensational basis, by Scofield in his popular reference Bible.

Newton wasn't alone in rejecting the new view as a flawed innovation. Notably Müller, Craik, Chapman and S. P. Tregelles firmly held to the view that certain events must take place before Christ's return – although that return (not death) remained for them the great hope of the Church. Among Anglicans, Archbishop Trench, Dean Alford, Bishops Ellicott and Ryle were among those upholding the ancient faith.

Sadly these emerging tensions between the early Brethren and particularly between Darby and Newton destroyed the tranquility of the Ebrington Street assembly. Soon after Darby returned from a lengthy visit to the Continent in 1845, a disastrous strife between him and Newton broke the peace of the church and almost stopped the progress of the work.

Darby began his own teaching sessions in Plymouth and began to attack both Newton's doctrines and Newton himself. He announced that he was withdrawing from the fellowship at Ebrington Street, a step which he later admitted had been precipitous.

In 1847, the emphasis of the conflict switched to a new point of doctrine, concerning the person and sufferings of Christ. It was not of course the first squabble in church history, and sadly has not been the last, brought about by finite minds attempting to grapple with both the humanity and deity of Christ. Darby condemned some views Newton had published in a tract as 'blasphemous doctrines' and Müller, who agreed with Newton on the second coming, observed that the views in Newton's latest tract seemed to imply 'that Christ himself needed a Saviour'. Craik suspected that Newton's errors were 'only those of a rash speculative intellectualist, who is yet sound at heart and seeking to honour Christ'. Later in the year, Newton realised the error of his thinking and published a statement readily admitting that he had erred in his tract. His statement ended: 'I trust that the Lord will not only pardon, but will graciously counteract any evil effects which may have arisen to any therefrom'.

It is a tragedy that the dispute didn't end at this point. Darby tried to show that Newton hadn't really renounced his errors despite Newton's vigorous profession to the contrary. The result was that the church at Ebrington Street virtually disintegrated, and Newton's connection with the Brethren ceased. He lived until 1899 retreating into a little circle of churches of his own; he still wrote articles and pamphlets which Müller later said were 'sound and scriptural' and which he and his wife read 'with deepest interest and profit'.

At the end of April 1848, Darby visited Bristol and called on Müller as was his usual custom. Müller invited him to preach the following Sunday at Bethesda, but he declined on the grounds of a previous engagement.

In May two members of the Ebrington Church came to Bristol and applied for communion at Bethesda. One of the men had been abroad during the Plymouth troubles and was therefore admitted but the other application was held over for consideration. Some of Darby's supporters within Bethesda raised objections to the gentleman's reception, and Craik then suggested that the three men most opposed to the applicant's reception should visit him.

They did this and pronounced both men clear of Newton's alleged heresy.

At a meeting in Exeter, Darby then publicly announced that he could never again go to Bethesda because the church had received 'Newton's followers'. He then confirmed this in a letter to Müller; and later alleged that Newton's followers had circulated his writings within Bethesda. Darby's followers at Bethesda now began to press for a formal investigation by the church into Newton's teachings (which had of course already been condemned and withdrawn by their author).

In June, one of Darby's followers, George Alexander, withdrew from Bethesda; and the elders were forced to summon a church meeting. At this meeting a statement (which became known as the *Letter of the Ten*) signed by ten of the elders, including, of course, Müller and Craik, was read and sanctioned by the majority of the church. Darby's sympathisers, however, promptly withdrew from fellowship.

The statement set out the view held at Bethesda concerning the humanity of Christ and stated that while Christ 'suffered outwardly the trials connected with His being a man and an Israelite – still in His feelings and experiences, as well as in His external character, He was entirely "separate from sinners"'.

The statement went on to give nine reasons why the elders felt themselves unable to comply with George Alexander's request that they should formally investigate and give judgment on Newton's errors. Their ninth reason introduced a welcome element of humour into the situation: 'We felt that compliance with Mr Alexander's request would be the introduction of an evil precedent. If a brother has a right to demand our examining a work of fifty pages, he may require our investigating error said to be contained in one of much larger dimensions; so that all our time might be wasted in the examination of other people's errors, instead of more important service'.

Darby didn't see the joke however and, on a visit to Yorkshire, found that Brethren assemblies there were sympathising with Bethesda. Thus on August 26th he issued from Leeds a circular excommunicating Bethesda 'en bloc' for allegedly receiving holders of Newton's views into the church! He urged Brethren assemblies everywhere to 'judge the Bethesda question'.

Müller and Craik showed no signs of panic and took no immediate action. One of Darby's followers wrote a paper attempting to show that one of Craik's publications was unsound. However Darby well knew that the able and experienced Craik was solidly orthodox and Darby was reported to have thrown his own supporter's paper into the fire.

On October 31st Müller decided to act. He publicly announced his personal condemnation of Newton's teachings and at a series of church meetings made clear that no one defending, maintaining or upholding Newton's (now retracted) views would be received into communion at Bethesda.

From that time on, Brethren assemblies who refused to apply Darby's decree against Bethesda came to be known as 'Open Brethren' (their late twentieth century successors prefer the title 'Christian Brethren') and those who followed Darby became known as 'Exclusive Brethren'. Anthony Norris Groves' son Henry maintained that more was done at Bethesda to judge and repudiate Newton's views than at any assembly acting under Darby's discipline. Darby's circle of churches came to believe in all sincerity that Bethesda had been cut off for holding Newton's views; whereas in fact Newton himself had repudiated the errors and the church at Bethesda had never entertained them for one moment.

Bethesda and the 'open meetings' which sided with her, steadfastly maintained the independence of each local church in deciding whom it received into fellowship; whereas exclusives argued that this wasn't 'practical unity of the body'.

Mrs Anne Evans continued to be a member of Bethesda throughout this sad and turbulent period. She described it as a 'time of agony of intense sorrow and upheaval'. Bethesda was, she wrote: for a time shattered from end to end. Friendships were broken up; families were divided

– husband from wife, children from parents, business relations were dissolved, health and even reason wrecked. We (at Bethesda) sadly needed humbling. We had begun to think too much of ourselves. We had increased rapidly in numbers and even in worldly standing, for many had joined us from the upper classes. Our leading brethren, too, were without any check.... All this was more than flesh and blood could stand, so Satan was permitted to come down on us and humble our pride in the dust.

But all was not lost. Anne Evans continued:

At this time of sorrow Mr George Müller was a grand stay to us; he did not lose his head; he held the reins with a steady hand; and when at last Bethesda emerged from the turmoil she was stronger, freer than ever before. We had increased in numbers (by the middle 1850s there were nearly seven hundred members). The orphan work, which was to have come to nought, was the 'wonder of the world'....

When the great Revival commenced the Open Brethren threw themselves with heart and soul into it. It was the reading of George Müller's book by two young men that led to it.

But that is a story for a later chapter.

13

MÜLLER'S SECRET TREASURE

By the time Darby had issued his circular excommunicating Bethesda, builders working at the new Orphan-House had completed the roof and part of the interior plastering. Over eleven thousand pounds had been given, and rather more than three thousands pounds were still needed in order to complete the work and fittings.

In February 1849 Müller spent long hours making final preparations before he could receive the first children and praying that the total cost would soon be met. Another fifteen hundred pounds came in mostly in two sizeable gifts.

'A visitor is here to see you,' he was told on the morning of February 11th.

'I had intended,' the visitor began after they were introduced, 'to leave your Institution money in my will, but I have now decided to give you this money in my life-time. I am particularly anxious that my name should be concealed and therefore have not written out a cheque so that even my bank will not know of my donation. Here is the money in cash.'

The visitor handed Müller two thousand pounds in cash.

'It is impossible to describe,' Müller wrote, 'the real joy I had in God when I received this sum. I was calm, not in the least excited, able to go on immediately with other work that came upon me...; but inexpressible was the delight which I had in God, who had thus given me the full answer to my thousands of prayers, during these eleven hundred and ninety five days.' The gift gave Müller the means to meet all the expenses for the new home plus some sixty pounds to spare. Altogether he received nearly sixteen thousand pounds for the new home including nearly seventy pounds from the sale of grass and turf from the field on which the home was built, and £750 interest: Müller took the view that 'as a steward of large sums, which were entrusted to me, I ought to invest the money, till it was actually needed'.

Monday June 18th 1849 – great excitement at Wilson Street: the first children were ready to move up to Ashley Down. How the first sight of this large new building took their breath away! How they enjoyed the sound of the birds singing, the sight of cows grazing in the fields, and the view across the valley towards Stapleton! Once inside, even the fresh paint and newly polished woodwork smelt good, and the whole place was bright and well ventilated. By Thursday everyone, including the teachers and staff, had moved in: one hundred and forty people under one roof. By Saturday Müller was able to report that 'there is already such a measure of order established in the house, by the help of God, as that things can be done by the minute hands of the time-pieces'.

During the first week, Müller was showing a visitor through the new home.

'These children must consume a great deal of provisions.'

As he spoke he took from his pocket a roll of bank notes amounting to one hundred pounds. On the same evening a large cask of treacle arrived at the home, with six loaves of sugar. A cooper made two large casks for treacle free of charge. Next day ten hundredweight of rice was delivered. 'After all the many and long-continued seasons of great trial of faith,' said Müller, 'within these thirteen years and two months, during which the orphans were in Wilson Street, the Lord dismisses us from thence in comparative abundance. His holy name be praised for it!'

'Mr J. N. Darby is waiting to see you downstairs,' an assistant told Müller the following month.

What actually occurred during the encounter which followed has since been hotly disputed: the following is based on Müller's account. At ten to one Müller entered the room where Darby was and shook him by the hand.

'As you have now judged Newton's tracts,' Darby said, 'the reason why we should not be united no longer exists.'

'I have only ten minutes now free,' Müller replied, 'having an engagement at one o'clock, and therefore cannot now enter upon this subject; for you have acted so wickedly in this whole affair, that many things have to be looked into before we could be really united again.'

At this Darby rose and left. The two men never saw each other again. Darby (who died in 1882) later denied that Müller's account of the interview was correct but there is apparently no record of Darby's version of the event. Professor F. F. Bruce, one of the leading figures among the Brethren today, has commented that 'a more gracious answer (by Müller) might have redeemed that never-to-be repeated opportunity. Like Müller, Darby had the qualities of his nationality, and his Irish impulsiveness might well have warmed to a less severe response'.

Every week Müller now took in five to eight new children, and by May 1850 over three hundred people sat down every day to meals on Ashley Down including a staff of over thirty. Every Wednesday afternoon parties of visitors were shown around the New Orphan-house, as it was known.

'We met at the door,' one visitor recalled, 'a little after two o'clock, a pretty numerous party of all ranks in life, waiting for admission. When the doors were opened, we found ourselves in a very small hall, from whence a stone staircase leads up into a spacious room in the central building, where visitors wait for their guide. This room is a perfect square, with the four angles taken off by the width of the windows, which we found looked into large pitched play-courts, with covered sheds for the children's use in wet weather. One court we saw was appropriated to infants of both sexes, a number of whom were toddling about under the charge of two or three older girls; another to girls; the third to boys; while the fourth window overlooks the part of the garden through which the visitors approach.

'Our guide entered, and took charge of the forty or fifty who had by this time assembled.... We proceeded into the Infants' Day Room, where we found a tribe of little things, under the care of the nurse. Ranged round one side of this room are a number of little basket beds, for the use of the youngsters when tired of play.

'We found in one room about a dozen boys, under the care of a female, quietly and busily engaged in the very necessary employment of darning stockings, which attracted the sympathy of the female part of the company most wonderfully. One lady, advanced in life, was quite carried away by her enthusiasm – "One thread up and one thread down, is the very perfection of darning." Some, perhaps, of these boys may at a future time be in the navy, others may chance to be emigrants; and we can hardly estimate the value of this humble but necessary art in such circumstances. Even in the very common experience of apprentices in this country, it will often prove of great advantage to them. In any case we admire the practical wisdom that insists, even in mending stockings, on teaching the best way. In the younger department are pigeon-holed cupboards for putting away their toys, when out of use. They were well-furnished with nearly every description that a general shop would supply.

'The washing-places, we observed, are furnished with baths, and on the walls is hung each child's little bag, numbered, with comb and hair-brush. The most scrupulous care is evidently bestowed to ensure thorough cleanliness of both persons and linen, as well as to guard against the communication of any infantile juvenile complaints from personal contact.

'In going through this most interesting establishment we were most forcibly impressed with the entire absence of a pauperised look in the dress and appearance of the children. The hair of the girls is beautifully neat, such as we could fancy a mother's love attended to; and there was a cheerful looking-up at the visitors, and a heart-smile on the young faces, which prove indisputably that both in Principal and Assistants the spring of action is Love, and that the presiding and pervading spirit which rules the entire establishment is the Law of Kindness. In fact, it is impossible to help being thoroughly convinced that the best of practical management exists in every department, and that everyone engaged in the work is admirably fitted for his duties, and has a hearty unselfish love of the work for its own sake.'

Although Müller now cared for three hundred children, he had a long and quickly growing waiting list of children seeking admission: in December 1850 the list ran to seventy-eight names (by 1856 it had grown to nearly eight hundred and fifty names). He found it distressing to turn even one child away.

There was still no other home in the United Kingdom with such a radical admissions policy. Most orphan homes made the admission of really destitute children, that is children who had lost both their parents, very difficult if not hopeless. Admission by means of votes from donors precluded the really poor from making use of orphanages as they normally didn't have the time or money needed to obtain the necessary votes. In the case of Müller's Home, nothing was necessary except application to Müller – no money, no subscribers, no votes were required. The very poorest people, without influence, without friends, without expense, wherever they lived in the United Kingdom, of whatever religious denomination or none, who applied on behalf of children who had lost both their parents could have the children admitted provided there were vacancies. Neither national nor local government made proper provision for orphans. An official report published in 1845 said that there were six thousand orphans in English prisons. 'By God's help,' Müller wrote, 'I will do what I can to keep poor orphans from prison.'

Müller began to consider the possibility of building another home large enough to accommodate seven hundred children so that he could care for one thousand altogether. He was particularly depressed by what he heard about conditions in workhouses. 'I have heard it again and again, from good authority, that children, placed in the Unions, are corrupted, on account of the children of vagrants, and other very bad young people who are in such places; so that many poor relatives of orphans, though unable to provide for them, cannot bear the idea of their going there, lest they should be corrupted.

In January 1851 Müller received the biggest donation for his work that he had been given to date: three thousand pounds. 'This donation ... like a voice from heaven, speaking to me concerning a most deeply important matter, respecting which I am seeking guidance from the Lord, the building of another Orphan-House.' For five months he continued to think about the matter, writing down eight reasons against enlarging the work, plus an answer to each objection and then eight reasons for building a new home for seven hundred children.

In April he received a donation to which a vicar, an archdeacon and one of the Queen's chaplains had contributed.

In May 1851 he finally decided to go ahead with his plans for expansion, and began to pray that God would provide him with the necessary means – about £35,000, he estimated. 'The greatness of the sum required affords me a kind of secret joy; for the greater the difficulty to be overcome, the more will it be seen to the glory of God, how much can be done by prayer and faith.'

In August, Müller received a cheque for five hundred pounds, but in the early months of the new venture he received few large sums. For several months in the summer of 1851 a report was doing the rounds that he already had thirty thousand pounds in hand for the building fund: it was a false report, the actual figure being less than twelve hundred pounds. Müller refused on principle to deny the rumour (he never commented on the state of the funds).

'Lord, You know how small an amount Your servant has,' he prayed, 'in comparison with what is needed. But You know that Your servant did not act rashly and under excitement in this matter, but waited upon You for six months in secret before he spoke about his intention. Now Lord, in Your mercy, sustain Your servant's faith and patience, and, if it please You, speedily refresh his heart by sending large sums, for which he is looking, and which he confidently expects.'

There was no immediate answer to the prayer and for some months it seemed that the persistent rumour about a very large sum being already in hand was affecting donations. By March 1852, funds were running so low in the day-to-day expenses account that on the 16th there was actually no money in hand except the balance in the building fund.

Müller was at his home in Paul Street expecting a member of his staff to arrive from Ashley Down for more money.

'Dear Heavenly Father,' he prayed, 'grant that I shall not have to withdraw money from the building fund for day-to-day needs.'

Just before the assistant arrived, he received 'from a noble lady' fifteen pounds which he passed on towards immediate urgent needs.

Next day, Müller received a donation of just under one thousand pounds of which he took two hundred pounds for current expenses, six hundred pounds for the building fund and the rest for school, Bible, tract and missionary expenses.

This was one of the worst periods in the history of the Homes for sickness. Over a period of nearly four months, more than one hundred children in the new Home became seriously ill with scarlet fever and five died.

Donations often arrived from far away. An Australian shepherd who had read Müller's *Narratives* while watching over his sheep sent a gift; a little girl in New Zealand set a hen apart for the orphans and sent the money from sale of the eggs; other donations came from the East and West Indies, the United States, Nova Scotia, Tahiti, Canada, India, Ceylon, Africa, the Cape of Good Hope, Turkey, France, Switzerland, Germany and Italy.

Towards the end of 1852 Müller prayed especially hard that God would send him some larger sums. At last, in January 1853, he received a promise that as the joint donation of several Christians, he was to receive eight thousand one hundred pounds. 'Day by day, for nineteen months,' he wrote, 'I had been looking out for more abundant help than I had had. I was fully assured that God would send help with larger sums; yet the delay was long. See how precious it is to wait on God! See how those who do so are not confounded! ... Have I then been boasting in God in vain? Is it not manifest that it is most precious, in every way, to depend upon God?'

By Monday June 13th the current account was down to about twelve pounds. Various things were needed including: flour – at that time about ten sacks were bought a week, three hundred stones of oatmeal, four hundredweight of soap; and there were a number of repairs being carried out in the house employing a number of workmen, besides the regular current expenses of about £70 a week. On top of this, the previous Saturday Müller had discovered a fault in the heating system which would cost about £25 to repair.

That morning, as Müller climbed the hill from Paul Street to Ashley Down, he prayed as he walked.

'Lord, it is a Monday when generally little comes in. But if it is Your will you can send what we need.'

On arrival at his room at the new Orphan-House he found a cheque for over £300.

> The joy which I had cannot be described. I walked up and down in my room for a long time, tears of joy and gratitude to the Lord running plentifully over my cheeks, praising and magnifying the Lord for His goodness and surrendering myself afresh, with all my heart, to Him for His blessed service. I scarcely ever felt more the kindness of the Lord in helping me.

Early in January (1854) Müller received the promise of a further large donation, this time of over five thousand pounds. A year later he again received from a number of Christian friends the promise of nearly six thousand pounds. These large sums brought the time much nearer when he could start work on the second building.

For some time Müller had been thinking that instead of putting up one enormous building for seven hundred children as he had originally envisaged it might be better to build two houses for four hundred in one and three hundred in the other. He therefore measured out the ground on each side of 'No. 1' and judged that the idea seemed feasible. He called an architect to survey the ground and make a rough plan for two Houses; this confirmed that the project was possible.

Thus Müller decided to make an immediate start on building a second Home to the south of No. 1 to house four hundred girls. In May workmen sunk four wells on the site and work began. The list of names of children who wished to enter the homes now numbered six hundred.

In February 1856, Müller received another large donation of three thousand pounds and in March a further four thousand pounds arrived.

People came with all sorts of ingenious explanations to account for the remarkable success which Müller achieved in raising these large sums of money without ever appealing for funds. Some said it was because he was a foreigner; others put it down to the novelty of the thing; some decided that Müller must have access to some secret treasure; but the most popular explanation was that it was all the result of the Annual Reports which Müller produced. Müller replied to these explanations with some wit.

> My being a foreigner, looked at naturally, would be more likely to hinder my being entrusted with such large sums than to induce donors to give. As to novelty procuring the money, the time is long gone by for novelty, for this is June 1856 and the work commenced in March 1834. As to the secret treasure to which I have access, there is more in this supposition than the objectors are aware of; for surely God's treasury is inexhaustible, and I have drawn that (though that alone) to go to, and have indeed drawn out of it, simply by prayer and faith, more than £113,000 since the beginning of the work.

As to the objection that the Reports were the means by which all the money was raised, Müller replied like this.

> There is nothing unusual in writing Reports. This is done by public Institutions generally, but the constant complaint is that the Reports are not read. Our Reports

are not extraordinary as to the power of language, or as to striking appeals to feelings. They are simply statements of facts. The Reports are not accompanied by personal application for means; but they are simply sent to donors, or to any individuals who wish to have or purchase them. If they produce results, which Reports generally do not, I can only ascribe it to the Lord.

...we doubt not that the Lord has again and again used the Reports as instruments in leading persons to help us with means. For as we continually stand in need of considerable sums; and as even hundreds of pounds go but a very little way, I entreat the Lord day by day, and generally several times every day, to supply me with means, to speak to the hearts of His dear children, and to constrain them by the love of Christ to help me out of the means with which He has entrusted them; and so it comes to pass, I doubt not, that the Lord again and again works by His Spirit in the hearts of those who have read or heard the Reports. But whether we are supplied with means through the Reports or irrespective of them; in either case it is God who is working for us....

The following letter arrived on Müller's doorstep.

October 11th 1856

Dear Sir,

In admiration of the services which you have rendered to poor orphans and mankind in general, I think it right that some provision should be made for yourself. I think it right to send you £100 as a beginning (which I hope many good Christians will add to), to form a fund for the maintenance of you and your family, and I hope you will lay out this as a beginning accordingly. May God bless you and your labours, as He has hitherto done everything connected with your institutions.

I am, dear Sir,

Müller saw the letter as a temptation to put his trust in something other than God Himself, and replied as follows:

> 21 Paul Street
> Kingsdown
> Bristol
> October 12th 1856

My dear Sir,

I hasten to thank you for your kind communication, and to inform you that your cheque for £100 has safely come to hand.

I have no property whatever, nor has my dear wife; nor have I had one single shilling regular salary as Minister of the Gospel for the last twenty-six years, nor as the director of the Orphan-House and the other objects of the Scriptural Knowledge Institution for Home and Abroad. When I am in need of anything, I fall on my knees and ask God that He would be pleased to give me what I need; and He puts it in the heart of someone or other to help me. Thus all my wants have been amply supplied during the last twenty-six years, and I can say, to the praise of God, I have lacked nothing. My dear wife and only child, a daughter of twenty-four years old, are of the same mind. Of this blessed way of living none of us is tired, but we become day by day more convinced of its blessedness.

I have never thought it right to make provision for myself, or my dear wife and daughter, except in this way, that when I have seen a case of need, such as an aged widow, a sick person, or a helpless infant, I have used the means freely which God has given me, fully believing that if either myself, or my dear wife or daughter, at some time or other, should be in need of anything, that God would richly repay what was given to the poor, considering it as lent to Himself.

Under these circumstances, I am unable to accept your kind gift of £100 towards making a provision for myself and family; for so I understand your letter. Anything given to me, unasked for, by those who have it in their heart to help supply my personal and family expenses, I thankfully accept; or any donation for the work of God in which I am engaged, I also thankfully accept, as a steward for the orphans; but your kind gift seems to me especially given to make provision for myself; which I think would be displeasing to my Heavenly Father, who has so bountifully given me my daily bread hitherto. But should I have misunderstood the meaning of your letter, be pleased to let me know it. I hold the cheque till I hear again from you.

In the meantime, my dear Sir, whatever your letter meant, I am deeply sensible of your kindness, and daily pray that God would be pleased richly to recompense you, both temporally and spiritually.

I am, dear Sir,
Yours very gratefully
George Müller

Two days later Müller received a reply, in which the donor asked him to use the one hundred pounds for the support of the orphans, and a few days later received a further two hundred pounds for the orphans from the same donor.

By November 1857 Müller was able to open Home 'No. 2' (as it became known) on Ashley Down: it lay immediately south of No. 1 at right angles to it. It had room for four hundred girls – two hundred infants and two hundred girls from eight upwards, and the first excited children arrived in the middle of November.

Sceptics doubted whether Müller would be able to provide for seven hundred children, and the large staff which he now employed. These doubts were confounded; and in the years which lay ahead Müller would startle the world by trebling the size of his work.

14

WHEN THE SOUTH WIND BLEW

Both new Orphan-Houses were fully centrally heated. Towards the end of November 1857, an assistant brought Müller some bad news.

'The boiler which feeds the radiators in No. 1 has a serious leak. We can't get through the winter if we do nothing about it.'

The boiler was entirely surrounded by brickwork and the location of the leak couldn't be identified without taking down the brickwork, an operation which would probably cause further damage to the boiler. For eight winters there had been no problems and this fault was quite unexpected. Müller firmly believed that to have done nothing and to have said, 'I will trust God regarding it', would have been careless presumption, and not faith in God. 'It would,' he said, 'be the counterfeit of faith.' Something, therefore, had to be done, and quickly.

'I am anxious that the children – especially the youngest – shouldn't suffer from the cold,' Müller said to his assistant. 'A new boiler would take many weeks to install. Could the present one be repaired?'

'We cannot be sure,' replied the assistant, 'but in any case it will take several days to dismantle the brickwork to identify the problem.'

'Could we use gas stoves temporarily?'

'We haven't enough gas to spare from the lighting system to heat the large number of stoves which would be required.'

'Could we use "Arnott's stoves?"?'

'They wouldn't be suitable because they need long chimneys to remove fumes.'

'Whatever the solution,' said Müller, 'we must not let finance stand in our way. I will gladly lay out hundreds of pounds rather than have the children suffer from the cold.'

Müller decided to have the brick chamber opened to see the extent of the damage and whether it would be possible to repair it to carry them through the winter. He fixed a date the following Wednesday for the workmen to come and make all the necessary arrangements. He knew that when the workmen arrived the fire in the boiler would have to be put out. The day after Müller made the arrangements, the first really cold weather of the winter began and a bleak north wind set in. It was early December. Müller knelt to pray.

'Lord, You know that I cannot put the repairs off. Dear Father, I ask for two things. Would You please change the north wind into a south wind; and will You give the workmen a "mind to work" as You did when Nehemiah rebuilt the wall of Jerusalem in fifty-two days because "the people had a mind to work"?'

On the Tuesday evening before the workmen were due to arrive, the north wind blew still; but on the Wednesday, the south wind blew exactly as he had prayed. The weather was so mild that no fire was needed. The workmen arrived on cue, removed the brickwork, found the leak in the boiler and began to repair it.

At about half past eight on the Wednesday evening, when Müller was going home, he was stopped at the lodge at the entrance to the Ashley Down Homes.

'The head of the firm,' the porter told him, 'which manufactured the boiler has arrived to see how the work is going and whether he can speed things up.

Müller returned at once to No. 1 and went down into the basement to meet the boss and see how the work was going.

'The men will work late this evening,' said the boss, 'and come very early again tomorrow.'

'We would rather, sir, work through the night!' said the foreman.

Müller remembered the second part of his prayer. God had certainly given the men 'a mind to work'!

In the morning the men completed the repairs, stopped the leak – though with great difficulty – and within about thirty hours had rebuilt the brickwork. Finally they re-lit the fire in the boiler.

And all the time the warm south wind blew.

Donations for the third home were still coming in: early in 1858, Müller received one gift of three thousand pounds and two others of £800 and £700. These and similar gifts meant that Müller had enough funds to begin work on No. 3. In September he bought eleven and a half acres of land on the other side of the road from Nos. 1 and 2. As the site was a large one, he decided to build No. 3 spacious enough to accommodate four hundred and fifty children. This would mean that he would be caring for one thousand, one hundred and fifty children. He would now need several thousand extra pounds. In December, a glass manufacturer told him that he would supply all the glass for No. 3's three hundred and fifty windows free of charge. Early in January 1859 Müller received seven thousand pounds, of which he took four thousand for the building fund.

During 1859 and 1860 gifts came in steadily and included numbers of very substantial donations towards the building. Even while No. 3 was being built and well before it was opened, Müller's thoughts turned towards a further dramatic enlargement of his work. After a long period of daily prayer and self-examination he decided to build two more large Homes on Ashley Down for eight hundred and fifty children so that he would eventually care for over two thousand children. What were Müller's reasons for such a daring expansion and was it really necessary?

As to the need, the number of applications for admission was, in the early 1860s, increasing all the time. Fresh applications arrived almost daily, sometimes three or four new ones a day. Moreover, Müller had until this time concentrated more on providing a home for girls than for boys. 'Girls,' he said, 'are the weaker sex; and are still more exposed than boys to utter ruin if neglected; and we can easily keep them till they are eighteen or nineteen years of age.' Thus the policy had been to take in more girls than boys. 'But now,' Müller continued, 'I was led to consider whether something more might be done for boys also, to prevent, if possible, the necessity of refusing the boys of a family, when the girls could be received.'

Accommodation in other orphan homes in the United Kingdom was still inadequate; and their admissions policy highly selective. 'Even if there were room in them,' Müller said, 'which is not the case, still, the existing rules of admission by votes, which are in use in most of them, make it difficult, if not impossible, for the poorest and most destitute persons to avail themselves of them ... Some time since I had an application for some orphans, whose mother, a widow, in attempting to obtain votes for one of her fatherless children, was actually so worn out that one day she came home, over-fatigued by canvassing for votes, sat down and died.' The only other alternative for these poor children continued to be the workhouses.

Many of the children – even teenagers – received by Müller since the beginning of his work had been quite unable to read when they arrived at the Homes. Müller reported that they had 'had the joy of educating hundreds, who otherwise might have had no mental cultivation; besides teaching them a great variety of other things which are profitable for this life in order to make them useful members of society'. But, he continued, 'all physical and mental improvement regarding them could never satisfy us. All would be exceedingly little in our estimation, if they were not spiritually benefited.... And this blessing has been granted to us, not concerning twenty or fifty of the orphans, but concerning hundreds.'

Looking back on nearly thirty years of the work, there was ample incentive for Müller to expand the Institution's activities. Increased administrative work would present little problem; by the early 1860s Müller already employed three full-time personal assistants who relieved him of much of the correspondence, accounting and so on. He could expand his staff as required. But the expense of looking after two thousand children plus staff would be enormous. Two new Homes with the necessary land would cost about fifty thousand pounds.

'And how,' people said, 'will you be able to keep up the work, provided you are able to accomplish the building, as then the regular current expenses will amount to about £35,000 a year?'

'I feel the force of all this,' Müller replied, 'looking at it naturally. I am not a fanatic or enthusiast, but, as all who know me are well aware, a calm, cool, quiet, calculating businessman; and therefore I should be utterly overwhelmed, looking at it naturally; but as the whole of this work was commenced, and ever has been gone on with in faith, trusting in the Living God alone for everything, so it is also regarding this intended enlargement. I look to the Lord alone for helpers, land, means, and everything else needed. I have pondered the difficulties for months, and have looked steadily at every one of them; but faith in God has put every one of them aside.'

Müller originally began his children's work to demonstrate what can be achieved through faith.

My chief object was the glory of God, by giving a practical demonstration as to what could be accomplished simply through the instrumentality of prayer and faith, in order thus to benefit the Church of Christ at large, and to lead a careless world to see the reality of the things of God, by showing them, in this work, that the Living God is still, as four thousand years ago, the Living God. This my aim has been abundantly honoured. Multitudes of sinners have thus been converted, multitudes of the children of God in all parts of the world have been benefited by this work, even as I had anticipated.

But the larger the work has grown, the greater has been the blessing, bestowed in the very way in which I looked for blessing; for the attention of hundreds of thousands has been drawn to the work and many tens of thousands have come to see it. All this leads me to desire further and further to labour on in this way, in order to bring yet greater glory to the name of the Lord.... That it may be seen how much one poor man, simply by trusting in God, can bring about by prayer; and that thus other children of God may be led increasingly to trust in Him, in their individual positions and circumstances, therefore I am led to this further enlargement.

At the end of May 1861 Müller announced his intention of enlarging his work to cater for two thousand children. By the end of the year not quite one thousand pounds had been received towards the fifty thousand pounds which would be needed to build houses Nos. 4 and 5. Müller calculated that at that rate it would take about twenty-five years before all that was needed for the building fund came in. But he wasn't discouraged: he kept trusting.

In the evening of January 11th, Müller spent several hours on Ashley Down praying for the various aspects of the work which he directed and for money to come into the building fund. When he got home to Paul Street, he found a crossed cheque for two thousand pounds with this note:

I enclose a cheque, value £2,000, which accept with my best love and the expression of my heartfelt thankfulness to God for the privilege of being a fellow-helper in the work of caring for the orphans. I would like it to be applied towards the building you propose (DV) erecting. I shall consider as though I had £1,000 in each building; but you are at liberty to use the whole for the first, if you wish. Inasmuch as it is done to the Lord, I know it is well spent.

Three days later he received another two thousand pounds and a fortnight later a further two thousand five hundred pounds.

The twenty-five-year wait before Nos. 4 and 5 were built began to look less likely!

In the early summer of 1861, the Townsend family moved to Bristol. Müller and John Townsend, who helped George in his Sunday School work in Bristol, became close friends. Townsend's daughter Abigail was not yet three when the family arrived in Bristol but she soon fell in love with Müller and often spent time at Ashley Down and with George and Mary at Paul Street. She was amazed at what she heard her parents say about the way God provided for Müller and his children.

'I want to be like George Müller!' she would often say.

Once at Paul Street she said, 'I wish Dod would answer my prayers like He does yours, George Müller.'

'He will, my dear.'

Taking Abigail on his knee, he repeated the promise of Jesus: 'Whatever you ask for in prayer, believe that you have received it, and it will be yours' (Mark 11:24).

'Now, Abbie,' he asked, 'what is it you want to ask God for?'

'Some wool.'

Clasping her hands together, Müller said, 'Now, you repeat what I say: Please God, send Abbie some wool.'

'Please Dod send Abbie some wool.'

Jumping down Abigail ran out into the garden to play quite sure that the wool would come.

Then she remembered that God didn't know what kind of wool she wanted, so she ran back to Müller.

'I want to pray again.'

'Not now, dear, I'm busy.'

'But I forgot to tell Dod the colour I want.'

Taking her on his knee again, Müller said, 'That's right, always be definite my child, now tell God what you want.'

'Please Dod, send it wa-re-gated,' said Abigail who possessed a wide vocabulary but couldn't pronounce her 'v's' any better than her 'g's'.

Next morning a parcel arrived addressed to Abigail containing a quantity of variegated wool. Her Sunday School teacher, remembering that her birthday was close although uncertain of the date, and remembering too that she was a keen knitter, had purchased some wool and sent it – not on her birthday – but on the right day to demonstrate to her delight that God hears and answers prayer.

One of the best loved Müller anecdotes also concerns Abigail Townsend. The story isn't recorded in Müller's journal but is included in a short biographical sketch, *The Adventures of Sister Abigail.*

Early one morning Abigail was playing in the garden on Ashley Down when Müller came out and took her by the hand.

'Come and see what our Father will do.'

He led her into the long dining room with the plates, cups and bowls all laid on the table. According to the account (which may have got somewhat distorted before being written down) there was nothing but the empty dishes on the tables. The children were standing waiting for breakfast.

'Children, you know that we must be in time for school,' said Müller. Lifting his hand he prayed, 'Dear Father, we thank Thee for what Thou art going to give us to eat.

Then they all heard a knock at the door. The baker stood there.

'Mr Müller, I couldn't sleep last night. Somehow I felt you didn't have bread for breakfast, and the Lord wanted me to send you some. So I got up at two o'clock and baked some fresh bread, and have brought it.'

Müller thanked the baker and praised God for His care.

'Children,' he said, 'we not only have bread, but fresh bread.'

Almost immediately they heard a second knock on the door. This time it was the milkman.

'Mr Müller, my milk cart has broken down outside the orphanage. I would like to give the children the cans of fresh milk so that I can empty the waggon and repair it.'

Müller thanked the milkman and the children enjoyed their breakfast.

After some delays in construction, the third Ashley Down Orphan-House opened on March 2nd 1862. The largest of the buildings erected by Müller on Ashley Down, No. 3's position was also the most prominent and it became (and remains) a familiar landmark in Bristol. A man living in Horfield, in sight of Ashley Down, said that, 'whenever he felt doubts about the Living God creeping into his mind he used to get up and look through the night at the many windows lit up on Ashley Down, gleaming out through the darkness as stars in the sky'.

But with a waiting list now of nearly a thousand children, Müller was anxious that still more stars should shine on Ashley Down. In October 1864 a donation of five thousand pounds brought the building fund to over twenty-seven thousand pounds and Müller set about buying the land to build his fourth home. For some years he had had his eye on a beautiful site on the same side of Ashley Down Road as Nos. 1 and 2, opposite No. 3. The site was about eighteen acres and had a small house and outhouses built at one end, close to the point where Sefton Park Road (then a narrow track) meets Ashley Down Road. Müller had prayed hundreds of times that he would be able to erect two large houses on this site.

Now that he had enough money to build the fourth Home, Müller saw the agent who acted for the owner of the land and asked him whether the land was for sale.

'It is,' replied the agent, 'but it's let until March 25th 1867.'

Müller wasn't discouraged by this news. He expected, through prayer, to come to an arrangement with the tenant, persuading him to leave early in return for fair compensation. Two other difficulties, however, now emerged. First, the owner of the land asked seven thousand pounds for the land which Müller judged to be considerably more than its value; second, he read that the Bristol Water Works Company intended to build an additional reservoir on the site, and to get an Act of Parliament passed to that effect.

Several times a day Müller now gave himself to special prayer about these three problems. He then went to see the committee of directors of the Bristol Water Works Company about their reservoir.

'Only a small area of land will be required for the reservoir,' the committee told him, 'not enough to interfere with your plans. If possible we shall endeavour not to take even this land if other sites become available.'

Relieved, Müller then visited the tenant and told him of his plans for the land and his hope that it might be possible to purchase it well before March 1867 when the tenancy expired.

'I hope very much,' Müller added, 'that we can settle the matter in a pleasant and friendly manner.'

'Please give me a few days to think things over,' replied the tenant.

While the tenant thought, Müller prayed. After a week, he paid a second visit to the tenant.

'I don't wish to stand in the way of the land being used for such a worthwhile purpose,' replied the tenant. 'But as I have spent a good deal of money on the house, I expect fair compensation for leaving early.'

'I am quite prepared and happy to do that,' said Müller.

So far so good. But now Müller had to tackle the last and most difficult problem: that of the price the owner wanted for the land. Typically, he combined ardent prayer with shrewd business sense – we see Müller, the tough negotiator. He knew well how much the land was worth to his Institution; but he took the view that its value to the Institution wasn't the same as the market value.

'Dear Heavenly Father,' he prayed, 'will You constrain the owner of the land to accept a considerably lower sum than he is at present asking?'

He visited the owner and politely but firmly told him why he didn't believe the land was worth what he was asking. They talked for a while and the owner was quiet for some minutes.

'I will accept £5,000 for the land rather than the £7,000 I originally asked.'

Müller accepted and agreed to pay this amount. He knew that because the land was level he would save money in laying the foundations for the two new Homes; a new sewer, completed a few months earlier, would greatly benefit the Homes; he would be able to continue to receive gas from the Bristol supply; and finally he realised that the great advantage to him was that building close to the other three Homes meant the whole institution could be easily directed. No other land in Bristol offered the same advantages: though it didn't show in the expression on his face, Müller had a bargain.

'The Lord has kindly given it to us,' he thought.

A missionary, who, despite his youth, greatly impressed Müller, paid a visit to Ashley Down in August 1865: James Hudson Taylor. From the earliest days of his Christian life, Hudson Taylor had been inspired by Müller's example; and now that – at the age of thirty-three, but already with six years' experience in China behind him – he had founded his own missionary society on similar principles to Müller's Homes, he valued more than ever the Bristol man of God's prayers, judgment and advice.

On August 22nd he arrived at Ashley Down with a party of young members of the new China Inland Mission and recorded in his diary:

> Had an hour with Mr Müller. He spoke most preciously on the call and spirit of the missionary; on the consecutive reading of the Scriptures; on prayer and faith in God; on obstacles and thorn hedges.

Next day Taylor recorded:

> Mr Müller spoke on communion with God being work for God; and on the need of not acting uncertainly; on mixing freely with people, and restraining the speaking of English among ourselves (in the presence of Chinese who could not understand); and finally promised to pray for the party.

As Müller showed the young missionaries around the three homes, and they watched the happy, healthy and well-clothed children, they reflected on the value of Müller's promise to pray. For the next twenty years, Müller's practical support of the China Inland Mission was to be crucial to its development.*

(* See *Hudson Taylor: A Man in Christ*, Roger Steer, OMF Books, 1990)

15

INDESCRIBABLE HAPPINESS

'I was going up Ashley Hill the other morning,' said a farmer, 'when I met Mr Müller walking towards the city. Had I not known him, I should have said he was a gentleman of leisure and without a care, so quietly did he walk and so peaceful and stately was his demeanour! The twenty-third Psalm seemed written all over his face.'

Müller was now (in 1865) in his sixtieth year; and still very much in his prime. His health was far better than it had been in his twenties and early thirties. Arthur Tappan Pierson, the American Bible teacher who knew Müller well, wrote:

His form was tall and slim, always neatly attired, and very erect, and his step firm and strong. His countenance, in repose, might have been thought stern, but for the smile which so habitually lit up his eyes and played over his features that it left its impress on the lines of his face. His manner was one of simple courtesy and unstudied dignity: no one would in his presence have felt like vain trifling, and there was about him a certain indescribable air of authority and majesty that reminded one of a born prince; and yet there was mingled with all this a simplicity so childlike that even children felt themselves at home with him. In his speech, he never quite lost that peculiar foreign quality known as accent, and he always spoke with slow and measured articulation, as though a double watch were set at the door of his lips....

Those who knew but little of him and saw him only in his serious moods might have thought him lacking in that peculiarly human quality, humour. But neither was he an ascetic nor devoid of that element of innocent appreciation of the ludicrous and that keen enjoyment of a good story which seem essential to the complete man. His habit was sobriety, but he relished a joke that was free of all taint of uncleanness and that had about it no sting for others. To those whom he best knew and loved he showed his true self, in his playful moods – as when at Ilfracombe, climbing with his wife and others the heights that overlook the sea, he walked on a little in advance, seated himself till the rest came up with him, and then when they were barely seated, rose and quietly said, 'Well now, we have had a good rest, let us go on.'

Müller was fond of Ilfracombe: he loved to wander around the harbour, protected from sea winds by Capstone Hill, or to explore the old town built on the cliffs above. Then, if the weather were fair, he would take his family with him to climb the wooded heights which form a semi-circle around the town.

In September 1865 he made one of his visits to Ilfracombe 'for a change of air'. On the morning of the 4th he climbed Capstone Hill with Mary and Lydia. While returning from the top, two men approached them.

'Please excuse me,' one of them said, 'aren't you Mr Müller?'

'I am.'

'I have to give you some money for the orphans.'

'Why don't you sit with me for a while on the bench, so that we can talk further?' said Müller.

'I live in the neighbourhood of M. I am a businessman, and what would be called a hard-working businessman. Some time ago one of your Reports fell into my hands, but, I honestly confess it, I couldn't believe that you did obtain your funds simply in answer to prayer; I questioned the truth of it. However, the thing came up into my mind again and again.

'While I was thus considering whether God was really with you, and whether you really obtained simply by faith and in answer to prayer these large sums of money, I heard of a certain property to be sold, which I thought I should like to buy, if it were disposed of reasonably. I looked it over and had it valued by a competent businessman, who told me it was worth so much. I then said to myself, in a kind of sceptical way, "I will now see whether God is with Mr Müller or not. If I get this property for so much (fixing a low price on it), I will give Mr Müller one hundred pounds."

'I then instructed a person to bid for me at the auction where this property was sold at a distant place; but so great was my curiosity to see whether God really would appear for you in this matter that by the next train I set off to the place where the auction was, that I might obtain as early as possible information how the matter would end.

'I found to my surprise that I had actually obtained this valuable property at the exact low price which I had fixed. I was astonished. But I began to reflect more on the principles on which you act, and I wondered that, as a Christian, I or anyone else could call into question what you say about answers to prayer. The more I consider the matter, and the more I read your Report, the more I see how right and proper it is to come to God for all we need, and to trust Him for everything.

'The conveyance having been made, and all being now settled about the sale, I felt it right to pursue my promise; so my friend, whom you saw just now with me, and I set out on a tour of Devonshire, and then, on our way home, called the day before yesterday at your house; but found you were from home. We stopped yesterday in Bristol, and having there learnt your address, we came here to Ilfracombe today, for I wished to know you personally.'

'Well,' said Müller, 'I am not at all surprised at God's working thus for me, since day by day I seek His help, and thus, in answer to prayer, obtain from the most unlikely persons, and entire strangers, donations for the work. For instance, I had a letter from a lawyer at M. where you come from, just recently, asking me to send him a proper form of legacy to be left to the orphans, as one of his clients wished to leave a legacy of one thousand pounds for the orphans. Now, as far as I know, I am not personally acquainted with a single person at M., nor do I know the name of the individual who purposes to leave this one thousand pounds.'

'About this legacy,' replied the stranger, 'I can tell you something. After I had got this property, and saw how wrong I had been in looking in such a sceptical way on your work, as if there were no reality in prayer, I decided on helping you further. I thought to myself, though I am a man in health, and of middle age, yet it might be well to make my will, and to leave you one thousand pounds for the orphans.'

Thus Müller discovered that this was the individual on whose behalf the lawyer had written to him. An hour later this one time sceptic called at Müller's lodgings with a cheque for one hundred pounds.

In 1859 Müller's friend and fellow-worker Henry Craik had been told by his doctor that he had a weak heart. From the summer of 1865 it was clear that Craik, who, like Müller, was sixty, was desperately ill. By January 1866, the man who had twice refused an honorary doctorate from St Andrews University, in recognition of his theological writings, was obviously dying. Among letters Craik received that January was an affectionate one from J. N. Darby calling him his 'dear brother' and regretting their 'ecclesiastical separation'.

Müller was often at his friend's bedside. On one visit, when Craik was very frail, Müller kissed him and was about to go when Craik, too weak to talk any more, said, 'Sit down' and also asked Craik's wife to sit down so that he could look at them, though unable to speak. Müller sat there silently for a while, and then left.

The next day, Müller caught a cold and was forced to stay at home for several days. During that period, Craik died. Both Müller and Craik had been Christians for just over forty years. Müller observed, 'My beloved brother and friend now had finished his course; I was privileged and honoured further to labour for the Lord, and to do this now without him with whom I had often taken counsel.' The immense crowds which gathered at Bethesda for Craik's funeral were a fitting testimony to the loss which was felt by the Christian community.

In May 1866 building work began on the fourth Orphan-House; and in January 1867, a further seven thousand pounds having been received, work began on No. 5. The contracts for both houses came to over forty-one thousand pounds. All the glass for the seven hundred windows was given freely by a firm of building contractors. On Guy Fawkes' Day 1868 the fourth Home was opened; and on January 6th 1870, the last of Müller's great buildings on Ashley Down, 'New Orphan-House No. 5' was duly opened.

Müller's vast expansion programme on Ashley Down was complete. Twenty-five years had elapsed since he had first announced his plans to build his own orphan-houses. But in no sense could he now sit back on is laurels. Every morning he rose at half past six and at a quarter to eight, after his usual period of prayer and Bible study, he began the task of going through his correspondence. Then, as *The Times* recorded some years later, 'at ten o'clock he was waited on by nine assistants, to whom he gave his instructions'. (Until the 1850s he had conducted a correspondence of about three thousand letters a year without a secretary.)

Expenses for the children's work now amounted to thirty thousand pounds a year. Two thousand children had to be fed and clothed; their clothes washed and mended; well over two thousand pairs of shoes had to be bought and repaired; each year hundreds of fresh children arrived who had to be fitted out with clothing and footwear; hundreds of boys and girls went out as apprentices and servants and had to be provided with suits of clothes at the expense of the Institution. Each boy who left the Homes as an apprentice had a premium paid for him to his master which was equal to about a year's support. When any child left, his or her travelling expenses were paid.

Keeping the five enormous buildings repaired, with more than one thousand seven hundred large windows and over five hundred rooms, was very expensive: painting, white-washing, colouring, repairing damage and faults. Thousands of articles of furniture had to be repaired or replaced.

When the children were ill, or even died, extra expenses had to be met. The large staff on Ashley Down including a school inspector, matrons, teachers, medical officers, nurses, Müller's personal assistants had their salaries paid out of money which was all prayed in. But, Müller recorded, 'we are able with as much ease, if not greater ease than very rich noblemen, to accomplish this simply by looking in our poverty to the infinitely rich One for everything'.

Mary Müller was the ideal wife for the director of five large children's homes.

'My darling,' Müller often said to her, 'God Himself singled you out for me, as the most suitable wife I could possibly wish to have had.'

During the years of trial from 1838 to 1846, when Müller sometimes had to use their own money in meeting expenses in the Homes, Mary never found fault with him but joined him in prayer that God would send help. And when He did, as He always did, they often wept together for joy.

In addition to a good general education, Mary was an expert at every kind of needlework and of the appropriate types and qualities of material for clothes and linen used on Ashley Down. For it was her responsibility to order hundreds of thousands of yards of all kinds of material. She would approve or reject the material when it was delivered. Every month she examined all the account books and checked hundreds of bills for the house matrons. It was said on Ashley Down that if any tradesman or a matron made the slightest mistake, Mary would be sure to spot it. She spent nearly every day on Ashley Down and paid special attention to sick children.

Of his marriage to Mary, Müller said:

Every year our happiness increased more and more.
I never saw my beloved wife at any time, when I met
her unexpectedly anywhere in Bristol, without being
delighted to do so. I never met her even in the Orphan-
Houses, without my heart being delighted to do so. Day
by day, as we met in our dressing room, at the Orphan-
Houses, to wash our hands before dinner or tea, I was
delighted to meet her, and she was equally pleased to see
me. Thousands of times I told her – 'My darling, I never
saw you at any time, since you became my wife, without
my being delighted to see you'.
Further, day after day, if anyhow it could be done, I spent
after dinner twenty minutes or half an hour with her in her
room at the Orphan-Houses, seated on her couch, which
the love of a Christian brother, together with an easy chair,
had sent her.... I knew it was good for her, that her dear
active mind and hands should have rest, and I knew well
that this would not be, except her husband was by her
side.... I spent these precious moments with my darling
wife. There we sat, side by side, her hand in mine, as an
habitual thing, having a few words of loving intercourse,
or being silent, but most happy in the Lord, and in each
other, whether we spoke or were silent.... Our happiness
in God, and in each other, was indescribable. We had not
some happy days every year, not a month of happiness
every year; but we had twelve months of happiness in the
year, and thus year after year. Often and often did I say, 'My
darling, do you think there is a couple in Bristol, or in the
world, happier than we are?'

Müller believed that one of the greatest secrets of their marital
bliss was that besides their times of private prayer, and family
prayer, he and Mary frequently prayed together.

For many years my precious wife and I had, immediately after family prayer in the morning, a short time for prayer together, when the most important points for prayer, with regard to the day, were brought before God. Should very heavy trials press on us, or should our need of any kind be particularly great, we prayed again after dinner, when I visited her room ... and this in times of extraordinary difficulties or necessities, might be repeated once or twice more in the afternoon....

Then in the evening, during the last hour of our stay at the Orphan-Houses, though her or my work was never so much, it was an habitually understood thing, that this hour was for prayer. My beloved wife came then to my room, and now our prayer, and supplication, and intercessions mingled with thanksgiving, lasted generally forty minutes, fifty minutes, and sometimes the whole hour. At these seasons we brought perhaps fifty or more different points, or persons, or circumstances before God.

Mary Müller was now (in 1870) seventy-two. For a year or two it had been obvious to Müller that her health was failing: she was growing thinner and tiring quickly. Müller tried unsuccessfully to persuade her to work less and eat more. Sometimes, Mary would lie awake at night for two hours or more and Müller would express his concern.

'My dear,' she would say, 'I am getting old, and old persons need not so much sleep.'

Two years earlier she had said to him, 'My darling, I think the Lord will allow me to see the New Orphan-Houses Nos. 4 and 5 furnished and opened, and then I may go home; but most of all I wish that the Lord Jesus would come, and that we might all go together.'

And indeed the Lord had allowed her to see both No. 4 and No. 5 opened; and throughout 1869 she had spent nearly every day at work in the five buildings.

Sadly she had worked too hard.

16

'No Place Ever Seemed So Dear'

'I never knew what it was for my mother to caress me, take me to church or teach me a child's prayer.' These were the words of William Ready who had been born in a London workhouse on January 23rd 1860. His father, an alcoholic, had been unable to support his wife and William's nine brothers and sisters; by 1865 both parents had died and the ten children were left as orphans.

William began the life of a waif, sleeping in dustbins or the dark corners of railway arches. 'Many times,' he said later, 'I have picked up a piece of orange peel as eagerly as if it had been a sixpence and I have even nibbled cigar ends to allay the pangs of hunger. Sometimes we went into public houses to sing the comic songs we had learned on the streets, which usually paid us well.... On Sunday mornings, at four o'clock, I used to carry the produce at Covent Garden Market, and my feet and hands were often frostbitten.'

In this state at the age of twelve, in 1872, William Ready was rescued by James Walk, a London City Missioner. Walk eventually arranged for Ready to go to Ashley Down. 'I was not happy I can assure you,' Ready recalled, 'when I found myself inside the block, with the great iron gates closing behind me. I didn't look on those as my friends who had interfered with my liberty of the streets. No sooner had the doors been closed when I began to feel I was in bondage and a real home-sickness came over me. I yearned for the streets of the Metropolis and the lights of London. I was as a bird in a cage and if anyone had said to me "You may go back" I should have said, "Thank you, Sir! You are my friend."'

The Ashley Down staff gave William a bath and dressed him in his uniform – corduroy trousers, a blue vest, coat and white collar. He never forgot the day when he was first shown into the dining-hall. The boys all gathered round him and began to pinch him and pull his hair. The bell rang and all the children took their places at table. For the first time in his life, he didn't feel hungry! Oh, to go back to his old haunts, to the rush of cabs and buses! They put two slices of bread and some treacle on a tin plate in front of him but he couldn't face eating it.

'Don't you want your tea?' a boy said to him.

'No!'

The boys on either side of him soon finished his share.

That evening, the other boys teased him until his Irish blood rose. He got into a fight with one boy and then a real tough guy, Curly Oliver, arrived on the scene anxious to join in. William took off his coat and vest and launched into a spirited attack on Curly. Just as he was beginning to enjoy the encounter, a master entered the room with his cane and led William to his dormitory.

'Your bed number is twenty-two,' he said.

Next morning at six, the bell rang to wake the boys up. At eight they went into breakfast. The tables were laid with plates of porridge and William didn't give the boys a chance to ask if he wanted his breakfast. His appetite had returned. At this breakfast William heard the Bible read for the first time.

The first lesson that morning was reading: William's master discovered he didn't know the letters of the alphabet. In the next few months, the master taught William to read well; they told him about God, Christ and salvation and he memorised passages from the Bible. He soon became popular with the other boys, and for a while conducted a secret class teaching eager pupils the tricks and acrobatics of London streets. A master discovered that he had been charging those able to pay a penny postage stamp a week tuition fees. However, as he discovered that the boys had paid of their own free will and without pressure, nothing more was said.

On one occasion, William led a gang of boys on an invasion of the masters' dining room in the dark to demolish the remains of their evening meal. He was caught and caned 'with the usual amount of preaching' and then suddenly, the master took pity on him and gave him some sweets.

'That,' said Ready, 'did more to drive the devil out of me than all the flogging and preaching. Towards the end kindness rather than punishment settled me down to reason and order.'

One morning in 1876 William was called out of school to see Mr French, the man in charge of the department which placed boys in apprenticeships.

'How would you like to be a flour miller, Ready?'

'I would, yes, Sir,' answered William no knowing in the slightest what the job involved.

Before long, according to the normal practice, he was measured for and provided with three suits of clothes at the expense of the Institution. Then came the final interview with Müller.

Müller received him kindly in his prayer room in No. 3 Orphan-House. He put half a crown into his left hand a Bible in his right.

'You can hold tighter with your right hand than with your left, can't you?' said Müller with a twinkle in his eye.

'Yes, sir.'

'Well, hold to the teaching of that book and you will always have something for your left hand to hold. Now, my lad, kneel down.'

Putting his hand on William's head, Müller committed him to God's keeping. Helping him to his feet again he said, 'Trust in the Lord and do good; so you shall dwell in the land and you will be fed (Ps. 37:3). Goodbye, my lad, goodbye!'

As he left Ashley Down, William Ready recalled that 'my belongings were my Bible, my clothes and half a crown and, what was best of all, the priceless blessing of George Müller's prayers.'

Ready was put on a train bound for Newton Abbot in Devon. A cheerful looking man with a flowing beard and a straw hat was at the station to meet him.

'Are you William Ready?'

'Yes, sir!'

'Well, I am your master, or your father if you like. Get into the trap, my son!'

Ready never forgot the seventeen mile drive through beautiful Devonshire countryside to William Perryman's home in Chagford: William's new father won his heart by his kind and friendly conversation. Perryman was a devout Christian, and before long Ready himself converted to Christ during his apprenticeship at Chagford. A few years later, he became a Free Church Minister, and, moving to New Zealand, became one of that country's most popular preachers.

Looking back on his years on Ashley Down he wrote, 'I can see now that it was just the place for me and what a blessing it was that I was sent there. If my own children were left orphans I could wish for nothing better than that they should be trained and cared for at Müller's.'

The Müller Homes today have long felt it right to come into line with current policy which is to accommodate children in small house groups so that life should conform as closely as possible to a normal home atmosphere. However, by nineteenth century custom and standards, George Müller must be considered both a pioneer and a radical. He, alone, offered modern homes to thousands of children who would otherwise have been either homeless, or sent to a workhouse or a debtors' prison, or grudgingly offered a corner in the over-crowded home of a relative. And there were no barriers to entry to Müller's Homes on grounds of poverty, class or creed.

Noting that admittance to other orphanages in the eighteenth and early nineteenth centuries was normally gained, not according to the relative needs of the child, but upon personal recommendation or by a majority of votes at periodic meetings of subscribers, Kathleen Heasman has credited Müller with leading the way in:

> giving priority to the needs of the child.... The fact that subscribers' meetings were not held, and the names and amounts given by particular donors were not made public,

meant that children were usually selected according to their need, for all who applied were admitted. Thus the system of voting was rarely found in evangelical children's homes, and this example (Müller's) gradually led to the abolition of the voting system altogether.

Müller's large homes did offer some advantages which smaller ones cannot. Life may have been regimented, and the routine predictable, but the shared fun of so many youngsters living and growing up together meant that it was often jolly. There was also a stability and security about them which were absent from smaller homes. An orphan who began life in a small London home and only arrived at No. 4 at the age of ten noticed the difference: in London the staff and children were constantly changing. But on Ashley Down 'a teacher who had done twenty-five years was just beginning'; some ex-Ashley Down children actually returned to Ashley Down with their grandchildren to find their old masters still there! Similarly smaller homes offered children a limited choice of friends, whereas if Ashley Down children quarrelled, they could always make new friends.

One former orphan wrote of her years on Ashley Down thus: 'I am glad to see a number of orphans remember the dear old Home, in which they spent their happiest days; for truly there have been none happier to me than those spent in the dear Orphan-House Number 3. How happy we were in our own little world, brought up in such a holy atmosphere.'

Another wrote: 'As I look back on my schooldays, just left behind me, I think they were the jolliest days of my life.' And yet another recalled: 'I was only a small child then, and am still a child when I think of Ashley Down. It was a lovely, lovely spot ... and no place ever seemed so dear'.

To impressionable teenagers, the experience of living under the care of people with a deep personal faith in Christ, together with the exhilaration produced when numbers of their contemporaries came to share this same faith, was never to be forgotten. The many hundreds who became Christians in this devout atmosphere felt an enormous debt of gratitude towards Ashley Down. One Christian girl soon after going into domestic service sent this letter to Müller:

> Beloved and respected Sir, I cannot feel grateful enough to you for all the kindness I received whilst under your fatherly care in the dear Orphan-house, and the years I spent there I can truly say were the happiest I ever spent in my life; for not only were we cared for temporally, but spiritually also; and I do indeed feel very thankful to the Lord that I was ever received there, and that He so soon brought me to a knowledge of Himself; and it is my heart's sincere desire to know more of Him, to become more like Him for He is truly to me the chiefest among ten thousand, and the altogether lovely ... I must thank you for the very lovely situation in which I am placed. My mistress is very kind to me, and I hope to give great satisfaction to her.... May you ever be the orphan's friend and protector; and many prayers for the conversion of the dear orphans who still remain unconverted.... I remain, dear Sir, yours very gratefully and respectfully.

Nancy Garton has written of the uniform worn by the children in Müller's day as giving 'the orphans a grace and a dignity, and as it became antiquated, a sentimental appeal, which the modern dress introduced in 1936, with its knee-length skirts and squashed-on hats, entirely lacked'.

According to Mrs Garton:

> The older boys wore a navy-blue Eton jacket, with a waistcoat buttoning up to the white starched collar, both of heavy serge; brown corduroy trousers; caps with a glazed peak; and in bad weather, short cloaks. Each boy had three suits.
>
> The small boys, up to about eight or nine years old, wore for everyday a garment which seems a strange choice from

the practical point of view. It was a plainly-cut smock, with no collar, in white or unbleached cotton. Possibly, being white, it could soon be boiled and restored to its original purity, but who, knowing boys, can help suspecting that it spent much of its time being anything but white. Blue serge shorts, socks and strap shoes completed the costume. For best wear, the little boys discarded their smocks, and wore Norfolk suits with broad Eton collars, in which they looked most attractive. Their caps were the same as the older boys.

The girls outdoor dress in cold weather was a long cloak in green and blue plaid; in mild weather a shepherd's plaid shawl took the place of the cloak; in hot weather, for best wear, the dress was a thin one of dull lilac cotton, over which was worn a small cape or tippet of the same material, a tiny ruff at the neck. Throughout the year the girls wore bonnets of natural coloured straw. To each bonnet was attached a long strip of thin material with a green and white checked pattern, which formed a band across the top, crossed at the back and was stitched at the sides, so that the two ends formed the strings by which the bonnet was tied on.

The everyday dresses for girls of all ages were of navy cotton covered with small white dots, to which for walking out was added a white tippet when the weather was too warm for cloaks or shawls. Indoors, the girls up to fourteen wore blue-checked gingham pinafores, cut high to the neck and buttoning behind. The girls over fourteen, who had left the schoolroom and were called 'House Girls', wore aprons with strings to distinguish them from their juniors. The most senior girls, those who were due to leave the Homes for situations within a few months, were known as 'Cap Girls', and wore caps, aprons to the waist and white collars. Every girl had five dresses.

The stockings were all hand-knitted by the girls; black wool for winter, and white cotton for summer. A pair of these white stockings is to be seen in the Museum at Müller House. The shoes were mostly of the ankle strap style.

With the old uniform, the girls had no waterproofs, and in doubtful weather there was one cotton umbrella for every two children. The privilege of carrying the umbrella was not one that was eagerly competed for. The walk on wet days was often a quiet squabble, as the more strong-minded of each pair in the crocodile pressed the umbrella into her partner's unwilling hand.

Nancy Garton has also given us a fascinating description of the children's hair-dos:

The girls' hair was managed rather cleverly, considering that hundreds of heads of hair had somehow to be made presentable every day. The tiny girls had theirs almost as short as a boy's, but beautifully glossy and well-brushed. Those from about eight years old up to eleven had a Dutch bob, with centre parting and fringe, such as they could comb into place themselves without assistance. The older girls, who were capable of doing their own hair, were allowed to grow it to shoulder length or longer, and hold it back with a velvet ribbon band. The most senior girls put their hair up.

Former Ashley Down children told me that children who came with their parents to visit the Homes were sometimes envious of the pretty hairstyles worn by the residents.

Müller also deserves to be regarded as a pioneer and a radical by virtue of his educational policy. He was actually criticised for educating children 'above their station'; not many years earlier, in his book *An Experiment in Education*, Dr Andrew Bell had written:

It is not proposed that the children of the poor be educated in an expensive manner, or even taught to write and to cypher ... there is a risk of elevating by an indiscriminate education, the minds of those doomed to the drudgery of daily labour, above their conditions, and thereby rendering them discontented and unhappy in their lot. It may suffice to teach the generality, on an economical plan, to read their Bibles and understand the doctrines of our holy religion.

Müller didn't agree. As well as religious education, he saw to it that his children were taught reading, writing, arithmetic, dictation, grammar, geography, English and world history, composition, singing, needlework and – for the girls – domestic science. The boys made their own beds, cleaned their shoes, scrubbed their rooms, were sent on errands, and dug, planted and weeded the gardens. The domestic science involved the girls in some work in the kitchens, sculleries, wash-houses and laundries at the five houses. Lewis Court has claimed that , even in Müller's day, if an aptitude were shown, a higher education for one of the professions was provided, but this seems to have been rare.

Müller employed a school inspector to maintain the educational standards at the school for his own children on Ashley Down and at schools financed and run by the Scriptural Knowledge Institution. 'The Annual Examination of the children was held during the months of February and March,' the inspector, at that time a Mr Horne, wrote in 1885. 'The children were examined and arranged in the second, third, fourth, fifth and sixth standards in many particulars according to the Government Code. Each child was examined separately in reading. Each child showed his or her copy-book to determine the mark for writing. Ten questions were put on each of the following subjects, viz, on Scripture, Geography, History and Grammar. The answers were given in writing. Six sums were given in Arithmetic. The answers were given on paper. The average percentage of all the marks the children received during the examination was 91.1.'

'To all who are acquainted with such matters,' commented Müller with some pride, 'the last sentence will show with what success our children are educated.'

Because of the duration of the education he provided, Müller was accused of robbing the factories, mills and mines of labour;

he was not deterred. In general girls remained under his care until they were seventeen and sometimes longer. They were then usually recommended to a suitable domestic situation and fitted out at the Homes' expense; some would go on to train as nurses. Generally the boys were apprenticed when they were between fourteen and fifteen years old. But Müller deliberately avoided fixed rules and maintained a flexible policy so that the needs of each individual were taken into account. In theory Müller allowed each boy to choose the trade he wanted to learn, although in practice the selection process was no doubt often similar to William Ready's case quoted above.

The Homes provided each boy with three suits of clothes and met any other expenses connected with his apprenticeship. Some boys left the Homes to become Post Office and Telegraph clerks, or clerks in other offices. Others among the brightest would go on to be teachers, perhaps in the Homes themselves – in which case they would do their training at a school in Purton, Gloucestershire, financed and run by the Scriptural Knowledge Institution.

As to discipline in the Homes, Nancy Garton has aptly summed it up as 'strict but not harsh'. A group of former Ashley Down children (there not long after Müller's death), told me, 'if we were punished we deserved it'. Just occasionally Müller had to expel a child who had become an unacceptably bad influence on the other children. But expulsion – that is, returning a child to a relative or guardian – was always a last resort after repeated warnings and attempts to reform the child; and after an offender had left, Müller and his staff followed him (or her) with their prayers.

Müller recalled the case of one boy who had arrived on Ashley Down in October 1849.

> He was then not quite eight years old; but though so young, it was soon found that he was old in sin, for he was a confirmed liar and thief. He gloried in it among the other boys, and told them that he had belonged to a juvenile gang of thieves, before he had been admitted into the Orphan-House, that he had often stolen from the ships

iron, brass and so on and sold it. We thought at first that he spoke thus merely in the way of boasting, yet it proved but too true that he was experienced in such matters; for twice he ran away from the Orphan-House, carrying off things belonging to other children. Moreover he could pick locks. We received him back twice, after having run away, hoping that by bearing with him, and using a variety of other means, he might be reclaimed; but all in vain. At last, having borne with him, and tried him for five years and four months, he was solemnly, with prayer, before the whole establishment, expelled, if by any means this last painful remedy might be blessed to him. Yet we follow even this poor young sinner with our prayers, and hope that the Lord may yet show him his evil ways, and give us even now joy concerning him, as we have had before in a similar instance.

Once, a boy was about to be dismissed before the whole company for repeated bad behaviour over a long period, when Müller placed his hand on his head and began to pray for him. To show how brazen and unconcerned he was, the boy turned to face Müller with eyes wide open. To his amazement, tears were rolling down Müller's cheeks. There and then, according to the story, the boy was converted to Christ and his life dramatically changed. Yet another boy, later in life, described his dismissal by Müller and Müller's final words, with tears of:

'I am sorry! God bless you.'

The Times once reported that amongst those who visited Müller's Homes, and expressed their admiration of the management and working, were the Earl of Derby, Lord Salisbury, Lord Hampton, and many others who were interested in social care.

Charles Dickens once visited Ashley Down. He had heard a rumour that the children were badly treated and sometimes hungry, and decided to investigate in person. Müller received him with courtesy, called for one of his assistants and handed him a bunch of keys.

'Please show Mr Dickens over any of the five houses he wishes to see.'

This was done and it was reported that Dickens went away entirely reassured.

Former Ashley Down residents whose memories go back almost to the Müller era recall having meat regularly on Mondays, Thursdays and Fridays while on Wednesdays and Saturdays they were served a broth with meat in it. On Tuesdays and Sundays (when many staff would be at Bethesda for the morning service) a dish of rice and raisins was a common lunch. Frequently the meat was Australian mutton, known to the children as 'og' or (more popular) corned beef; the children incidentally often referred to bread as 'toke' due to the wording of a favourite Ashley Down grace, 'We thank thee Lord for these tokens of Thy love'. Bristol's situation as a port meant that it was not unusual for the children to receive fresh fruit, particularly bananas and oranges. Occasionally, at times of surplus, large quantities of free fruit would be delivered to Ashley Down to prevent it from rotting. Eggs were regularly on the menu, but to some extent also seasonal: on his or her birthday every child was entitled to two eggs, one for himself and one for his best friend. The usual beverage was milk and water.

If the predictability of the menus and the routine of events tended to make life on Ashley Down somewhat monotonous, there were a number of annual events which interrupted the routine and provided the children with both happy memories and highlights to which they could look forward (in addition to their own birthdays).

First, the annual summer treat was the outing to Pur Down, when the children set off in the morning armed with either a pink or blue cotton bag filled with sweets and sweet biscuits to eat on the journey. On this day, on arrival at the field, the children of the five houses could mix as they pleased. The picnic lunch (of bread and cheese) and tea (bread and butter and cake) was transported to Pur Down in large hampers. A group of now elderly former Ashley Down children, who could never remember it raining on Pur Down, proudly showed me an old oak tree under which they used to play many years ago on that great day. The outing ended with the launching of five fire balloons, one for each House.

Probably the event which children anticipated with the greatest excitement was Christmas. Well before the time, they began to prepare for the celebrations – learning to sing carols and other songs from the Ashley Down Song Book (often in parts without accompaniment), making the decorations, and memorising poems, sketches and plays to be recited and performed at the parties.

Each December, Müller's journal took on a seasonal tone:

December 23rd 1878. From Clifton we received for the children a number of dolls, some fancy boxes, albums, games, balls, tops and a great variety of other play-things – From Durdham Down, as Christmas presents for the orphans, dressed dolls, boxes and packets of chocolates and sweets, some drums, tops, balls, marbles, whips and guns, boxes of toys, books, fancy cards, paint boxes, transparent slates, pocket-handkerchiefs, wool ties and ruffs, baskets and boxes, pencils, trumpets and other play-things.... From a Bristol wholesale house, fifteen boxes of fruit, ten boxes of oranges, ten boxes of figs, and a sack of nuts for the orphans' Christmas Treat.

December 16th 1884. From a Bristol wholesale house eight barrels of flour, one barrel of currants, and sixteen quarter boxes of Valencias for the children's Christmas puddings.

One Christmas, one hundred and fifty pheasants were sent to Ashley Down from a donor in Cornwall.

And so a former orphan could recall, 'Well do I remember the happy Christmases spent at No. 4; the start of the preparations for the decorations; the arrival of the great big Christmas tree, nothing on it, but I knew before Christmas it would be loaded with toys and presents; and somewhere amongst the many there would be one for me!' And another, who wrote to the Homes one Christmas, 'I expect the times are just as exciting as when I was there. I imagine the decorations being got ready, and the secrecy of it all, and then learning the lovely carols, and the Christmas Shop! I would love to peep in, to see if it is really like it used to be. I don't think it could possibly be better.' The Christmas Shops were little sweet shops, opened in each wing of the Houses, managed by members of the school staff who bought the sweets from the large Bristol sweet manufacturers on special terms. In time these shops came to be opened in other seasons as well.

After the founder's death, and perhaps during his lifetime as well, another annual treat was Müller's birthday, September 27th. At this time the children took a week's holiday from school and, as one old girl recalled, 'we used to go out most days, blackberry picking. How we all enjoyed it!' The day itself was always marked by special helpings of Müller-cake, made with sultanas, and an enormous apple dumpling for each child.

We cannot of course pretend that every child was happy on Ashley Down; some clearly weren't. The experience was especially unhappy for children who had known for a while the love of their own parents and a normal life; for these children – arriving on Ashley Down perhaps aged eleven, twelve or more – the five great buildings naturally appeared particularly barrack-like and uninviting. And no doubt mistakes were made in the appointment of staff, with the result that kindness and understanding were sometimes in short supply. As a pioneer in the field, Müller was forced to learn by his mistakes: and mistakes there were. Almost certainly the children's existence on Ashley Down was too sheltered, too remote from the realities of the outside world. Today, Müller's children attend normal local authority schools and mix freely with other boys and girls. But in the founder's day Bristol didn't offer free education for some two thousand children and it is difficult to suggest the alternatives which were open to him.

In the event, however, the children received a sound education which they would have been fortunate to have obtained elsewhere. They received, too, a treasure of immeasurable value: teaching which was able to make them 'wise unto salvation' and which offered to those who would accept it, 'life more abundant'.

17

SAFE TO GLORY

Not many days after the opening of No. 5 in January 1870, Mary Müller – now in her seventy-third year – caught a heavy cold which left her with a troublesome cough.

'My darling, you must allow Dr Pritchard to see you,' said Müller.

Mary agreed, reluctantly.

'You must give up walking from Paul Street to Ashley Down, I'm afraid,' said the doctor. 'Take a cab from now on. And you must set aside time for a daily rest after dinner.'

At night Müller would feel Mary's pulse and find it feeble and irregular; but Mary wouldn't agree that much was the matter with her. Towards the end of January, she felt a pain across the lower part of her back and right arm. Although the pain grew worse, Mary travelled to Ashley Down with Lydia and directed affairs at the Homes as usual. At tea-time she drove back to Paul Street with her sister Miss Groves and Lydia; Müller went off to the prayer meeting at Salem Chapel. When he arrived home, he found that their doctor, Josiah Pritchard, had ordered Mary to bed.

'She must stay in bed,' Dr Pritchard told Müller, 'and have a fire lit in her bedroom. She has rheumatic fever.'

Müller expected the worst. But, he said, 'though my heart was nigh to be broken, on account of the depth of my affection, I said to myself, "The Lord is good, and does good; all will be according to His own blessed character. Nothing but that which is good, like Himself, can proceed from Him. If He pleases to take my wife, it will be good, like Himself. What I have to do, as His child, is to be satisfied with what my Father does that I may glorify Him."'

Next day, on the Tuesday evening, Müller sat alone in his wife's room at No. 3. Mary was at home in bed for the first time in nine years; on the wall was a day-to-day calendar *The Silent Comforter*, Müller looked at the text for the day: Psalm 119:75, 'I know, O Lord, that your judgments are right, and in faithfulness you have afflicted me.' Müller read the words again and again.

'Yes, Lord,' he said to himself, 'Your judgments are right, I am satisfied with them. You know the depth of the affection of Your poor child for his beloved wife, yet I am satisfied with Your judgments; and my inmost soul says that You in faithfulness have afflicted me. All this is according to Your love with which You have loved me in Christ Jesus, and whatever the issue, all will be well.'

Underneath this text, *The Silent Comforter* had the words, 'My times are in Your hands' (Ps. 31:15).

'Yes, my Father,' thought Müller, 'the times of my darling wife are in Your hands. You will do the very best thing for her and for me, whether life or death. If it may be, raise yet up again my precious wife, You are able to do it, though she is so ill; but however You deal with me, only help me to continue to be perfectly satisfied with Your holy will.'

During that week, the words of the hymn 'One there is above all others', kept coming into Müller's mind:

> Best of blessings He'll provide us,
> > Nought but good shall e'er betide us,
> Safe to glory He will guide us,
> > Oh how He loves!

'My heart,' he said, 'continually responded – "Nought but good shall e'er betide us".'

On the Wednesday, Mary felt less pain, and before he left Paul Street for Ashley Down, Müller sat on her bed and read a verse from Psalm 84, 'The Lord God is a sun and shield: the Lord will give grace and glory: no good thing will be withheld from them that walk uprightly.'

'My darling,' Müller said to Mary, 'we have both received grace, and we shall therefore receive glory; and as, by God's grace, we walk uprightly, nothing that is good for us will He withhold from us.'

Later in the day, Mary told their daughter Lydia the verse which George had read and how it had comforted her. And as Müller went about his work on Ashley Down he said to himself again and again, 'I walk uprightly, and therefore my Father will withhold nothing from me that is good for me; if therefore the restoration of my dearest Mary is good for me, it will surely be given; if otherwise, I have to seek to glorify God by perfect submission to His holy will.'

'Every two hours through the night,' Dr Pritchard said to Müller that evening, 'I want you to give your wife a small quantity of beef tea or a teaspoon full of wine in a tablespoon of water.'

Müller did this, and each time he prayed with Mary.

'I should feel easier,' Dr Pritchard told Müller, 'if my colleague Dr Black could see Mrs Müller as I must tell you that the situation is now very grave.'

'I am perfectly satisfied with your treatment,' replied Müller, 'but if you would feel happier please make the appointment.'

On Saturday morning, Müller stayed at home with Mary. After lunch he said:

'My darling, I am sorry to have to leave you, but I shall return as soon as I can.'

'You leave me with Jesus,' said Mary.

That night her pains grew worse. Müller spent the night trying to make her as comfortable as he could. Mary was now unable to move any of her limbs.

In the morning Doctors Black and Pritchard called.

'All hope of recovery has gone,' Dr Black said to Müller.

Müller went into their bedroom.

'The Lord Jesus is coming for you,' Müller said to Mary.

'He will come soon!' said Mary.

At half past one, Müller gave Mary her medicine and a spoonful of wine in water. Mary had difficulty in swallowing and her speech became indistinct. George sat quietly beside her and noticed that 'her dear bright eyes were set'.

He left the room for a moment.

'Mary is dying,' he said quietly to Lydia and Mary's sister.

The two ladies joined George at Mary's bedside and were soon joined by another of Mary's sisters. The four of them sat there for two and a half hours. At twenty past four on Sunday February 6th 1870 Mary Müller died.

'Thank you for releasing her,' said Müller as he knelt down by the bed. 'Thank you for taking her to be with Yourself. Please help and support us now.'

George and Mary had been married for forty years.

On February 11th 1870, Müller himself conducted the funeral service at Bethesda and at the cemetery. About one thousand two hundred children followed in the procession; they were joined by the staff from Ashley Down and hundreds of members of Bethesda Chapel. Before he preached his funeral sermon Müller sat in the vestry repeating again and again:

'Oh Mary, my Mary!'

He took his text, 'You are good, and what You do is good' (Ps. 119:68). He recalled that Mary had become the first member of Bethesda church when it reopened under Craik's pastorship in 1832; that she had lived to see two thousand seven hundred believers received into communion; and that when she died there were nine hundred and twenty members. He gave a detailed outline of her life and work.

'Perhaps all Christians who have heard me,' he said towards the end of his address, 'will have no difficulty in giving their hearty assent that "the Lord was good, and doing good" in leaving her to me so long; but I ask these dear Christian friends to go further with me, and to say from their hearts, "The Lord was good, and doing good" in the removal of that useful, lovely, excellent wife from her husband, and that at the very time when, humanly speaking, he needed her more than ever. While I am saying this, I feel the void in my heart. That lovely one is no more with me, to share my joys and sorrows. Every day I miss her more and more. Every day I see more and more how great her loss to the orphans. Yet, without an effort, my inmost soul habitually joys in the joy of that loved departed one. Her happiness gives joy to me. My dear daughter and self would not have her back, were it possible to produce it by turn of the hand. God Himself has done it, we are satisfied with Him....'

But, despite these brave words at the funeral, in the months that followed Mary's death, Müller felt the loss deeply. He recorded that 'my earthly joy was all but gone'; and about ten days after the bereavement he became, for a while, very unwell. As he recovered from this illness he found that when 'now between eight and nine o'clock in the evenings, I went home from the Orphan-Houses, instead of in the company with my beloved Mary, as for so many years past (for she was always with me) I said to myself: "I shall not meet my beloved wife at home, but I shall meet the Lord Jesus, my precious Friend; He will comfort me"; and I thanked God that he had left my beloved daughter to me, who always watched for my arrival to greet me, and did all she could to soothe my bereaved heart. But the loss was great, the wound was deep, and, as the weeks and months passed on, while continuing habitually not only to be satisfied with God, but also to praise Him for what He had done in thus bereaving me, the wound seemed to deepen instead of being healed, and the bereavement to be felt more and more....'

The loss was felt too by the children and old boys and girls who had passed through the Homes; Müller received hundreds of letters of sympathy, even months after the event. One such came from one of the first Wilson Street children:

Dear Mr Müller, Not from ingratitude is it, I have not written before, but because I knew you had so many letters; but not a particle do I love dear Mrs Müller less than those who have written. I think I loved her with you as my parents.

True I never knew my parents, to know what it was to love them; but I do know what it is to love you and her, and from my heart I mourn her loss. I know you miss her daily. I miss her going by the House; for I always watched you go by; but now you are alone. I trust it may please God to spare you for years to come to us all, as well as to your own dear child and family; for oh! It would be blank, indeed, were you removed from us. I remain yours very respectfully.

The writer of this letter was not alone in her anxiety as to what would happen if Müller were taken.

'What, Mr Müller, will become of the Orphan-Houses when you are removed?' people asked.

'The Orphan-Houses,' Müller would reply, 'and the land belonging to them, are vested in the hands of eleven trustees, and therefore the Institution stands on the same footing, in this particular, as other charitable Institutions.'

'But where will be found the man who will carry on the work in the same spirit in which you do, trusting only in God for everything that in any way is needed in connection with the work?'

'When the Lord is pleased to remove me from my post, He will prove that He was not dependent on me, and that He can easily raise up another servant of His to act on the same principles on which I have sought to carry on the work.'

'You should pray that God will raise up a successor to carry on the work after you,'

'I do this regularly,' Müller always replied.

'Would you ask Mr James Wright to come to see me?' Müller said to an assistant not many months after Mary's death.

Since Wright's boyhood, Müller had watched his 'consistently godly deportment', and for nearly twelve years he had been one of Müller's most valued helpers in all aspects of the work of the Scriptural Knowledge Institution including the children's work. For some years George and Mary had prayed specifically that God would fit him to become the successor.

'I have to tell you,' Müller said to James Wright, 'that I consider it to be God's will that you should succeed me as the director of this Institution.'

Wright produced a number of reasons why he considered himself unfit for the job, none of which Müller would accept as valid.

'I feel that you find the task a great burden. I beg you not to accept Mr Müller's invitation,' Wright's wife said to her husband. After some weeks, however, she changed her mind and Wright went to see Müller again.

'I now feel that it would not be my duty to refuse to accept your invitation any longer.'

'Then it is agreed,' said Müller, smiling, 'if I am taken, you will succeed me.'

Shortly after this, Wright's wife died.

They said of Wright that his 'beautiful face and radiant smile showed, better than any words possibly could, that peace and joy ruled his heart. His dignified yet gracious demeanour at once won the respect of all. Of his faith and love his works bear witness, but his humility was equally apparent to an observing mind.'

Wright was fond of music and for many years his beautiful bass voice led the singing at Bethesda. He loved to join a group gathered around a piano or organ and sing hymns from the *Bristol Tune Book*.

Eighteen months later, in August 1871, Wright asked to see Müller about a personal matter.

'I have come to ask for the hand of your daughter in marriage.'

We don't know how Müller replied, but he recorded: 'I knew no one to whom I could so willingly entrust this my choicest earthly treasure.'

For two weeks Lydia agonised about her own response to Wright's proposal. Müller discovered that her only difficulty was that she would have to leave her father.

'I beseech you not to let this stand in your way,' Müller said to Lydia. 'It would be a great comfort and joy to me to see you united to such a husband.'

They were married at Bethesda on November 16th 1871: Wright was forty-five and Lydia thirty-nine. Wright later described their life together as a time of 'unbroken felicity'.

Bethesda was soon to see another wedding.

18

Return to the Rigi

Nearly two years after Mary's death, Lydia's engagement, among other things, finally persuaded Müller to marry again – a decision reached, he said, 'in the fear of God, and in the full assurance that I had the sanction and approval of my Heavenly Father'. He recorded that he had known Miss Susannah Grace Sangar, a governess from Clifton about twenty years his junior, for 'more than twenty-five years as a consistent Christian, and regarding whom I had every reason to believe that she would prove a great helper to me in my various services.' They were married on November 30th 1871.

For the next two years, Susannah Müller learned more and more about the work and sought to relieve her husband of as much as she could. And then, in March 1874, she developed a heavy fever: it was typhoid. At first it seemed the attack wasn't too serious.

On Thursday March 26th, Müller left Susannah with Lydia at Paul Street better than she had been for several days. After lunch, Lydia came to fetch Müller from Ashley Down.

'Susannah has had a haemorrhage.'

Müller rushed home to find that his wife had sustained a very serious loss of blood. Dr Williams arrived. 'My dear wife,' he recalled, 'looked as pale as death, and the perspiration was on her brow; but by the means used, after a while seemed brought back again to life.'

On Sunday April 5th, Susannah became delirious; the fever was at its peak. In the evening Dr Williams consulted Dr Black.

'Mrs Müller may recover if she can sleep,' said Dr Black.

Susannah hadn't shut her eyes for more than thirty hours. A third nurse was sent for so that two others could rest. Müller did his best to see that all the medical instructions were carried out correctly. 'But my hope was in God alone. I knew Him, and I knew He would do what was best for me. My heart was satisfied with him. I delighted myself in Him.' Susannah's condition was now known in many countries and thousands of prayers were offered up on her behalf.

That night the crisis came and passed. She slept for five hours and through most of Monday. From that day Müller began to see small signs of improvement. But still Susannah's pulse was about 120 and very weak.

'I have never known a patient recover after such a massive haemorrhage as that sustained by Mrs Müller,' a distinguished London consultant said – Müller described him as 'the most eminent and most experienced London physician'.

'For the third time now,' Müller wrote, 'my inmost soul sought to be satisfied with God, to delight myself in God, to kiss the hand which smote me; and, by His grace, I did so.... I know what a lovely, gracious Being God is, from the revelation which He has been pleased to make of Himself in His Holy Word; I believe this revelation; I also know from my own experience the truth of it; and therefore I was satisfied with God, I delighted myself in God; and so it came, that He gave me the desire of my heart, even the restoration of my dear wife.'

By the beginning of May, Susannah was well enough to be wheeled in an easy chair out of her bedroom to a sitting room to be on a sofa for short periods; by the middle of the month she made her first short trip out into the open air in a carriage. By the end of May the couple were able to travel to Burnham, Somerset, so that Susannah might enjoy the benefit of sea air. In September they travelled to Ventnor on the Isle of Wight where she made a complete recovery.

Since coming to Bristol in 1832, Müller had preached almost exclusively in that city; his position as a pastor of the large church at Bethesda and a director of the orphan-houses and literature distribution work had tied him to Bristol. But the situation at Bethesda was changing: there were several gifted and experienced men who could shoulder responsibilities. And James Wright had already proved himself an able co-director of the work on Ashley Down and of the Institution generally. So after much prayer, Müller decided to devote his closing years to a world-wide work of preaching and teaching.

He was convinced that there were many people who were perfectly genuine in their desire to be right with God, but who lacked peace because they relied upon their feelings. After more than half a century of daily, systematic and consecutive study of the Bible, Müller would now aim to share with a wider audience the truths that he had discovered and to encourage Christians to become lovers of the Bible themselves; and to test everything by the word of God.

Another of Müller's aims in embarking on his preaching tours would be (in the true spirit of Groves and the best of the early Brethren) to break down barriers of denominationalism and to promote, as he put it, 'brotherly love amongst true Christians'.

> Though not agreeing at all with some of their opinions and practices, I nevertheless preach amongst all, having seen for many years how greatly the heart of the Lord Jesus must be grieved by the dis-union that exists among His own true disciples. On this account, therefore, I have sought (in my feeble measure) to unite all real believers; but, as this cannot be done, by standing aloof from our brethren in Christ, until they see eye to eye with us in every point, I have gone amongst them, and have united with them, in so far as nothing has been required of me which I could not do with a good conscience.

Susannah Müller loved travel and would make an ideal companion. Although George's health was still good it would have been impossible for him to complete the arduous programme of world-wide engagements which lay ahead without Susannah at his side to act as nurse-cum-secretary. She would ensure that the tours wouldn't be all work and no play: for, no doubt partly due to her influence, the couple took time off from George's numerous engagements to visit tourist attractions, beauty spots and places of historic interest.

Their first tour – not leaving English shores – was a short one in the spring and early summer of 1875. Müller was in his seventieth year and Susannah about fifty. Spurgeon asked Müller to preach for him, and, in the famous Metropolitan Tabernacle, the man whose pioneering work in Bristol had made him well known in London, addressed a large congregation. He spoke in Newcastle and, returning to London, at the Mildmay Park Conference – the interdenominational forerunner of the Keswick Convention which was itself just getting under way.

Gavin Kirkham, himself a gifted evangelist, and first secretary of the Open-Air mission, wrote at that time:

Mr Müller's appearance is striking; he is tall and commanding. He is in his seventieth year. He has a strong German accent, though he is easily understood by any English hearer. In his public ministry, he is emphatically a *teacher*, yet he frequently brings in the way of salvation, in a clear, sweet, persuasive manner. Preachers may learn from his *method* of preaching. He first of all gets a message from the Lord: that is he waits upon the Lord, by reading the Scriptures, meditation and prayer, till he realises that he has the mind of the Spirit as to what he shall say. He has sometimes been in doubt till almost the last minute, but never once has the Lord failed him. He strongly advocates and practises expository preaching. Instead of a solitary text detached from its context, he selects a passage, it may be of several verses, which he goes over consecutively clause by clause. His first care is to give the meaning of the passage, and then to illustrate it by other Scriptures and then to apply it. This is done sentence by sentence, so that it is definition, illustration, and application all the way through. Yet there is no uncertainty to his hearers as to when he is coming to a close, as he intimates at the outset how many verses he purposes to consider. His illustrations are occasionally taken from history, biography, or nature, but chiefly from Scriptures or his own personal experience.

One of the most striking things about Mr Müller's preaching is the way in which he induces his hearers to *reconsider* what has already been said. He frequently says: 'Let us ask ourselves, Have I understood this? How does it apply to *me*? Is this *my* experience?'

The first tour was a relatively short one, with Müller preaching seventy times; but it was already obvious that wherever he went in the years ahead, he would be assured of eager and attentive audiences.

In August 1875 Moody and Sankey arrived back in New York after a campaign in Britain which had made them famous. Moody had described Müller as one of three men in England he longed to meet; he had duly visited Bristol, in his biographer's words, 'to imbibe a heady draft of Müller's faith'.

On the day that Moody and Sankey returned to New York, George and Susannah set off on their second tour of Britain which would last until July 1876. Müller said that his special aim was to 'help forward the work of the devoted brethren, Moody and Sankey.... These dear brethren, from having been able to stay on a comparatively short time in each place, were unable to lead on the young converts in knowledge and grace; I therefore sought to follow up their labours, and, in my feeble measure, to do what I could to supply this lack of service.' Anxious to instruct new converts he held fourteen meetings at the Mildmay Park Conference Hall in London, often speaking to three thousand people at once.

On then to Scotland where he preached at a Convention in Glasgow to five thousand people on the power of the Spirit; not all who came could get into the hall, and Müller accepted an invitation to speak at an overflow meeting of about one thousand two hundred in a neighbouring church. During a month in

Glasgow he preached nearly forty times, and every Sunday evening addressed three thousand people in the Prince of Wales Theatre.

Then, after three weeks in Dublin, including a number of meetings at a packed Merrion Hall, the Müllers travelled to Liverpool. There Müller spoke at the immense Victoria Hall which had been built for Moody and Sankey. 'In this vast audience,' W. H. Harding recalled, 'sits a bronzed weather-beaten man, now the captain of a merchant vessel, who in other days was an inmate of the Orphan-House. How can this man, still unconverted, sit in peace while this old benefactor, grey and obviously ageing, delivers once again, as in the long ago, the blessed message of eternal life? The scarred captain listens, weeps, apprehends spiritually the motive of Müller's life, and steers straight for the haven of soul rest.'

Müller preached over fifty times in Liverpool, on Sundays to between five and six thousand people. On then for a busy tour of Scotland during which Susannah recorded that while at Crathie 'we became acquainted with a Christian housekeeper living at Balmoral Castle, who kindly conducted us one afternoon through the Queen's residence in Scotland; and, a short while before we left Crathie, Her Majesty arrived at the Castle, whom we saw driving out occasionally, accompanied by the Princess Beatrice'.

The third tour took the couple to Europe and they spent the last two weeks of August 1876 in Paris. In September they arrived in Berne where Müller preached in German for the first time in thirty-six years. One afternoon they went to Die Enge, a hall on the side of a steep hill outside Berne where Colonel von Buren had invited about one hundred and fifty people to meet them. As they sat drinking coffee looking across to the distant Alps, whose snow-covered peaks appeared rose coloured in the light of a setting sun, someone said:

Le bon Dieu l'a fait expres pour vous donner plaisir.

Before embarking on an extensive series of meetings, George and Susannah boarded a steamer at Lucerne and crossed Lake Geneva to Vitznau at the foot of the Rigi. More than half a century had passed since Müller had climbed to the summit with Beta and his other student friends in the summer of 1825. Fortunately, in the intervening years someone had thoughtfully built a cog-wheel railway and the Müllers travelled to the top in relative comfort. But the view across the Bernese Oberland to Geneva to the south and up to the Black Forest in the north had hardly changed.

As snow began to fall, the couple were glad to find shelter in a hotel beneath the summit. 'At half-past four the next morning,' wrote Mrs Müller, 'we rose and ascended the Rigi Kulm, whence splendid ranges of innumerable snowy mountain peaks and distant glaciers could be seen extending far and wide, to which, illuminated as they were by the bright beams of the rising sun, a gorgeous prismatic colouring was imparted; and there we stood for a considerable time, gazing round upon that grand, wild, solitary, silent region with an interest that could scarcely be exceeded.'

At the top of the St Gothard Pass, nine thousand feet above sea level and enveloped in a thick fog, the former governess from Clifton and her husband were 'thankful to accept the very poor accommodation afforded at the Hospice, and, in spite of the smoke of some Italians that filled the only room with a fire in it which the house contained, were glad to be allowed to share it with them, and with any other travellers who happened to come in'.

In Zurich, Müller preached twice at the Anna Kapelle to congregations which overflowed into the staircases and doorways. In Constance, the Müllers visited the Council Chamber in the Merchants' Hall where John Huss had been tried and sentenced to be burned at the stake for his outspoken views on the corruption of the pre-Reformation church.

At Stuttgart in Germany, the Queen of Wurttemberg sent for Müller and at the palace asked him a number of questions about the children's work in Bristol. At Darmstadt he held a drawing-room meeting at the house of the Court preacher: four drawing rooms were thrown open, and Princess Karl (mother of Prince Louis of Hesse, husband of Princess Alice of England), Princess von Battenberg, and several people from the royal court turned up.

At Dusseldorf, the City Missioner approached Müller in some distress.

'I have six sons and have been praying for their conversions for many years. They do not respond. What should I do?'

'*Continue* to pray for your sons,' Müller told the Missioner, 'and *expect* an answer to your prayer, and you will have to praise God.'

In the spring (1877) George and Susannah visited Wartburg Castle near Halle where Martin Luther had been imprisoned in 1521. They saw the sitting-room where the reformer had translated the Bible into German. At Halle, Müller preached at Francke's Orphanage, the Institution which had inspired him in his early days in Bristol. Müller was delighted to find that his old tutor, Professor Tholuck was still alive and now Counsellor of the Upper Consistorium of Prussia. The two men had a joyful reunion and a long conversation.

On the way to Berlin, at Wittenberg, they saw the church on whose door in 1517 Luther had nailed his ninety-five theses against indulgences; and at an old monastery they visited the room where he had lived as an Augustinian monk.

During three weeks in Berlin, Müller preached to large congregations. Count Bismarck (a cousin of the famous statesman), came 120 miles just to see and hear Müller.

'Your *Narratives* have been a great blessing to my soul,' Bismarck told Müller.

After speaking at meetings in most towns in Holland, Müller brought his European tour to an end after preaching over three hundred times. Back at Paul Street, a letter was waiting for him from the United States signed by the Rev. E. P. Thwing and four other pastors begging him to come to America to preach.

The invitation was the most recent of many he had received inviting him to the States. This time he decided to accept.

19

To the White House

The Müllers set off for the United States in August 1877 aboard the 4,000 ton ship the *Sardinian*. For some reason they had been allocated the chief officer's deck room for their cabin, which Susannah found to be 'tolerably comfortable'.

Although the Atlantic was rough, the ship remained on schedule until running into thick fog off Newfoundland. Captain Dutton had been on the bridge for twenty-four hours when George Müller appeared at his side.

'Captain, I have come to tell you that I must be in Quebec by Saturday afternoon.'

'It is impossible,' said the captain.

'Very well,' said Müller, 'if your ship cannot take me, God will find some other way – I have never broken an engagement in fifty-two years. Let us go down into the chart-room and pray.'

Captain Dutton wondered which lunatic asylum Müller had escaped from.

'Mr Müller,' he said, 'do you know how dense this fog is?'

'No, my eye is not on the density of the fog, but on the living God who controls every circumstance of my life.'

Müller then knelt down and prayed simply. When he had finished the captain was about to pray, but Müller put his hand on his shoulder.

'Do not pray. First, you don't believe He will answer; and second, I believe He has and there is no need whatever for you to pray about it.'

Captain Dutton looked at Müller in amazement.

'Captain,' Müller continued, 'I have known my Lord for fifty-two years, and there has never been a single day that I have failed to get an audience with the King. Get up, captain, and open the door, and you will find the fog is gone.'

The captain walked across to the door and opened it. The fog had lifted.

Captain Dutton retold the story many times during many times as master of the *Sardinian*; a well-known nineteenth century evangelist subsequently described him as 'one of the most devoted men I ever knew'.

As they drew near to Quebec, the Sardinian fired her guns as a signal of her approach. At the Hotel St Louis, a pile of letters awaited them inviting Müller to preach. But before travelling south to New York, they found time to visit the Niagara Falls.

The couple were rather disappointed by their first distant view of the Falls. After driving to a bridge just above the American Falls, they climbed a staircase to Luna Island, and then, standing by a railing close to the edge of the precipice, they began to appreciate the size and grandeur of the American Falls.

'This,' they thought, 'surpasses everything; surely this must be the grandest cataract in the world!'

But it wasn't; after a few more steps they came into full view of the great Horse Shoe Fall, on the Canadian side of the river, gushing eighty-five thousand cubic feet of water every second over the cliffs into a huge, boiling cauldron at the bottom. They looked at the Rapids where the Niagara descends, as Susannah put it, 'over rough ridges of rock, great masses of stone and large boulders', and where 'its waters surge and foam, in ten thousand fantastic shapes, and in the wildest turmoil, as though frantically eager to rush over the precipices into the abyss below'.

On Sunday morning, September 9th, at Dr Talmage's Tabernacle – said, at that time, to be the largest church in the United

States – the Rev. Professor E. P. Thwing introduced Müller to the congregation. The visitor from Bristol preached for three-quarters of an hour. After an evening meeting, a former Ashley Down girl, now married and settled in America pressed forward to greet the Müllers.

Müller preached about fifty times in the Brooklyn and New York area, including several times in German to the large German population. Then they travelled to Boston where Müller's first engagement was at Moody's Tabernacle – an enormous building which held seven thousand people.

Müller preached twice at the Old Presbyterian Church Newburyport, founded by George Whitefield, and caused a stir by reading from the Bible which had belonged to the great man whose biography he had read forty years earlier; the Bible wasn't normally opened. Müller spoke from the pulpit which stands just above the spot where Whitefield is buried.

'God sent you to America, dear brother!' a pastor said to Müller after he had preached at Dr Mitchell's Church in Washington. 'That's just the kind of teaching we want; something that will rouse and wake up Christians as well as the unconverted. God sent you to America, Sir; of that I'm certain.'

On the morning of January 10th 1878, at half-past nine, the Müllers had a very special appointment. They had been invited to the White House to meet President Hayes and his wife. 'They received us with much courtesy,' said Susannah, 'and, after making some enquiries about our work in England, the President entered for half an hour into conversation with Mr Müller. Mrs Hayes afterwards conducted us through the White House, a large old mansion, and showed us the State apartments, with the various objects of interest which this residence contains.'

Müller had a gruelling three weeks in Washington, often preaching twice a day, but they found time to climb the four hundred feet to the top of the dome on the Capitol Building and to admire the view.

From Washington, they travelled to Salem, Virginia, in the Allegheny Mountains, and Müller's fame had preceded him. At the Lutheran church, 'hundreds of young men were present, most of them students from Roanoke College and the Theological Seminary, many of whom were standing at the entrance closely packed together; whilst others sat upon the pulpit side by side. The gallery was thronged. At the back of it several young men were standing upon forms, with their heads near the ceiling, and upon the edge of the front seats in the gallery a few boys were perched, with their legs hanging over the pews, in a somewhat dangerous position.'

'This good man,' said the *Roanoke Collegian* in its leading article in January 1878, under the heading 'Rev. Geo. Müller', 'so widely and favorably known as the founder of the Orphan's Home at Bristol, England, and the author of the *Life of Trust* has just paid us a visit.... He is about six feet high, quite erect, his locks are silvered with age; his face bears the distinctive outlines of the refined German, while his *personel*, at once classic and military, impresses rather by the expression of joy and holy confidence that play upon the countenance.... Asking amiss, and asking aright were the two themes in his sermon. Asking amiss is asking from selfish motives. Asking aright has three elements: 1. Desiring God's glory. 2. Confessing our unworthiness and pleading the merits of Jesus. 3. Believing that we do receive the things for which we ask.'

The next journey took the couple four hundred miles to Columbia in South Carolina where they stayed with Chief Justice Willard. Mr Willard took them to the State House and introduced them to the Governor and the Secretary of State for South Carolina. Müller opened the day's proceedings at the state House of Representatives with prayer.

At the end of February the Müllers boarded a river steamer for a tedious journey down the river Savannah to Jacksonville during which the *City of Bridgetown* ran aground several times. At Jacksonville, a vast audience gathered to hear Müller – said to be the largest congregation ever known in the town.

After meetings in Montgomery and New Orleans, the intrepid pair boarded the steamer *John Scudder* for the long voyage up the Mississippi to Memphis. Although the food provided on board was excellent, George and Susannah were disturbed to discover that no drinking water was available except the unfiltered water of the river. This was so full of impurities and muddy sediment that it formed a thick deposit in the bottom of any glass or cup into which they poured it. Poor George and Susannah couldn't make up their minds whether to drink it cold or in the form of tea or coffee. At last they hit upon the expedient of getting hold of a jug filled with ice, melting the ice, and then mixing a little wine with the water to take off the chill: this made a palatable drink. Müller preached to 'passengers, coloured servants and as many of the ship's company as were able to attend' but he found that the passengers were 'chiefly worldly people, who amused themselves with music, singing, dancing and card playing, from which there was no escape, as from our cabin we could see and hear all that was going on'. If the Müllers had made the journey ten years later, New Orleans jazz bands, which by then had become popular, would have been added irritation.

On April 18th (1878) the Müllers rose at half-past five, and set off on the long journey from St Louis to San Francisco nearly two thousand four hundred miles away. They travelled in the reserved compartment of a Pullman carriage, which even Susannah conceded was comfortable with good sleeping arrangements. On the first morning, when they pulled into Council Bluffs for breakfast, they were surrounded by a crowd of emigrants to California, amongst whom the Müllers distributed tracts. After Omaha, Nebraska, their journey took them through the prairies, and for a while Susannah couldn't understand why the train was only travelling at fifteen miles an hour. At last she realised (perhaps her husband told her) that they were gradually climbing thousands of feet above sea level; the climb was actually so long and steep that the engine broke down and the passengers tumbled out to admire the spectacular view. Müller and his wife saw this as an opportunity to distribute more tracts. With a partially repaired engine they crawled on at an even slower pace to Sherman, the highest railway station in the world, where the cold was intense and the snow deep.

Arriving at Wells, they saw groups of Indians wrapped in scarlet blankets and striped woollen mantles dyed with brilliant colours; and (before the day of televised westerns), Mrs Müller was intrigued by their 'curious-looking hats, trimmed with feathers and wide ribbons'; and noticed that they 'had their faces painted with patches of vermillion'.

As dawn broke on the morning of April 23rd they had their first sight of California. 'A magnificent prospect of indescribable grandeur suddenly burst upon our view. Far above (Summit) station innumerable mountain peaks were towering towards the sky; the sun, which shone brilliantly, lighted up the snow to a whiteness that was dazzling; deep abysses, chasms and ravines surrounded us; millions of pine and fir-trees were growing up the mountains' sides; and thousands of feet far down below, valleys clothed with the richest verdure added beauty to the scene.'

At eight o'clock the conductor threw open the door of the carriage.

'Cape Horn!' he shouted.

The passengers jumped up, looked out of the windows to find the train travelling slowly along the edge of a precipice nearly two thousand five hundred feet high. Through 'Emigrant's Gap' they began to descend further into California. The weather grew warmer and Susannah saw that 'the fields were covered with grass, intermingled with brilliant masses of wild flowers; lupins, eschscholzias, wild roses and geraniums were flourishing ... and millions of Californian poppies of an intense yellow, deepening into orange colour, outshone all the rest'.

'I never saw flowers till I saw them in California,' cried a passenger.

At Oakland station, San Francisco, they were met by two friends who took them on board the *El Capitan* which ferried them across San Francisco Bay and then to the Palace Hotel where they were shown a suite of rooms which, Susannah was quick to point out, their friends had engaged for them.

On their first Sunday in California, Müller preached to two thousand people at the Tabernacle Presbyterian Church in Tyler Street. On the Tuesday, a friend called in his carriage and took them on a sightseeing drive. They walked along the beach and felt the Pacific breeze against their faces. Then, Susannah recalled, 'our friend conducted us to Cliff House, an hotel built upon a high rock overlooking the ocean where, from a balcony we had the opportunity of observing the sea-lions by which the rocks that stand out in the sea are frequented. Hundreds of these curious amphibious creatures were there with their pointed heads and bodies shining with salt water. Some were basking in the sunshine on dry portions of the cliffs, others were plunging into the sea, several were climbing up sloping places on the rocks and others were barking discordantly.'

At Cliff House, a waiter came over to their table.

'Mr Müller, I must introduce myself. I am the brother of Emma Evans, a child who you cared for on Ashley Down. I often heard you preach when I was in Bristol years ago. I had heard you were in the United States, and just now to my delight I recognised you.'

Before the Müllers left, the waiter presented George and Susannah with a bouquet of flowers.

At Oakland, all the principal churches closed so that their congregations and ministers could hear Müller preach at the First Presbyterian Church. Due to the crowds who came, hundreds couldn't get in and missed hearing Müller preach from Lamentations 3:22-26.

'We have had a glorious meeting,' a pastor told Müller afterwards.

At San Jose, a letter arrived for Müller from a woman whose daughter had been converted at fourteen, but two years later had become mixed up in spiritism to which she had remained attracted for nine years. At San Francisco, however, she had heard Müller preach several times and was profoundly impressed by one sermon in particular. 'You are the first person who has found the way to her heart for these nine years,' the woman wrote to Müller, 'she says she would not have lost that sermon for a hundred dollars'.

After constant preaching at San Jose and Stockton, Müller needed a break and the couple accepted a suggestion that they should visit the Yosemite Valley. They had been warned that travelling by Californian stage-waggon would prove a never to be forgotten adventure. 'Our coachman drove furiously,' Susannah recorded after she had recovered from the experience. 'Rough and smooth, hill and dale, all were alike to him. Now we were driven over one great stone, and then came into collision with another; and as for a drag (brake) going down hill, such a thing was never thought of. The man was doubtless an experienced driver, or at any rate he was a fearless one; but, being ourselves soberminded persons, unaccustomed to such go ahead proceedings, we should have been thankful to take things more quietly; and besides this, desired greatly to reach our journey's end with no bruises and without broken bones. Through the Lord's kindness, however, we reached Priest's Hotel in safety, where we alighted for the night; and after a journey of eleven hours and a half, retired immediately to rest.'

After three days in the Yosemite Valley they rose at half past four to set off for the return journey with ten other passengers in a stage-waggon drawn by five horses. At four in the afternoon a cart approached carrying a man and woman who drew up on one side of the road to let the larger carriage pass. Suddenly the woman jumped to her feet.

'Is that George Müller?'

'It is.'

'Then I must shake hands with you, sir! I have read your *Life of Trust*, and it has been a great blessing to my soul.'

George and Susannah leant out of the window to shake hands with the woman and her husband.

'Pray for me!' shouted the woman as the two carriages pulled away from one another.

At Salt Lake City, the great stronghold of Mormonism, they visited Lion House, the former home of founder Brigham Young. 'His body lies buried in a miserable, neglected piece of ground – a sort of back yard – and his grave is covered by a large, flat stone bearing an inscription; but,' Susannah added sardonically, 'what the epitaph was, we did not care to ascertain.' Müller preached at the Methodist Church to a large congregation which included several Mormons.

At the end of June, they boarded the *Adriatic* for Liverpool after Müller had preached over three hundred times and travelled over nineteen hundred miles. The tour had lasted a year and, on July 8th, 'upon arriving in an open carriage at the top of Ashley Hill at half-past four, found a little army of boys and girls with almost all our helpers at the Orphan-Houses waiting to receive us. There, as we slowly drove along, the boys cheered heartily, and the girls waved their handkerchiefs, determined (as a by-stander remarked) to give us "a right royal welcome"; and at the entrance of New Orphan-House No. 3, a crowd of children closed around us, with loving, friendly greetings.'

20

SIMPLY BY PRAYER

Over forty years had now elapsed since Müller first sought to demonstrate, by founding and maintaining a children's home according to certain defined principles, that there is 'reality in the things of God'. During that period many had been convinced by the demonstration and were brought from scepticism to faith. The response of those who were already Christians had often been to commit themselves more wholeheartedly to lives of prayer and service to God. Most remarkable of all was the effect that a knowledge of Müller's life had on a young Irishman, James McQuilkin, and subsequently through him on the 1859 revival.

Soon after becoming a Christian in 1856, McQuilkin saw an advertisement for the first two volumes of Müller's' *Narratives*. He managed to get hold of a copy in about January 1857 and was amazed by what he read.

'See what Mr Müller obtains simply by prayer,' he thought. 'Thus I may obtain blessing by prayer.'

The following autumn McQuilkin spoke to a small group of young men who used to pray regularly with him in Connor.

'God has really blessed me through reading the *Narratives of some of the Lord's dealings with George Müller*. I now realise the power of believing prayer. I suggest that we should meet to pray regularly for an out-pouring of the Holy Spirit on this district. You will have heard about the great revival which is sweeping through many parts of America. Why shouldn't we have such a blessed work here seeing that God did such great things through Mr Müller, simply in answer to prayer?'

In March 1859 these young men organised a series of meetings near Ballymena; the atmosphere in the area became electric, with hundreds falling to their knees to pray and repent in the streets. In May the movement reached Belfast and began to affect churches of all denominations. In the revival which followed, the lives of hundreds of thousands of people were affected.

Before the end of the year the flames spread through the United Kingdom and then on into Europe. One result of the revival was that thousands of men felt that God was calling them to become full-time evangelists. In England, one such was an Exeter shoemaker named George Brearley who devoted his life to preaching and working on the Blackdown Hills on the Devon and Somerset border. He built or re-opened village chapels, was active as a pastor and established Day Schools.

The schools which George Brearley and his son Walter established on the Blackdown Hills were – like so many other schools in Britain and throughout the world – financed by Müller's Scriptural Knowledge Institution. The last of these schools – at Bishopswood – wasn't closed until 1947 when State education services finally made it redundant.

In the 1870s and early 1880s, the Scriptural Knowledge Institution entirely financed nearly eighty Day Schools for children and half a dozen Adult Schools; in addition, from five to ten schools were partially financed. In Müller's financial year 1879-80, the Institution was entirely responsible for the education of over seven thousand children in seventy-six schools throughout the world as well as seven Adult Schools. Of these schools, fourteen were in Spain, four in India, one in Italy and six in British Guiana; the rest were in England and Wales.

Another convert of the 1859 revival, later to become famous, was a young man from Manchester named Henry Moorhouse, who, in 1861, as a gambler and heavy drinker rushed into a revival meeting in the Alhambra Circus in Manchester, looking for a fight, only to be arrested by hearing the name – Jesus; he 'who had entered to fight remained to praise and pray'.

In 1867, Moorhouse met D. L. Moody in Dublin, and later Moody heard Moorhouse preach while on a visit to Chicago. 'I have never forgotten those nights,' recalled Moody. 'I have preached a different gospel since, and I have had more power with God and man since then.' Moorhouse became a close friend of Moody and Sankey; it was said that Moorhouse was 'the man who moved the man who moved the world'; and that he taught Moody that God hates sin, but loves the sinner.

During the last year of his life, Moorhouse sold Bibles and tracts from a Bible carriage and conducted evangelistic campaigns in the industrial districts of Lancashire, Yorkshire, and Leicestershire. In two years Moorhouse sold over one hundred and fifty thousand Bibles and Testaments, and gave away millions of books and tracts; all his literature was supplied by Müller's Scriptural Knowledge Institution in Bristol.

In August 1878, Moorhouse wrote to Müller from Blackpool:

Beloved Mr Müller, We are having a glorious time here, selling about one thousand copies of the New Testament a week, and preaching to thousands in the open air. Enclosed is a Post Office Order for £12 10s. Please send us three thousand twopenny Testaments. Many thanks for your kindness in giving them at half price to us. God bless you, dear Mr Müller.

In acknowledging receipt of the Testaments sent, Moorhouse wrote again from Blackpool:

Beloved Mr Müller, The New Testaments have arrived safe from London. I thank you very much for giving them to me at one penny each. The expenses of the Gospel Carriages, for horses, lights and rent of ground will average about £3 a week; and I trust the sale of Bibles etc will cover this.

I wish you could see the thousands of people listening to the preaching of the gospel in the open air, and sometimes hundreds of people weeping. You would say this is the Lord's work. I wish there were a dozen more carriages out in the villages – I met a great many, in the States, who were much blessed by your ministry, out there; and many ministers told me how much they loved you.

Four years earlier in 1876, Moorhouse – who was never strong – had been told by doctors that his heart was weak; he had continued his work in the same cheerful energetic spirit as before. In September 1880, Müller received his final letter from Moorhouse:

Beloved Mr Müller, We have had a glorious time at Darlington and Stockton-on-Tees. Tens of thousands at the latter place heard the glorious gospel of our Lord Jesus. We took the carriage to the races, and never had such a week before at such a place.... Could you see the hundreds listening with upturned faces, and many with tearful eyes to the simple story of Calvary, your heart would rejoice, and you would feel repaid for all the loss you sustain in giving us the Scriptures and the little Gospel books at so cheap a rate. May God bless you, beloved Mr Müller.

A few weeks later, Henry Moorhouse was dead. In the year he died (1880), Müller's Scriptural Knowledge Institution sold nearly a hundred thousand Bibles and New Testaments at reduced prices and gave away over four thousand. As well as English the Bibles were in Welsh, Danish, Dutch, French, German, Italian, Portuguese, Spanish, Russian, Swedish, Greek and Hebrew. In the same year, the Institution circulated nearly three and a half million tracts and small books.

During Müller's life, the Institution which he and Henry Craik had founded in 1834 laid out nearly half a million pounds on objects other than the orphan work. Of this Müller spent nearly £115,000 on the school work throughout the world, nearly £90,000 on the circulation of Bibles, Testaments, tracts and books, and over £260,000 on world-wide missionary work. In the peak years of the missionary work in the early 1870s, Müller sent £10,000 abroad annually to nearly two hundred missionaries. By the mid-1880s expenditure was running at about £5,000 a year and rather more than one hundred and thirty missionaries were supported. All this expenditure was quite apart from the sum of nearly one million pounds which Müller spent during his life on the residential children's work at Wilson Street and on Ashley Down.

'See what Mr Müller obtains by simple prayer,' James McQuilkin had said. 'Thus I may obtain blessing by prayer.' And, as we saw, he did. There is indeed a simplicity about prayer – 'Ask, and it will be given you; seek and you will find; knock and the door will be opened to you. For everyone who asks receives; he who seeks finds; and to him who knocks, the door will be opened.' This was the simple promise from Matthew 7:7-8 with which Müller began a sermon on prayer in 1880.

'Had it been left to us to make promises regarding prayer,' Müller said in his sermon, 'I do not know that you or I could have done more than say, "Ask, and you will receive". Yet, while the promise is so full, so deep, so broad, so precious in every way, we have here, as becomes us with other parts of the word of God, to compare Scripture with Scripture, because in other parts additions are made, or conditions given, which, if we neglect, will hinder our getting the full benefit of prayer.'

During the sermon, Müller outlined a number of conditions on which successful prayer depends. First, he said, our requests must be according to God's will. Second, we mustn't ask on account of our own goodness or merit, but 'in the name of the Lord Jesus Christ' – John 14:13-14. Müller was careful to remind his congregation, however, as he often did, of the verse in Psalm 66:18 'If I had cherished sin in my heart, the Lord would not have listened.' 'That is,' he said, 'if I live in sin, and go on in a course hateful to God, I may not expect my prayers to be answered.'

The third condition was that we must exercise faith in the power and willingness of God to answer our prayers. 'This is deeply important,' Müller said. 'In Mark 11:24 we read, "Whatever you ask for in prayer, believe that you have received it, and it will be yours". "Whatever you ask for" – of whatever kind – "believe that you have received it, and it will be yours". I have found invariably that in the fifty-four years and nine months during which I have been a believer, that if I only believed I was sure to get, in God's time, the thing I asked for. I would especially lay this on your heart that you exercise faith in the power and willingness of God to answer your requests. We must believe that God is able and willing. To see that He is able, you have only to look at the resurrection of the Lord Jesus Christ; for having raised Him from the dead, He must have almighty power. As to the love of God, you have only to look to the cross of Christ, and see His love in not sparing His Son, in not withholding His only begotten Son from death. With these proofs of the power and love of God, assuredly, if we believe, we shall receive – we shall obtain.'

The fourth condition was that 'we have to continue patiently waiting on God till the blessing we seek is granted. For observe, nothing is said in the text as to the time in which, or the circumstances under which, the prayer is to be answered. "Ask, and you will receive." There is a positive promise, but nothing as to time.... Someone may say, "Is it necessary I should bring a matter before God two, three, five, or even twenty times; is it not enough I tell Him once?" We might as well say there is no need to tell Him once, for He knows beforehand what our need is. He wants us to prove that we have confidence in Him, and that we take our place as creatures towards the Creator.

'Moreover, we are never to lose sight of the fact that there may be particular reasons why prayer may not at once be answered. One reason may be the need for the exercise of our faith, for by exercise our faith is strengthened. We all know that if our faith were not exercised it would remain as it was at first. By the trial it is strengthened. Another reason may be that we may glorify God by the manifestation of patience. This is a grace by which God is greatly magnified. Our manifestation of patience glorifies God. There may be another reason. Our heart may not yet be prepared for the answer to our prayer. I will give an illustration....' Müller gave some illustrations from the lives of those known to him and then drew on his own vast experience.

'If I say that during the fifty-four years and nine months that I have been a believer in the Lord Jesus Christ I have had thirty thousand answers to prayer, either in the same hour or the same day that the requests were made, I should not go a particle too far. Often, before leaving my bedroom in the morning, have I had prayers answered that were offered that morning, and in the course of the day I have had five or six more answers to prayer; so that at least thirty thousand prayers have been answered the self-same hour or the self-same day that they were offered. But one or the other might suppose all my prayers were thus promptly answered. No; not all of them. Sometimes I have had to wait weeks, months or even years; sometimes many years.

'In November 1844, I began to pray for the conversion of five individuals. I prayed every day without one single intermission, whether sick or in health, on the land or on the sea, and whatever the pressure of my engagements might be. Eighteen months elapsed before the first of the five was converted. I thanked God, and prayed on for the others. Five years elapsed, and then the second was converted. I thanked God, and prayed on for the other three. Day by day I continued to pray for them, and six years more passed before the third was converted. I thanked God for the three, and went on praying for the other two. These two remain unconverted. The man to whom God in the riches of His grace has given tens of thousands of answers to prayer, in the self-same day or hour in which they were offered, has been praying day by day for nearly thirty-six years for the conversion of these two individuals, and yet they remain unconverted; for next November it will be thirty-six years since I began to pray for their conversion. But I hope in God, I pray on, and look yet for the answer.

'Therefore, beloved brethren and sisters, go on waiting upon God, go on praying; only be sure you ask for things that are according to the mind of God, for He does not desire the death of the sinner. This is the revelation God has made of Himself – "Not willing that any should perish, but that all should come to repentance". Go on, therefore, praying; expect an answer, look for it, and in the end you will have to praise God for it.'

Of the two individuals still unconverted at the time of this sermon, one became a Christian before Müller's death and the other a few years later.

21

THE SCENT OF HONEYSUCKLE

A highlight of the fifth preaching tour, to Europe from September 1878 to June 1879, was a visit to schools in Spain which for the last ten years had been entirely financed by the Scriptural Knowledge Institution. Müller addressed one hundred and fifty boys at a school in a poor district of Barcelona, speaking very slowly so that an interpreter could translate his words.

'My dear children,' he said, 'I love you all very much, and pray for you every day. I long from my inmost soul to meet everyone of you in Heaven; but, in order that you may go to that happy place, as poor, lost, guilty sinners, you must put your trust in the blessed Lord Jesus Christ who was punished instead of us; for His blood alone can cleanse us from our sins.'

Müller went on to tell the Spanish children about the boys on Ashley Down. Close to the boys' school was a school for girls, also entirely supported by SKI. After Müller had spoken to the girls, and they had sung a hymn for him, 'a pretty little girl, about six years old, with black hair and very bright eyes, was mounted on a form, when she repeated the 128th Psalm in Spanish with great ease, and apparently without missing a word.' The couple went on to visit other schools in Barcelona and Madrid all of which were entirely supported by SKI.

After leaving Spain, the Müllers spent some months in the south of France, Müller preaching many times in French. At a church linked with a home for mentally retarded and epileptic children, the director wouldn't hear of an interpreter because, he said, *Monsieur Müller est admirable*.

George and Susannah spent March in Menton and held meetings daily at the Eglise Française and the German Church. On Sunday mornings the little hall of the Free Church of Scotland was crowded, and its doors and windows left open; several people would sit outside on the balcony and listen to Müller in the spring sunshine. Among them on three Sundays was an Englishman in his middle forties, there for the benefit of his health: Charles Haddon Spurgeon – the most popular English preacher of the nineteenth century. On several occasions that spring, the Müllers drove out in an open carriage with Spurgeon. One afternoon they drove along the Turin road leading to Castiglione.

'When in the midst of landscapes such as these,' said Spurgeon, as they wound slowly up a hill, 'from the crown of my head to the sole of my foot, I feel as though I could burst out into one song of praise.'

We don't know whether he did so, or if he did whether Müller and Susannah accompanied their friend.

Dr Henry Bennet lived in Menton and during his convalescence from an illness Spurgeon was able to come and go in Bennet's garden as he pleased. That same spring, Spurgeon recorded that Mr and Mrs Müller spent a day with him there. 'Dr Bennet came up,' Spurgeon recalled, 'and I was amused to hear Müller teaching him the power of prayer.'

'I want to buy a terrace near my home,' Dr Bennet said to Müller, 'but the owner is asking a hundred times its value.'

'You should pray about it,' said Müller.

'It is too trifling a matter to take to the Lord,' said Bennet. 'You may very properly pray about your orphanages, but as to this terrace to complete my garden – I couldn't make a good case about it!'

'But,' Müller responded, 'it encourages people in sin if we yield to covetous demands, and so I think you might pray that the owner should be kept from exorbitant claims.'

'As simple country folk,' replied Bennet, 'they are in my opinion very excusable for trying either to keep their land, or to get all they can from an Englishman whom they imagine to be a living gold mine!'

Müller smiled. Spurgeon commented later that the 'spirit of both was good; but of course, the simple, childlike, holy trust of Müller was overpowering. He is not a sanctimonious person; but full of real joy, and sweet peace and innocent pleasure.' Charles Spurgeon Junior once wrote in a letter that his 'Father declares himself far better able to "trust and not be afraid" through intercourse with Mr Müller'.

After a journey through north and central Italy, where Müller preached in San Remo, Florence and Rome, they arrived in Naples. Here, some English seamen from Bristol, hearing that Müller was in the area, invited him to address them, which he did in the harbour aboard a ship. As their tour continued, they climbed Vesuvius and admired the view; took a trip in a gondola in Venice; and travelled to the Waldensian Christians, or Vaudois, tracing their origins back to Apostolic times, had lived in the quiet seclusion of their mountain villages, almost unaffected by developments elsewhere in the world-wide church.

In the two principle valleys of St Martin and Lucerne, the members of the little churches, Susannah wrote,

...are obliged to walk many miles in order to attend the meetings. These Waldensian Christians are generally very poor, and many of them live in houses roofed with rough, flat stones loosely put together, instead of slates or tiles. In the windows, too, of a few of their abodes, paper occupied the place of glass. At Pomaret some of the people were standing at their doors to gaze at us, because our visit was expected; and as we drove along *Monsieur le pasteur* Georges Müller had many respectful bows and salutations.

At five o'clock we reached the house of the pastor at Villa Seche, and in the evening accompanied him to his church, a very ancient Vaudois place of worship, situated at a great height upon a mountain, many hundreds of feet above his residence. A steep, rugged, winding pathway, covered in places with loose stones, led up this mountain towards the church; and as some rivulets streamed over the ascent, it was difficult to avoid getting ankle-deep in water. The silence and solitude of the whole region, too, were striking. At length, warm, tired and almost breathless (Müller was now seventy-four), we reached the church, a large old-fashioned building, which was crowded with a rustic congregation, who (the meeting having been announced for five o'clock, though circumstances did not allow of our getting there until seven) had been sitting there two hours patiently waiting our arrival. The service, which was in French, was opened with singing and prayer after which Mr Müller addressed the audience for an hour, throwing himself heart and soul into their circumstances. At the close of the meeting we distributed little French and Italian books amongst the people shook hands with many of them; and soon after nine reached the pastor's cottage down below, a Swiss chalet, with a projecting roof, and two wooden galleries outside. In this mountain home the domestic arrangements were of the simplest most frugal character possible, many of the comforts and conveniences of life (often considered indispensable) being wanting; but we were most kindly entertained, and greatly enjoyed our little visit.

At a school of St Jean, near La Tour, the largest Vaudois settlement, Müller preached in French again to a large congregation. At the close of the meeting the pastor prayed *que le discours excellent de notre frère soit grave sur nos coeurs*; and another gentleman said *Monsieur Müller nous a dit precisement ce qu'il nous faut; le sermon était admirable.*

Müller had ended his first tour of the United States with over a hundred written invitations to preach not yet accepted.

Therefore, after spending ten weeks in Bristol following their return from Europe, the Müllers set sail again for the States aboard the *Germanic* towards the end of August 1879.

On Sunday evening, September 14th 1879, at the Methodist Episcopal Church, South Second Street, Brooklyn, the pastor introduced a guest speaker to his congregation.

'My dear friends, I rejoice to tell you that we are about to hear the gospel from the heart and lips of our venerable friend, who, though now aged seventy-four, has preached the gospel upwards of one thousand four hundred times in the last four years, in the various cities and countries he has visited. Hear this, you young men, and remember that he is no smoker, nor lover of alcoholic drink; but we see how God can strengthen for His blessed service those who trust in Him, and seek to live to His honour and glory. I have now great pleasure in introducing you to Mr George Müller, of Bristol, England.'

Müller preached powerfully from Isaiah 3:10-11.

In December Müller was one of the speakers at a large conference in the Shaftesbury Hall, Toronto, speaking on Christ in the Scriptures and on the second coming. On the final afternoon, Müller publicly replied to nine questions one of which was as hotly debated then as it is in some quarters today.

'Are we to expect,' the questioner asked, 'our Lord to return at any moment, or must certain events be fulfilled before He comes again?'

Hundreds of pulses beat a little faster as Müller rose to his feet to deliver his reply.

'I know that on this subject there is great diversity of judgment and I do not wish to force on other persons the light I have myself received. The subject, however, is not new to me; for having been a careful, diligent student of the Bible for nearly fifty years, my mind has long been settled on this point, and I have not a shadow of doubt about it. The Scriptures declare plainly that the Lord Jesus will not come until the apostasy shall have taken place, and the man of sin, the "son of perdition" (or personal Antichrist) shall have been revealed, as seen in 2 Thessalonians 2. Many other portions of the Word of God distinctly teach that certain events are to be fulfilled before the return of our Lord Jesus Christ. This does not, however, alter the fact that the coming of Christ, and not death, is the great Hope of the Church, and, if in a right state of heart, we (as the Thessalonian believers did) shall "serve the living and true God, and wait for His Son from Heaven".'

Müller preached his last sermon in Toronto to an immense congregation in the Great Metropolitan Church on the subject of the indwelling and power of the Holy Spirit from John 14:16-17. During this tour Müller preached three hundred times.

They returned to Liverpool on June 16th, arriving on Ashley Down the following day. The children had all assembled ready to greet them and as they caught their first glimpse of the returning couple they broke out into noisy cheering. A small girl stepped forward and presented Susannah with an enormous bunch of honeysuckle while Müller stood beaming. Many years later (in 1939) the same girl then in her sixties, wrote:

> I always follow the scent of honeysuckle, but have never yet found any to come near my memory of that bunch – each and every one looks smaller and less lovely ... I've just returned from a fortnight's work in Wiltshire. I did so hope to have time to visit Bristol. Perhaps it is as well I couldn't get time.... Perhaps the dear old house would have looked changed. It was so very beautiful, and my eleven years so very happy. I'd rather keep my memories.

George and Susannah, too, were glad to be back in the dear old home.

Müller had left North America with over one hundred and fifty invitations to preach still unaccepted, and therefore in September 1880 George and Susannah left again for Quebec. Glad to resume his friendship with Captain Dutton, he held eight meetings aboard the *Sardinian*, led three Bible studies and distributed about two hundred small books to the passengers and crew. Fog didn't delay the Sardinian this time.

During a stay in the Boston area, Müller visited Plymouth and preached at the Church of the Pilgrims erected by the Pilgrim Fathers on arrival there in December 1620. George and Susannah looked at the first house ever built in New England and visited a museum of relics brought over to America by the *Mayflower* party.

At New Haven, Connecticut, Müller spoke several times to staff and students at Yale University, a task in which, he said, 'I take the deepest interest, from having been converted myself while a student at the University of Halle.'

George and Susannah spent the winter months from December 1880 to March 1881 in New York. In the coldest winter the city had known for thirty years they frequently made ferry crossings through ice which was so thick that the ship could only force its way through with difficulty. Müller held nearly one hundred meetings including nearly forty among the half a million Germans in the New York, Brooklyn area.

On their eighth missionary tour, George and Susannah visited Egypt, Palestine, Turkey and Greece, taking time off in Egypt for an excursion to the pyramids.

Travelling south through Palestine in an open Russian waggon drawn by three horses they found that the land spoken of in Old Testament as 'flowing with milk and honey' had grown barren, rocky and uncultivated and Susannah decided that God's curse appeared to rest not only upon the Jews but also upon their land. (It is not clear whether her husband shared this view which would be strongly contested today.) But, she thought, 'at the return of the Lord Jesus, when Israel as a nation will be converted and restored, "The desert shall rejoice, and blossom as the rose".'

At the Mediterrranean Hotel in Jerusalem they moved into a pleasant corner room on the first floor with a fine view of the Mount of Olives; and throughout their stay they took daily walks on the terrace on the flat roof of the hotel to admire the splendid panorama.

Müller held many meetings in Jerusalem preaching in English and German with interpretation into Arabic when necessary.

The population of Jerusalem was at that time less than thirty thousand and included about eight thousand Jews living in the poorest part. 'At the present time,' Susannah observed, watching signs of the fulfilment of Biblical prophecy which we have since lived to see, 'there is no indication whatever of any gathering Jews on an extensive scale from other countries to their own land.'

In December Müller (now in his seventy-eighth year) and Susannah joined a party of English friends and rode on donkeys to Bethany. On their way they crossed the Brook Kidron and visited the cave, hewn out of a rock, where it is thought Lazarus was buried. They saw an old ruined house, where they were told Martha, Mary and Lazarus lived. From the summit of the Mount of Olives they could see the plain of Jordan, the well-watered plain which Lot chose for himself, the Mountains of Moab in the distance, the country around the Cave of Adullam and the point where the river Jordan flows into the Dead Sea. The weather was magnificent; after sunset the whole scene was lit up by a full moon which shone brilliantly, and coming down the Mount of Olives, they enjoyed the magnificent view of Jerusalem. They passed the Garden of Gethsemane, some of whose olive trees may date back to our Lord's day.

On another day they rode on donkeys to Bethlehem, six miles from Jerusalem; and, after lunching in a cloister of the Latin Convent, they visited the church erected on the spot where (according to tradition) our Lord's manger stood. During their stay in Jerusalem, they visited the *Via Dolorosa*, the Mosque of Omar (built on the site formerly occupied by Solomon's Temple), the Church of the Holy Sepulchre (erected, according to tradition, on the spot where our Lord was crucified), Absalom's Pillar, the Pool of Bethesda, the site of Herod's palace, the ruins of the Castle to which Paul was taken and the Pool of Siloam.

After over nine weeks in Jerusalem the Müllers returned to Jaffa for a week's stay before climbing into a small boat which, it was intended, would take them out to the Austrian steamship *Flora*, bound for Haifa and anchored some way from the shore. A heavy gale was blowing, and,

After riding over heavy breakers, and getting clear of the rocks, our boat was tossed about upon the waves for nearly half an hour; and, after at last we reached the ship, a favourable opportunity of getting a foothold on board (to be seized just at the right moment as the boat was lifted upwards by the waves) had to be closely watched for, when one after the other, at the risk of our lives, we had to spring on to the steep ladder staircase, that led up towards the deck.

At Haifa, some German Christians met them and drove them in an open waggon through torrential rain to the Hotel du Mont Carmel. It was said that Müller's preaching at Haifa brought about a spiritual revival among the large colony of German settlers there.

In February they rode on donkeys to Mount Carmel and stopped at a monastery near the summit where the monks entertained them with cups of black coffee and glasses of mulberry wine. The monks took them into a church where they showed them a cave where they said Elijah had lived; and then led them to a lighthouse standing on a rock so that they could see the magnificent view. The sun shone brightly, the atmosphere was clear; here, they recalled, Elijah, by prayer, brought down fire from Heaven to burn up his sacrifice on the altar.

Later on the tour, Müller preached many times at Constantinople and with Susannah visited the barracks at Scutari where Florence Nightingale attended the casualties of the Crimean War. While walking a few minutes away from their hotel, The d'Angleterre, they were intrigued to watch some dancing Dervishes. 'There were eighteen performers altogether,' Susannah recalled, 'who wore brown mantles, and high, round caps made of felt. At a particular signal, they all fell flat upon their faces; but afterwards rose, and walked a few times round the room, with folded arms, bowing and turning slowly many times. Their mantles were then suddenly cast off, when they appeared in long, full bell-shaped petticoats and jackets, and, after stretching out their arms to the utmost, began gravely and deliberately to dance and revolve (that is to spin round and round like a top) for about fifteen or twenty minutes as rapidly as possible.'

Müller addressed a busy schedule of meetings in Athens, but they also found time to visit the Areopagus, or Mars Hill, and to stand on the spot where Paul preached his famous sermon. They explored the Acropolis, and saw the ruins of the many ancient idol temples which had so stirred the heart of the Apostle eighteen hundred years earlier.

Home then to Ashely Down via Corinth, Rome and Florence after a journey which had lasted over nine months.

22

Loved by Thousands

Whenever he returned from a long preaching tour, Müller found that his son-in-law, James Wright, assisted by an efficient staff, was running Ashley Down well. Moreover when a problem arose during a foreign tour which required Müller's special judgment, Wright would include the issue in his frequent letters. Fears that donations would decrease in Müller's absence had been allayed in the third year after Müller had begun his work abroad when the total income received had been greater than in any previous year.

Müller therefore had no hesitation in setting off again with Susannah in August 1882 for their ninth tour – of Europe. At Dusseldorf Müller was delighted to be greeted by the City Missioner whom he had met six years earlier.

'I resolved to take your advice,' the Missioner told him, 'and give myself more earnestly to prayer for my sons. Two months after you left, five of my six were converted to faith in Christ and now the sixth is thinking seriously about trusting Him.'

From Dusseldorf the Müllers travelled down the Rhine to Heidelberg, Mannheim and then to Vienna for a number of meetings. They visited Budapest and Prague before returning via Leipzig to Halberstadt where Müller had spent many of his school days. Here they wandered around the cathedral where Müller had taken communion for the first time sixty-two years earlier. Next morning they drove along the road to Kroppenstadt.

'This road looks much the same as it did when I was a boy,' Müller said to Susannah, 'except that where there were poplar trees on either side now there are fruit trees.'

It was the first time Müller had returned to Kroppenstadt since his childhood; he held two meetings in a large hall. The locals flocked to hear their most famous son give an account of his life and work. Müller found that the house where he had been born was still standing; and he was able to show Susannah the house in Heimersleben to which the family had moved when he was four.

From Heimersleben they travelled to Berlin for a number of addresses to large congregations as well as some – ever popular at that time – drawing room meetings. Moving on to Danzig, Müller met two friends from his days as a student in Halle both of whom had been ministers for fifty years. At Koningsberg, on Christmas Day, Müller addressed an immense congregation of three thousand people who had gathered that morning to hear him at the Tragheimer Kirche.

At the end of December they boarded a Prussian train bound for St Petersburg, settling into a comfortable sleeping compartment heated with warm air. In the morning they awoke to find themselves travelling through a 'vast wilderness of snow'. At St Petersburg (Leningrad) station they were met by Her Highness the Princess Lieven and Colonel Paschkoff, an officer in the Imperial Guards and a wealthy nobleman whom Müller described as 'one of the most active Christians in the whole vast empire'.

'Will you please stay with me while you are in Russia?' said the Princess, whom Susannah described as 'a beloved sister in the Lord'.

'However,' said Müller, 'as we rarely accept invitations to stay with friends, because I require as much rest and time to myself as possible, we declined the proposal, and went to an hotel where we remained two nights. Finding, however, that the Princess greatly desired we should be her guest, and that she would have been much disappointed if we had continued to refuse her kind offer of hospitality, on Monday January 1st, we went to her mansion, and were most kindly entertained there, for upwards of eleven weeks.

The Princess had allocated the Müllers a room known as the Malachite Hall, because of its magnificent malachite mantelpiece, pillars and cornices. The malachite – a hard, green stone, beautiful when polished – had been mined on the Urals. Despite the splendid luxury of the accommodation, however, Müller's stay at St Petersburg was to be neither idle nor without its excitement. He preached sixteen times at the British and American Chapel; eight times in German at the German Reformed Church, eleven times in German at the Moravian Church; held three meetings for Swedes at the British and American Chapel, with translation into Swedish, attended three pastors' meetings, held five large drawing-room meetings at Colonel Paschkoff's mansion, conducted two at the home of Count Korff and held thirty-five at Princess Lieven's. On top of this, he received visitors and enquirers every day, and had about forty private interviews with small groups of Christian workers. He spoke in hospital wards and children's homes.

Tolstoy in his *Resurrection* captured the fascination St Petersburg society had for drawing-room meetings in the late nineteenth century. Nekhlydov's aunt, Countess Katerina Ivanova, is portrayed as a 'fervent adherent of the doctrine which teaches that faith in the redemption is the essence of Christianity'. Tolstoy described the elegant carriages which brought the faithful to a meeting which had been arranged in the Countess's ball-room.

Ladies in silk, velvet and lace, with false hair, tightly laced waists and padded figures, sat in the luxuriously furnished ball-room. Between the ladies were men in uniforms and evening-dress, and five or six of them from the lower classes: two house-porters, a shopkeeper, footman and a coachman. Kieseweter (the preacher), a thick-set man with hair just turning grey, spoke in English, and a thin girl wearing pince-nez translated quickly and well. He said that our sins were so great, and the punishment they deserved was so great and unavoidable, that it was impossible to live, anticipating such punishment.

It is possible that Tolstoy's somewhat unsympathetic portrayal of Kiesewetter was based on Müller, although it is more likely to have been Dr F. W. Baedeker, cousin of the 'Baedeker' of Continental Guide-Book fame, and himself a contributor to several of the Guides. Bedeker, whose home was in Weston-super-Mare, had since the 1860s been a close friend of Müller and also stayed with Princess Lieven on his frequent visits to St Petersburg. He used to tell of a long conversation he once had with Count Tolstoy in Moscow about England and life in Russia.

Müller obtained permission from the Russian Minister of Interior to preach in the German churches in St Petersburg, and also to Swedes in the British Chapel. The permit from the Minister was in Russian which Müller couldn't understand – but he was told that the desired permission had been granted.

On Friday evening, February 9th, the Müllers were startled to receive unexpected visitors at Princess Lieven's mansion. It was the police.

'You are required to appear tomorrow morning before the chief officer of police.'

Next morning, the chief police officer treated Müller courteously, shook hands, and half apologised for acting as he did.

'You are charged with holding meetings with translation into Russian for which no permission has been granted from the Ministry of the Interior.'

From that time the police banned the meetings at Colonel Paschkoff's house. A few years later, Colonel Paschkoff was exiled to Siberia by Tsar Alexander III for his persistent evangelism, drawing-room meetings and tract distribution.

The Müllers found the cold more intense than they had found it in Canada or the United States. However, they didn't allow the weather to deter them in their search for a little adventure. In March they visited by sledge a settlement of Laplanders camped on the ice of the Neva. Mrs Müller records:

A party of Lapps (clothed in skin and furs, with the warm side turned inwards and looking as if sewn up in their garments) were standing near a tent. They wear no under linen (we were told), and never wash themselves or change their clothes, except when they fall off from dirt and constant use. The interior of a Laplander's hut too, upon the ice, presented a miserable, uncomfortable appearance. It consisted of a tent made of skins, with the fur turned inwards, and had an opening at the top, which answered the double purpose of chimney and of window. An iron pot, containing soup, was suspended over a small fire in the centre of this tent, and the floor of ice in the hut was covered by rugs; but the domestic arrangements inside were of a most repulsive character....

They returned to England via Poland, where the highlight of their stay was Müller's success in touching the hearts of the citizens of Lodz, an industrial town. After a week of crowded meetings in the town, Müller received a note of which this is a translation:

I, and almost the whole population of this town, in the name of the Lord Jesus, entreat that you will have the kindness to remain with us until after next Sunday. In the name of many thousands I thank you for your ministry.

The crowds at Müller's meetings continued to be as large as the German Baptist Church could hold, about one thousand two hundred people, and Mrs Müller noted that 'the preaching too was the theme of conversation in the factories, public houses and in many private families'. So they extended their visit as long as they could.

Returning to England in May, Müller preached seven times at a crowded Mildmay Conference. Then, when they returned to Ashley Down in June, the huge crowd of children waiting to greet them all but melted the Müllers to tears.

In September 1883, the Müllers left Tilbury aboard the *Siam* bound for Madras, India. They set foot on Madras Pier at the end of

October and Müller preached many times in Madras including an address to four hundred Hindus at the Free Church of Scotland. They engaged an Indian servant named Abraham to travel with them throughout India: Abraham could speak Hindustani, Tamil and Canarese.

In December a 'tonga' – a covered carriage on two wheels, drawn by ponies – took them up into the Nilgiri Hills to Coonoor. Then they travelled to Benares, chief of the Hindu sacred cities where they stayed with the Rev. John Hewlett of the London Missionary Society. To explore the city, an early start was necessary to avoid the midday heat and on February 22nd they rose at five to set off in an open carriage for a drive through the city and its suburbs. They visited a well-known Hindu School of Philosophy where many Brahmins, pundits and their pupils were busy. Then they climbed into a small steam boat for a trip along the River Ganges and a magnificent view of the city; they saw numerous bathing-ghats, a burning-ghat, for burning dead bodies, temples, mosques and sacred wells. As they watched from the deck of the boat they saw three dead bodies floating down the river with crows perched on them pecking at the flesh.

'The Indian poor can't afford to pay for the wood needed to burn their dead,' George and Susannah's guide told them, 'and so they throw them into the river instead.'

At Allahabad and Agra, from where they were able to visit the Taj Mahal, Müller's busy programme continued unabated. After staying at Government House in Lahore with Sir Charles Aitchison they travelled to Delhi and Poona. They took an early morning drive to Parbuttee, a hill four miles from Poona. Getting out of their carriage at the bottom of the hill, they walked to the top and admired the view. A temple at the summit housed a representation of the god Shiva and other gods and goddesses. Their guide, a Hindu, was about to tell them about these deities, when Susannah, never a woman to mince her words, nor prone to see a great deal of light in other religions, interrupted.

'We do not believe in Shiva in the least,' she said, 'but in the true and living God, who made heaven and earth, and who sent His Son to die for poor lost sinners, as revealed in the Holy Scriptures.'

'I, too, believe in a supreme Being,' said their guide.

'Did you ever hear of Jesus Christ?'

'Never.'

'Can you not then ask some kind of missionary to teach you about Jesus, for without faith in Him you will never go to Heaven?'

'I must try to learn about Him,' said the guide, 'I must try, I must try.'

A hectic schedule in Bombay brought the Indian tour to a close. Before they left, Susannah received a letter which referred to Müller as 'loved by thousands in India, and I believe hundreds of thousands in other lands'.

Early in May they bid their servant Abraham a reluctant farewell and boarded the *Indus* for Aden and home. On June 5th they caught an express from Paddington which made Bristol in two and a half hours, and returned to No. 3 House after a journey of over twenty thousand miles.

The next three tours were all in the British Isles.

The fourteenth tour took the Müllers (via the States) to countries they had never previously visited. On January 23rd 1886 the couple sailed into Port Jackson harbour, Sydney, aboard the *Australia*; there they stayed at Perry's Hotel until early March. Müller held many meetings and was introduced by Sir Alfred Stevens to Lord Carrington, the Governor of New South Wales and also called on Sir James Martin, Sydney's Chief Justice.

Next stops on the tour were at Bathurst and Melbourne, where Müller twice addressed an audience of three thousand at the Theatre Royal and on one occasion preached to about five thousand at Melbourne Town Hall.

In August they travelled on to Java; Hong Kong (many meetings); and on into the heart of China for meetings in Shanghai, Hankou and Nanjing. On this visit to China, Müller met Hudson Taylor and many of the missionaries working with him in the China Inland Mission whom he had been supporting through good times and bad for many years.

In Japan, huge audiences turned up to hear Müller in Yokohama, Tokyo, Kobe, Kyoto and Osaka.

George and Susannah's next tour (from August 1887 to March 1890) was their last beyond European shores. They travelled first, via the States, to Adelaide, Australia, and Tasmania where Müller held many meetings during a stay lasting some months. In New Zealand their tour began with a series of meetings in Queenstown. Then they caught a train in Kingston bound for Dunedin. Opposite them, in a long saloon carriage, a gentleman sat with a newspaper in his hand. He began to read aloud from the newspaper to his fellow passengers.

'The Rev. George Müller of Bristol, England,' he read, 'is about to make a visit to Dunedin. I would give a great deal indeed to see *him*.'

'Mr Müller is sitting opposite you,' said a passenger helpfully.

The newspaper reader was delighted. He took off his hat, shook hands warmly with George and Susannah, and began a long conversation in which, Susannah observed, 'our fellow passengers seemed greatly interested'.

At Dunedin they stayed at the Grand Hotel and all Müller's meetings were crowded including those at the large Garrison Hall, which held nearly three thousand. The New Zealand tour took them on to Port Chalmers, Oamaru, Timaru and Wellington. On Monday February 27th 1888, one Wellington newspaper stated that, 'Yesterday evening the Rev. George Müller of Bristol, England, preached at the Opera House to the largest congregation ever packed into the building, for not only were all seats crowded to the utmost, but hundreds of persons were obliged to stand.' On his third visit to Sydney, Müller preached eighty-six times.

At the end of December they arrived in Calcutta for the start of their second visit to India and once again engaged an Indian servant to accompany them on their travels – not Abraham, but a native of Madras, John Nathaniel. Müller worked hard in

Calcutta, preaching many times despite the heat which grew intense even for India. The mosquitoes were a menace by day and night; and though coolies worked punkahs continually in drawing room, dining room and even through the night in their bedroom, nothing really cooled them down.

Müller was eighty-three, and Susannah grew alarmed for his health.

'You must seek the advice of a doctor,' she told George.

'You must not,' the doctor said to George, 'remain in Calcutta a day longer than is absolutely necessary on account of the intensity of the heat. If you do, you will do so at the risk of your lives.'

So they left Calcutta by train at half past four on 29th April; but it wasn't soon enough. Müller became very ill. Susannah thought he was going to die; there were no hotels in the area nor any railway stations with any comfortable facilities.

Müller lay gasping for breath on the long seat of their compartment. Susannah put a pillow under his head; kept all windows wide open; and fanned him repeatedly. She persuaded him to drink a little wine and water and to eat a few sandwiches.

'Now try to sleep,' she said.

They stopped at a station.

'Please fetch a cup of tea for Mr Müller,' Susannah said to John Nathaniel, 'or a glass of lemonade.'

Susannah prayed fervently and managed to keep life in Müller until they reached Damookdea Ghat at nine in the evening. Finding that Müller's pulse was good, Susannah took courage and went on board a ferry-steamer. She found two chairs on deck so that her husband would get the benefit of the night breezes blowing over the Ganges; at Sara Ghat they went ashore.

At the station John Nathaniel secured a comfortable sleeping compartment in another train. Müller slept and they reached Silgari at nine the following morning. From there they travelled by steam tramcar up into the Himalayan Mountains to Darjeeling where Müller was helped into a jin-rickshaw; two Nepalese coolies carried Susannah in a dandy on their shoulders up a very steep, long road to Rockville. Here, in a boarding house in a beautiful situation with a fine view of the Himalayas, Müller recovered from his ordeal.

23

ADMIRING HIS KINDNESS

During some of the tours (wrote Müller) we have for many weeks together been exposed to cold from fifty to fifty-six degrees below freezing point; and at other times to heat from ninety to one hundred and ten degrees and upwards, discomforts which must have been experienced in order to know the full force of them. Then, on the sea, again and again, very heavy gales, and even a typhoon, have overtaken us, when the trials thus occasioned were severe. On the land we have had to travel, on a stretch, not merely for twenty or thirty hours uninterruptedly, but more than once we have been on the railway six days and six nights in succession. Though, on the whole, we have had excellent accommodation during our long journeys, yet sometimes we have been obliged to put up with the most trying and inferior kind. Twice, though in the best cabins, on board large, first-class steam-ships, we have been exceedingly tried by insects; in the United States, in New South Wales, in Ceylon, and in India, the mosquitoes were most grievous; and in two first-class steam-ships rats so abounded that they ran over us by night. Yet hitherto God has helped us and, we doubt not, will help us to the end.

And indeed He did. Within a few days of coming close to death on the train from Calcutta to Darjeeling, Müller was able to resume a typically busy schedule – preaching regularly, delivering lectures, conducting Bible readings and writing the fiftieth annual report of the Scriptural Knowledge Institution.

The Indian tour took them on to Simla, Mussorie, Dehra Dun, Agra, Cawnpore and Allahabad where Müller preached to seven hundred Indian Christians from five different churches who had gathered in the open air for a love feast.

At Jubbulpore, Müller was handed a telegram from his son-in-law, James Wright: Müller's only child Lydia Wright had died on January 10th 1890, in her fifty-eighth year. He had had no previous inkling of her illness and he described the news as a 'heavy blow'; but he took comfort from Romans 8:28: 'And we know that in all things God works for the good of those who love Him, who have been called according to His purpose.' The Müllers decided to return to England by the first suitable steamer from Bombay.

Even at Bombay – while waiting for the first ship to leave – Müller preached fifteen times, and once in German to the sailors aboard a Prussian man-of-war. When he returned to Bristol he had 'great cause for praise that the whole work was going on so well under the direction of (the bereaved) Mr Wright'.

For more than four months in the summer of 1890 Müller worked on Ashley Down. He badly needed a rest, however, and so he and Susannah left England in August for a river trip down the Rhine past picturesque ruins set amid lovely wooded country. At Heidelberg, feeling rested and invigorated, Müller preached four times in the German Evangelical Chapel. He extended his break into a lengthy preaching tour addressing large audiences in Germany and Switzerland.

Moving east Müller preached in Vienna and there met up with his friend F. W. Baedeker. Müller laid his hands on sixty-eight year old Dr Baedeker's head.

'Heavenly Father,' Müller prayed, 'separate your dear servant to the special ministry to the banished brethren. I commit him to your loving care.'

In the previous year the Russian Orthodox Church had resolved that Baptists, Stundists and those following 'Paschkoffist heresies' should be sternly dealt with; Colonel Paschkoff was one of many thousands banished to Siberia, Transcaucasia or other remote parts of the Empire. Baedeker travelled across Siberia and into Sakhalin Island, visiting and encouraging these groups of persecuted Christians.

Moving further south into Italy, Müller preached in Florence, Rome and Naples. In May he and Susannah arrived back in England and travelled straight to Ashley Down after an absence of twenty-one months.

The preaching tours were over. In seventeen years, George and Susannah had travelled about two hundred thousand miles visiting forty-two countries; Müller was now eighty-seven.

The financial year that ended a few weeks after the Müllers arrived back on Ashley Down – the year ending in May 1892 – was the second only in the history of the Homes in which expenditure had exceeded income. The first occasion had been the year 1881-2 when the expenses of the children's work had exceeded income by nearly five hundred pounds; but in less than a month after the opening of the new financial year a sum was received from the payment of legacies which was three times greater than the deficiency: and this had occurred before the publication of the annual accounts.

On this, the second occasion, expenditure was nearly two thousand pounds in excess of income. Sixteen legacies, however, which had been left were due and might be paid on any date, worth nearly three thousand pounds. In addition between forty and fifty other legacies had been left to the Homes, worth nearly two thousand six hundred pounds, but the payment of them depended on the testators' widows or other relatives. Further, the five Houses on Ashley Down had been built and furnished at a cost of one hundred and fifteen thousand pounds; none was encumbered by a mortgage. Finally, the Institution owned about nineteen acres of valuable building land worth thousands of pounds. On the strength of all this, Müller hadn't the slightest difficulty in borrowing from the bank for a short period to cover the deficit.

On the other hand, Müller didn't feel happy even to *appear* to be in debt. He wrote: 'The Lord's dealings with us during the last year indicate that it is His will that we should contract our operations, and we are waiting upon Him for directions as to how, and to what extent, this should be done; for we have but one single object in connection with this Institution, viz, the glory of God. When I founded it, one of the principles stated was, "that there would be no enlargement of the work, by going into debt"; and, in like manner, we cannot go on with that which already exists if we have not sufficient means coming in to meet the current expenses.'

In the event, the only actual contraction of the work took place in the Day School activities; at the end of July 1892 Müller announced that most home and foreign Day Schools would be closed on October 31st. The school at Purton in Gloucestershire, the premises of which were owned by the Institution, and where young teachers were trained before working on Ashley Down, carried on as usual. Also all the Spanish and Italian schools, as well as three United Kingdom ones, continued to exist independently of SKI, the Institution assisting them whenever it could still do so. Sunday Schools would be supported as usual.

With regard to the children's work, after some months of prayer, Müller and his staff finally interpreted God's will to be that the work shouldn't expand further. Originally, Müller had bought over ten acres of land on which he planned to build two more houses opposite Numbers 4 and 5. In March 1893, however, he sold this land at one thousand pounds.

By the end of the century, the social problem which Müller had sought to alleviate was itself easing. Leaders of national opinion such as Charles Dickens and the Earl of Shaftsbury had aroused interest in the care of children throughout the country. And others, besides Müller, had entered the field – Barnardo, Fegan, the Church of England Children's Society and so on. Following Müller's example, there was now none of the eighteenth century style barriers to entry; and the system of admission by election of subscribers had, thanks to Müller, all but disappeared.

Susannah Müller was now seventy-three. On January 13th 1894, Müller's journal notes without warning that:

> It pleased God to take to Himself my beloved wife, after He had left her to me twenty-three years and six weeks. By the grace of God I am not merely perfectly satisfied with this dispensation, but I kiss the hand which administered the stroke, and I look again for the fulfilment of that word in this instance, that 'in all things God works for the good of those who love Him' (Rom. 8:28).

Müller was again a widower. 'My loneliness,' he wrote, 'after sixty-two years and five months of a happy married life has been great and is great; but I continually praise God for what He gave me, for what He has left me for a long time, and for what He has now taken; for it is all good for me. By constantly admiring the Lord's kindness to me in this very thing, and that He has now entirely freed my beloved departed one from all bodily and spiritual infirmities, and made me unspeakably happy in His presence; He overpowers my loneliness, and is doing more than merely supporting me.'

With the last preaching tour over, Müller rarely left Bristol. Now that he was alone, he gave up No. 21 Paul Street and moved into a suite of rooms in No. 3 House on Ashley Down which became his home for the rest of his life.

In September 1895, on his ninetieth birthday, a presentation was made to him in Bethesda Chapel.

'My voice is stronger,' he said during the course of his speech of thanks, 'than it was sixty-nine years ago and my mental powers are as good as ever.'

The same day he wrote in his journal that, 'my mind is as clear and as capable of work as when I passed my examinations for the University in March 1825 (seventy-one years ago)'.

He still took regular part in the Sunday morning services at Bethesda, Alma Road and Stokes Croft Chapels. He no longer preached, however, at evening services, though he continued to play his normal part in the running of the Orphan-Houses including writing the Annual Reports.

24

Precious Prospect

Early in the summer of 1897 Charles Parsons visited Müller in his study at No. 3. Müller received him with a cordial handshake.

'You are very welcome,' he said.

'You have always found the Lord faithful to His promise?' Parsons asked.

'Always,' replied Müller. 'He has never failed me! For nearly seventy years every need in connection with this work has been supplied. The orphans from the first until now, have numbered nine thousand five hundred, but they have never wanted a meal. Never! Hundreds of times we have commenced the day without a penny in hand, but our Heavenly Father has sent supplies by the moment they were actually required. There never was a time when there was no wholesome meal. During all these years I have been enabled to trust in God, in the living God, and in Him alone. One million four hundred thousand pounds have been sent to me in answer to prayer. We have wanted as much as fifty thousand pounds in one year, and it has all come by the time it has been really needed.

'No man on earth can say that I ever asked him for a penny. We have no committees, no collectors, no voting and no endowments. All has come in answer to believing prayer. My trust has been in God alone; He has many ways of moving the hearts of men to help us all over the world. While I am praying He speaks to this one and another, on this continent and on that, to send us help. Only the other evening, while I was preaching, a gentleman wrote me a cheque for a large amount for the orphans, and handed it to me when the service was over.'

'I have read your life, Mr Müller, and have noticed how greatly, at times, your faith has been tried. Is it with you now as formerly?'

'My faith is tried as much as ever, and my difficulties are greater than ever. Besides our financial responsibilities, suitable helpers have constantly to be found, and suitable places have to be provided for scores and hundreds of orphans who are constantly leaving the Homes. Then often our funds run very low; we had come nearly to the end of our supplies: I called my beloved helpers together and said to them "Pray, brethren, pray!" Immediately, one hundred pounds was sent to us, then two hundred pounds, and in a few days one thousand five hundred pounds came in. But we have to be always praying and always believing. Oh, it is good to trust in the living God, for He has said, "I will never leave you nor forsake you". Expect great things from God, and great things you will have. There is no limit to what He is able to do. Praises be for ever to His Glorious Name! Praise Him for all! Praise Him for everything! I have praised Him many times when He has sent me sixpence, and I have praised Him when He has sent me twelve thousand pounds.'

'I suppose you have never contemplated a reserve fund?'

'That would be the greatest folly,' Müller answered with great emphasis. 'How could I pray if I had reserves? God would say, "Bring them out; bring out those reserves, George Müller." Oh no, I have never thought of such a thing! Our reserve fund is in Heaven. God, the living God is our sufficiency. I have trusted Him for one sovereign; I have trusted him for thousands, and I have never trusted in vain. "Blessed is the man who trusts in Him".'

'Then, of course you have never thought of saving for yourself?'

Charles Parsons never forgot the way Müller answered this question. Until this point, Müller had been sitting opposite him with his hands clasped and eyes which looked quiet, calm and thoughtful. Most of the time he leaned forward, his gaze directed to the floor. But at this question, he sat erect, and looked for several moments into Parsons' face. 'There was a grandeur and majesty about those undimmed eyes,' Parsons recalled, 'so accustomed to spiritual visions, and to looking into the deep things of God.' Parsons wasn't sure whether the question seemed to Müller a sordid one, or whether perhaps it touched a lingering remnant of Müller's 'old self'. At any rate, the question seemed to arouse his whole being.

After a pause, during which 'his face was a sermon' and 'his clear eyes flashed fire', Müller unbuttoned his coat and took out of his pocket an old fashioned purse, with rings in the middle separating the various types of coin. He gave it to Parsons.

'All I am possessed of is in that purse – every penny! Save for myself! Never! When money is sent to me for my own use I pass it on to God. As much as one thousand pounds has thus been sent to me at one time, but I do not regard these gifts as belonging to me; they belong to Him, Whose I am, and Whom I serve. Save for myself! I dare not save; it would be dishonouring to my loving, gracious, all-bountiful Father.'

Parsons handed the purse back to Müller, who told him how much it contained.

'How much time do you spend on your knees?'

'More or less every day,' Müller replied. 'But I live in the spirit of prayer. I pray as I walk about, when I lie down and when I rise up. And the answers are always coming. Thousands and tens of thousands of times have my prayers been answered. When once I am persuaded that a thing is right and for the glory of God, I go on praying for it until the answer comes. "George Müller never gives up!"'

Müller got up from his seat and walked around to the side of a table.

'Thousands of souls have been saved in answer to the prayers of George Müller. He will meet thousands, yea, tens of thousands in Heaven!'

There was a pause. Parsons said nothing.

'The great point is,' Müller continued, 'never to give up until the answer comes. I have been praying for fifty-two years, *every day*, for two men, sons of a friend of my youth. They are not converted yet, but they will be! How can it be otherwise? There is the unchanging promise of Jehovah, and on that I rest. The great fault of the children of God is, *they do not continue in prayer; they do not go on praying; they do not persevere.* If they desire anything for God's glory, they should pray until they get it. Oh, how good, and kind, and gracious, and condescending is the One with Whom we have to do! He has given me, unworthy as I am, immeasurably above all I had asked or thought! I am only a poor, frail, sinful man, but He has heard my prayers tens of thousands of times, and He has used me as the means of bringing tens of thousands into the way of truth. I say tens of thousands, in this and other lands. These unworthy lips have proclaimed salvation to great multitudes, and many, very many, have believed unto eternal life.'

'I cannot help noticing the way you speak about yourself,' said Parsons.

'There is only one thing George Müller deserves, and that is – hell! I tell you, my brother, that is the only thing I deserve. I am indeed a hell-deserving sinner saved by the grace of God. Though I am by nature a sinner, I do not live in sin; I hate sin; I hate it more and more; and I love holiness; yes, I love holiness more and more.'

'I suppose through all these long years in your work for God, you have met with much to discourage you?'

'I have met with many discouragements,' Müller replied, 'but at all times my hope and confidence has been God. On the word of Jehovah's promise has my soul rested. O, it is good to trust in Him; His Word never returns void. He gives power to the faint, and to them that have no might He increases strength. This applies also to my public ministrations. Sixty-two years ago I preached a poor, dry, barren sermon, with no comfort to myself, and, as I imagined, with no comfort to others. But a long time afterwards I heard of nineteen distinct cases of blessing that had come through that sermon.'

Müller fetched from another room a copy of his life story and signed it for Parsons. While Müller was out of the room, Parsons looked around at his study. The furniture was simple and useful; on the desk lay an open Bible, with clear type, without notes or references. *This then*, thought Parsons, *is the abode of the mightiest man, spiritually, of modern times – a man specially raised up to show a cold, calculating, selfish age the realities of the things of God, and to teach the Church how much she might gain, if only she were wise enough to take hold of the arm of Omnipotence.*

Just once while Parsons was with Müller, there was a knock at the door. Müller opened it, and one of the orphans stood there – a fair-haired girl.

'My dear!' said Müller. 'I cannot attend to you just now. Wait a while, and I will see you.'

That summer, Müller's ninety-second, also marked the Diamond Jubilee of Queen Victoria's long reign. On June 16th, a gift of fifty pounds arrived on Ashley Down from the Mayor of Bristol. A note read: 'From the City Jubilee Fund, for the purpose of providing treats for the orphans, in commemoration of Her Most Gracious Majesty the Queen.' Müller spent the money by arranging for the children from the five Houses to visit Clifton Zoo. He said that the children greatly enjoyed the trip: 'Besides inspecting the interesting and instructive collection of animals, the children were supplied with tea and an abundance of suitable provisions.'

June 20th 1897 was Jubilee Sunday, and Müller broke his recently self-imposed rule by preaching at the evening service at Bethesda. How eagerly the large congregation watched as the tall, erect figure mounted the pulpit stairs and turned to address them! This was to be a sermon from the man who founded his Scriptural Knowledge Institution three years before the teenaged Princess had become Queen and who had begun to care for thirty children in Wilson Street, fourteen months before her accession. In the sixty years that had elapsed, his name had become a byword for faith throughout the world; this was the man who claimed in a letter to the British and Foreign Bible Society to have read the Bible through well over one hundred times. This would be a sermon worth listening to!

'Our meditation this evening,' he began, 'as the Lord may help us, will be on the short but precious 23rd Psalm, "The Lord is my Shepherd; I shall not want".'

Müller went on to expound and apply the Psalm verse by verse. When he came to the last verse he said:

'Now comes the last verse, "Surely goodness and mercy shall follow me all the days of my life, and I shall dwell in the house of the Lord for ever." The poor one has been invited as a guest by the Rich One. He goes and he finds it very pleasant there, and is happy. All that is just what he desires naturally. Now, what conclusion does he come to? "I find it very pleasant to be here, I will remain here, I will not go away any more." This brings before us what the child of God finds, in acquaintance with Christ Jesus; not merely having to say, "My cup runneth over; I am brimful of happiness." But, "I have almost more than I can bear. I find it so pleasant, so exceedingly pleasant, this way of going on, I can never get into another position any more. I remain in the house of my Heavenly Father for ever."

'That is the position to which we are brought as believers in Christ! And as assuredly as we are honestly walking in the ways of the Lord, and truly surrendering the heart to God, this is the result to which we come. We find it so pleasant, so precious even for this life, that we have no desire to depart from the ways of the Lord. In our natural worldly condition, we seek after happiness; but we do not get it. Nothing but disappointment is the result, for after a few hours all this worldly happiness is gone. But the position into which we are brought by faith in the Lord Jesus Christ not only ensures us happiness for a few days, or a few months, or a few years, but for ever and ever. So that our heart says, "I will remain in this way; I am happy in this way; I will never forsake this way."

'Not merely so. But "Goodness and mercy shall follow me all the days of my life". I shall now be for ever and ever a happy man, and I will remain in the presence of my Father; I will not leave His House any more, because I found it so very, very precious to be a child of God.'

'What is the secret of your service for God?' someone once asked Müller.

'There was a day when I died, utterly died,' he replied, and as he spoke he bent lower and lower until he almost touched the floor, 'died to George Müller, his opinions, preferences, tastes and will – died to the world, its approval or censure – died to the approval or blame of even my brethren and friends – and since then I have studied to show myself approved only unto God.'

During that summer Müller was persuaded to take a few weeks' rest at Bishopsteignton in Devon.

'What opportunity is there here for service for the Lord?' he asked on the evening of his arrival.

'But you have just come from continuous work. Isn't this a time for rest?'

'Now that I am free from my usual labours,' Müller promptly replied, 'I must be occupied in some other way in the service of God; to glorify Him is the object of my life.'

So meetings were quickly arranged for him to preach in Bishopsteignton and Teignmouth.

Müller returned to Bristol; the leaves on Ashley Hill turned golden and then fell. Summer gave way to winter. In his rooms in No. 3, Müller continued to work and pray; as the weather grew colder he still ventured out from time to time to preach in Bristol. One weekday evening that winter, a huge crowd gathered to hear him in Old Market Street Chapel. It is said that, as he spoke, he seemed full of the Holy Spirit.

'My text,' he said, 'is from Lamentations 3:22-23 "Because of the Lord's great love we are not consumed, for His compassions never fail. They are new every morning; great is your faithfulness."

'While all things change here below,' he said towards the end of his address, 'the precious Jesus our Friend is "The same yesterday, and today, and forever". What He was millions of years ago, He is now. What He was when He walked through Judea, Samaria and Galilee, He is now – His heart full of tenderness, of pity, of compassion.

'Though you be the greatest, the oldest, the most hardened sinner, though you have sinned again and again against light and knowledge, if you now trust in Christ, you will for His sake be forgiven, for there is power in the blood of Christ to take away the greatest sins.

'Learning itself gives no happiness – no real, true happiness. Christ, and Christ alone, gives real, true happiness. I know seven languages, and with all this I should have gone to hell if it had not been that I knew Christ, Christ, Christ. Oh! The blessedness of being a disciple of the Lord Jesus!

'I am a happy old man; yes, indeed, I am a happy old man! I walk about my room, and I say, "Lord Jesus, I am not alone, for You are with me. I have buried my wives and my children, but You are left. I am never lonely or desolate with You and with Your smile, which is better than life itself!!'

Sunday morning, March 6th 1898: the sea breezes above the Avon gorge seemed a little less chilly; the residents of Clifton watched for signs of approaching spring. At Alma Road Chapel, latecomers at the morning service quickly noticed: Bristol's most distinguished citizen was present. Fervently they hoped he would take part. He did. Shortly before the time when it was customary to 'break bread', the aged saint rose to his feet.

'May we read from Isaiah, chapter six?'

He read the chapter and then asked the congregation to turn with him to the Gospel of John 12:37-41.

' "Isaiah said this because he saw Jesus' glory and spoke about him." This last verse,' said Müller, 'settles the matter, that what we were reading in Isaiah 6 all refers to the glory of our adorable Lord Jesus Christ. In the whole of divine testimony we do not find a single portion which speaks more of His majesty and glory. We will now read it once more, verse by verse, in reference to our precious, adorable Lord Jesus.'

In his own inimitable style, Müller read the passage again, making clear, concise comments on each verse: drawing lessons where there were lessons to be drawn, but never imposing on the text unintended meanings.

'O how pitifully,' he concluded, 'how mercifully, how tenderly, how graciously the Lord has been dealing with us in Christ Jesus! And what He has been doing and is doing, He will continue to do to the end of our earthly pilgrimage – He will never leave us nor forsake us, and a little while, and then He takes us home to Himself. O the bright, glorious prospect which we poor, miserable sinners have through faith in Christ Jesus! And at last taken home to be for ever with the Lord, and to see that lovely One who laid down His life for us, ourselves being permitted to kiss His feet.

The two men had enjoyed sixty-eight years of close friendship.

On the Tuesday, Müller worked as usual. On Wednesday morning he said to James Wright:

'When I got up this morning I felt weak and had to rest three times as I got dressed.'

'Do you think you should have an attendant in your bedroom to help you dress in future?' asked Wright.

'After tomorrow,' said Müller.

Later in the day he said to Wright:

'I feel quite myself again.'

In the evening, he led the usual weekly prayer meeting in No. 3 and concluded by announcing the hymn 'We'll sing of the Shepherd that died'. He joined in the singing of the last verse:

> We'll sing of such subjects alone,
> > None other our tongues shall employ;
> But better His love will be known
> > In yonder bright regions of joy.

Müller said 'Good night' to James Wright and began to climb the stairs to his bedroom.

Close behind, but not knowing who was ahead of her, a young student teacher then living at No. 3 ran up the stairs singing 'I know not what awaits me, God kindly veils my eyes'.

When she reached the top of the first flight, she became conscious of a dark figure standing quite still. It was Müller. He waited until she reached him and shook hands with her.

'I am so glad to see you so happy,' he said, 'but you must not run up the stairs two at a time, you may hurt yourself. Good night.'

Müller retired to his room. For some time, he had been in the habit of having a snack during the night, and as usual that evening someone had put a glass of milk and a biscuit on his dressing table, in case he needed it.

Next morning he awoke between five and six o'clock. He got up and walked towards his dressing table.

And then, in a moment, that bright prospect of which he had spoken just four days earlier came – for him – glorious reality. George Müller saw his lovely One.

25

REBUKING SCEPTICS

At about seven on the Thursday morning, Müller's attendant knocked on his door with a cup of tea. On entering, she found him lying dead on the floor beside his bed. On his desk were the unfinished notes of a sermon he would never preach.

The news created a sensation in Bristol. On the Sunday reference was made from virtually every pulpit, Anglican, and non-conformist, to the city's late philanthropist, man of prayer and preacher.

Next day, Monday March 14th 1898, was the day of the funeral. It is said that nothing like it has been seen in Bristol before or since. Firms closed or gave their employees time off to witness the event and pay their respects; thousands of people lined the route of the procession; on Bristol cathedral and other churches flags flew at half mast and muffled peals were rung; in all the main streets they put up black shutters or drew their blinds. The city mourned.

After a short service at No. 3 House, a procession formed to walk to Bethesda for the main service. Four of the occupants of Müller's first home in Wilson Street joined the column: they remembered the day in June 1849 when they had marched up to Ashley Down to see their spacious new quarters.

Hundreds couldn't get in to the service at Bethesda. Among those who did squeeze in to the main area of the chapel and its galleries were many Anglican clergymen and free church ministers. After addresses from James Wright and Benjamin Perry, nearly a hundred carriages including the mayor's state coach joined the procession across the river to the cemetery where a crowd of about seven thousand people had gathered at the main gates. With considerable difficulty, stewards cleared a way for the bearers to carry the coffin up the hillside to the spot under a yew tree where Mary and Susannah had been buried. The service at the graveside concluded with the massive congregation joining to sing the last hymn which Müller had chosen at his last prayer meeting less than five days earlier – ending, as he would have wished, not in sadness, but in anticipation of those 'yonder bright regions of joy'.

Obituary articles appeared in most national newspapers; one of the longest and most detailed – in *The Times* – has already been quoted in chapters fifteen and sixteen, and will be further cited below. Several of the newspapers contrasted the unequivocal facts of Müller's life with the rationalism of the age. 'Mr Müller,' said the *Bristol Evening News*, 'occupied a unique position among the philanthropists of the nineteenth century. In an age of agnosticism and materialism, he put to practical test theories about which many men were content to hold profitless controversy.'

The *Liverpool Mercury*, noting that thousands of children 'have been fed, clothed and educated out of funds which have poured in without any influential committee or organisation, without appeal or advertisement of any sort,' asked: 'how was this wonder accomplished? Mr Müller has told the world that it was the result of "Prayer". The rationalism of the day will sneer at this declaration; but the facts remain, and remain to be explained. It would be unscientific to belittle historical occurrences when they are difficult to explain, and much juggling would be needed to make the Orphanages on Ashley Down vanish from view.'

The *Daily Telegraph*, in similar vein, said: 'Mr Müller's life and example, by their eloquent and touching beauty, cannot fail to impress even a sceptical and utilitarian age.' Writing of Müller's far-reaching social achievements, the *Telegraph* noted that he had 'robbed the cruel streets of thousands of victims, the gaols of thousands of felons, the workhouse of thousands of helpless waifs.'

In a sense the tributes of the Bristol press are of greater significance than those of the national papers. For it was in Bristol that Müller sought to demonstrate that God answers prayer. Hundreds of Bristolians were or had been permanently employed at the Homes; many more worked there temporarily teaching, nursing, carrying out repairs or making deliveries; others took the weekly opportunities to visit the five Homes. Had Müller's principles failed, the truth could scarcely have been shielded from Bristol's watchful eyes. The West Country has never lacked its sceptics nor the nineteenth century its cynics. The news of under-fed, ill-clothed or cruelly treated children would have quickly travelled from Ashley Down to the heart of Bristol and beyond. And yet the *Bristol Times*, devoting its first leader as well as a separate news item and obituary article to Müller's passing, commented: 'It may be taken as substantiated that nearly all which has been said about Mr Müller is absolutely true'. The paper spoke of Müller's 'rare and stupendous intellectual gifts' and genius, and concluded that he was 'raised up for the purpose of showing that the age of miracles is not past, and rebuking the sceptical tendencies of the time.'

How are we to assess George Müller 114 years after his death?

Some of his personal qualities were by themselves unusual, and when combined in one man, are rare to say the least. We may point, first, to the outstanding administrative ability of the man (himself the son of a civil servant) who founded a home for thirty children and over the years undertook to expand the operation, becoming responsible for the welfare and education of ten thousand children and the direction of a full-time staff of several hundred people. That same man, as a director of the Scriptural Knowledge Institution, controlled expenditure of hundreds of thousands of pounds to aid and encourage missionary work overseas, and to provide education for children and adults at home and abroad in schools financed and run by his Institution. His supervision of all this activity was characterised by a consistent attention to detail: he maintained accurate accounts of every aspect of his work; he was renowned – even when the work was at its peak – for his knowledge of many of the children by name (in the early days he knew them all); he took a similar personal interest in the affairs of his large congregation at Bethesda and in the missionaries all over the world he supported.

In his decision-making as the work grew he was scrupulously correct: whether the decision was to expand or not to expand, whom to appoint to his staff, he would carefully set out the pros and the cons in true managerial style – but with this in addition, long hours would be spent in thoughtful prayer. And yet with all his attention to detail, he was, as we have seen, neither inflexible nor lacking in vision.

Then we may point to the man's remarkable energy, which he demonstrated as a student at Halle and London by regularly working for between twelve and fourteen hours a day, and in his seventies and eighties by travelling about two hundred thousand miles to preach and work in forty-two countries.

Müller was an individualist. He preferred to direct than be directed, to be the employer rather than the employee. His early connection as a trainee with a London Missionary Society didn't last: he found their restrictions unacceptable and preferred to go his own way – though the break was friendly enough. But there was a master whom he delighted to obey, and it was in the service of Christ that he found his life's work. From that summer in Devon when, as he put it, he 'found his all in God', his life was one of total commitment to Him. 'Honour, pleasure, money,' he wrote, 'my physical powers, my mental powers, all was laid down at the feet of Jesus.'

He wasn't therefore a selfish individualist. The evidence corroborates his testimony that there was a day when he died, 'died to George Müller, his opinions, preferences, tastes and will'. His energy and abilities were directed into selfless channels in the service of God and his fellow men. (During his life he received about ninety-three thousand pounds for his personal expenses: of this he gave away over eighty-one thousand; and at his death his sole estate was valued at about one hundred and sixty pounds.)

Combined with the undoubted stubbornness of the Prussian, there was a surpassing graciousness of character which won him the affection and loyalty of friends and staff, the love and admiration of hundreds whom he met on his preaching tours, and obvious respect of the citizens of Bristol. Charles Parsons, who knew him well, recorded: 'In himself George Müller was one of the most lovable of men: his heart overflowed with love. To the orphans whether singly or in groups he spoke in the tenderest manner imaginable. Said one of the schoolmasters to me one day, himself brought up an orphan in the Homes, "Mr Müller is more than a father to us all".'

I have read all his writings (which amount to well over a million words) and I have never found a harsh or caustic comment: as shrewd a judge of character as any, for Müller it was the good and wholesome aspects of men which were worthy of note; as for the rest he was content to remain silent.

Some will say he was narrow-minded. He certainly seems to have thought of 'the world' as *disordered* and in the grip of the evil one – a view he would have defended on the basis of both observation and Scripture – calling in aid verses like 1 John 5:19, 'We know that we are children of God, and that the whole world is under the control of the evil one.' Twice after his conversion he went to the theatre (except to preach) and once to a concert, but felt 'that it was unbecoming for me, as a child of God to be in such a place'. Even had he been fond of the normal forms of entertainment, there would have been little time for this in his busy life – or, perhaps, he would have achieved less. Narrow-minded or single-minded? – you must decide. His attitude to the world didn't prevent him from going 'into all the world' to preach the gospel. And as for his attitude to Christians who held differing views from his, we saw that one of his aims on the preaching tours was to discourage sectarian attitudes amongst Christian denominations and, as he said, to 'preach amongst all' (ch. 18).

The reference in the *Bristol Times* to Müller's 'rare and stupendous intellectual gifts' is somewhat surprising. Certainly he was gifted intellectually: he shone at school, despite his wild life; he left Halle with a good degree; and spoke seven languages. But on the whole he was happier in the field of action rather than in the realm of ideas. When he taught Christians, his ministry was mainly either *practical* (how they might live the Christian life, find reality and know definite answers to prayer), or such as would inspire his hearers to greater commitment. This interested him far more than abstract theological debate: it was only with reluctance (and of necessity) that he was drawn into the controversy in the 1840s on the humanity and sufferings of Christ. He well understood the issues involved: indeed his comments on the debate are strikingly penetrating; but he refused to indulge in unedifying tract warfare on the subject.

His most notable intellectual quality was his ability to *think clearly*. In 1839, for instance, when a separation threatened at Bethesda over a dispute on points of church order, Müller and Craik went into retreat for a fortnight, to think, study and pray. They returned to Bethesda for a series of meetings at which they explained their findings. The paper which Müller produced containing the substance of what they said is something of a masterpiece of concise, logical thought. It outlined their findings on eldership, discipline and the Lord's Supper, carefully distinguishing between what could be 'expressly proved from Scripture', and what Scripture seemed 'rather in favour of'. Primarily a man of action rather than a philosopher or controversialist, Müller was nevertheless capable of sustained and objective thought. *Accuracy* was the feature which struck him most about Newton's later writings.

What has intrigued and inspired people for over a century now, is not simply what George Müller *was* but what he *did*: if his personal qualities were unusual, his achievement was in one respect unique, perhaps since apostolic times and possibly even since Elijah's finest hour on Mount Carmel (see 1 Kings 18).

For Müller embarked on his project with the stated aim of demonstrating God's reality, and of proving to those who cared to observe that He answers prayer. There have always been those who claim to have proved this power for themselves or who have trusted in God alone to support them; Müller's uniqueness lies not in his exercise of faith, or in the importance he attached to prayer, but in his announcement, as he embarked on the undertaking, that he was setting out to demonstrate that God is real. In 1837, recalling the reasons which had led him to establish his first home (in 1836) he wrote:

Now, if I, a poor man, simply by prayer and faith, obtained *without asking any individual*, the means for establishing and carrying on an Orphan-House; there would be something which, with the Lord's blessing, might be instrumental in strengthening the faith of the children of God, besides being a testimony to the consciences of the unconverted, of the reality of the things of God.

So Müller issued his challenge to unbelievers to watch the work he had begun and see whether there was a God who would finance it; he invited believers not only to see what God would do, but to consider their response if He proved faithful.

The preceding pages have told what happened. In brief: during the next sixty-three years, Müller received nearly one and a half million pounds (to be precise: £1,453,513 13s 3d); and the many branches of his work included the care of some ten thousand children. He claimed that neither he nor his staff ever issued an appeal for funds or asked any individual to support his work. No evidence has been produced to disprove this. (There was once an allegation that Müller had prayed publicly that God would send money to the Homes; Müller described this as 'entirely false'.) According to Müller, for over sixty years God provided the means – and thus demonstrated His reality.

What will be the reaction to this in the second decade of the twenty-first century?

We cannot claim that the events of Müller's life constitute scientific proof either of the existence of God, or, if He exists, of His willingness or ability to answer prayer. I believe however, that what Müller described as 'the Lord's dealings' with him constitute – not proof of these things – but evidence which deserves to be taken seriously.

Leaving aside for the moment the issue of *how* the money was raised, you can verify the visible facts of the case by taking a trip to Bristol. Those five great buildings still stand on Ashley Down. Now used by Brunel Technical College, No. 3 – where the founder lived and died – is clearly and suitably named: *Müller House*. When in Bristol, you should visit the other *Müller House* at Cotham Park, headquarters of the work of the George Müller Foundation today (see ch. 26), to enquire whether Müller's principles have stood the test of time. There has been departure from them.

Müller believed that God exists; that in the nineteenth century He was still the living God; that this living God answered his prayers and 'put it into people's hearts' to give to the work that he directed. To argue that God didn't answer his prayers, as he believed, or that there is and was no God to support his work, is to say that he was deluded. (This assumes that he sincerely believed that God was providing for him: an alternative view – though more difficult to sustain – that he was a deceiver is discussed later in this chapter.) The view that Müller was deluded can be held without malice, and can be maintained alongside an admiration, even affection, for the man: he was a good, perhaps a great man of considerable achievement – but he was wrong, sincerely wrong. It is my conviction, however, that the evidence of Müller's life lends no support to this position. The evidence points not to a deluded or disillusioned man, but to someone who daily had his faith confirmed and strengthened.

It's true that Müller's faith was tried. Chapters 9 and 10 described the period from 1838 to 1846 when – although the children knew nothing of this – there was rarely an excess of funds. The need was supplied by the day, even by the hour.

Just once during this period, Müller became – in his words – 'tried in spirit' (ch. 9). 'For the first time, the Lord seemed not to regard our prayer.' But an hour or so later, having been handed a gift by a visitor from London who had been staying for several days next door to the Boys' home in Wilson Street, and who had been entrusted with this donation by her daughter in the Metropolis, Müller was able to 'burst out into loud praises and thanks the first moment I was alone'. To Müller, the fact that the money had been so near the orphan homes for several days without being given, was proof that it was in God's heart to help them, 'but because He delights in the prayers of His children, He had allowed us to pray so long; also to try our faith, and to make the answer so much the sweeter'.

Müller apparently saw this early period as a test of his obedience, and of that of his helpers. 'It can only be ascribed to the especial mercy of God that the faith of those who were engaged in this work did not altogether fail, and that they did not entirely grow weary of this way of carrying on the Lord's work, and go, in despair of help from God, back again to the habits and maxims of this evil world.' It was a period when his character was moulded, prepared for his life's work.

And can we not agree that the very fact that for long periods enough was sent, but no more than enough, was evidence of the hand of God? Isn't this as remarkable in itself as the total receipt of one and a half million pounds? Doesn't a rejection of Müller's version of events involve the acceptance of an incredible alternative? It would mean that for over sixty years, his sympathisers, for various reasons excluding divine intervention, not only sent him sufficient funds in total to enable the vast expansion of the work, but also for periods – particularly in the early years – sent just enough to supply the need, but never, even for one day, too little.

We have noted that an alternative to the view that Müller was deluded is that he was a deceiver, in other words that, despite his assertions to the contrary, there were periods when the children were in need. But this is a view which it is impossible to reconcile with Müller's popularity in Bristol, and the respect which, as we have seen, the citizens of that city – with the evidence before them – held for him.

If, as I believe, there is little evidence to support the hypothesis that Müller was either deluded or a deluder, there is even less to suggest that, as the years passed, he grew disillusioned. He never struck his contemporaries as a man who was anxiously striving to preserve a myth, or who had reason to doubt that the needs of over two thousand people would be met. 'A peaceful and stately demeanour ... without a care' was the testimony of a West-Country farmer. 'The twenty-third Psalm seemed written all over his face.'

Müller's longevity is surely consistent with his profession of an inner peace: a delight in God cradled in the experience of answered prayer. 'I cannot tell you how happy this service in which I am engaged makes me. Instead of my being the anxious, careworn man so many persons think me to be, I have no anxieties and no cares at all. Faith in God leads me to roll my burdens, all my burdens, upon God. Not only burdens concerning money, but burdens concerning everything, for hundreds are my necessities besides those connected with money. In every way I find God to be my helper, even as I trust in Him for everything ... I have found invariably, during my long life as a believer, that if I only believed, I was sure to get in God's time the thing I asked for.'

The incident described in chapter 19, when – anxious to honour an engagement in Quebec – Müller prayed successfully for fog to be lifted is, while authentic, not typical of the man.

> We do not pretend to miracles (he wrote at another time). We have no desire that the work in which we are engaged should be considered as extraordinary, or a even remarkable one. We are truly sorry that many persons, inconsiderately, look upon it as almost miraculous. The principles are as old as the Holy Scriptures. But they are forgotten by many; are not held in living faith by others; and by some they are not known at all; nay, they are denied to be scriptural by not a few, and are considered wild and fanatical.

The particular relevance of the fog incident to our present discussion is Müller's comment to Captain Dutton, 'for fifty-two years, there has never been a single day that I have failed to get an audience with the King'. This, surely, was the confidence of a man in the habit of seeing his prayers answered.

Another indication of his calm assurance that God would meet the needs of his children was his readiness to send thousands of pounds abroad to missionaries and lay out large sums of money on his educational work in England and abroad. He didn't think it necessary to put every penny to the Ashley Down account. Here was a man who discovered that his God was a rich God.

The obituary writer in *The Times* was struck by the loyalty that Müller commanded in his staff. 'His reliance upon a Higher Power in the great crises of life was regarded on the part of many as simple fanaticism; but the results he obtained were marvellous; and though misunderstood in some quarters, he was able to kindle in those around him a devotion and enthusiasm which was as extraordinary as they were unique.' Could the explanation of this 'extraordinary enthusiasm' be that these people like Müller had discovered for themselves the reality of the things of God?

The Times observed, and Müller frequently conceded, that there were those who dismissed his principles as (in Müller's words) 'wild and fanatical'. The dictionary defines a fanatic as a 'person filled with excessive and mistaken enthusiasm, especially in religion'. Was Müller a fanatic? Not according to the *Western Daily Press:*

> Never was there a philanthropist with less of fanaticism and more of method. His bearing and speech were not those of an emotional enthusiast who would incur heavy liabilities with a light heart; indeed, had he been such a man, his life would have been less surprising than it was; it was his calmness and confidence, associated with the most careful watchfulness over expenditure and most businesslike habits, that presented a combination of qualities altogether unique and wholly surprising.

And, of course, Müller himself denied it. 'I am not a fanatic or enthusiast, but, as all who know me are well aware, a calm, cool, quiet, calculating businessman.' And won't most businessmen agree that someone who successfully raised one and a half million pounds at nineteenth century values, and directed its outlay, can't easily be dismissed as 'filled with ... mistaken enthusiasm'?

Müller wasn't of course, a political reformer and didn't like Lord Shaftesbury, seek to improve social conditions by influencing legislation in Parliament. Nor did he strive to awaken the social conscience of Victorian Christians. He was though an interested member of the 'Reformatory and Refuge Union' of which the President was Lord Shaftesbury, and Quintin Hogg a prominent member. It was perhaps in this connection that Shaftesbury visited Ashley Down. Müller's diaries indicate an awareness of the findings of official reports on poverty, of conditions in the work-houses and prisons. But his main concern was to do what he could by direct action to offer children a better start in life rather than seeking to reform the existing Poor Law Institutions. His reaction to the revelation in an official Report that there were six thousand young orphans in the prisons of England was to say: 'By God's help, I will do what I can to keep poor orphans from prison'; he was content – in the main – to leave to others the attempt to change the system itself.

It may be that the reaction of some to the re-telling of the Müller story will be to wish that they themselves were similarly gifted with faith. And to be sure, Müller was a great man of faith. But in his lifetime, he used to deny that he had been given a special gift of faith.

'My faith,' he said, 'is the same faith which is found in *every believer*. Try it for yourself and you will see the help of God, if you trust in Him.'

'But what can we do to have our faith strengthened?' people used to ask him.

'First,' he would reply, 'read the Bible carefully and thoughtfully. Then you will learn more and more about God's character – how kind, loving, merciful, wise and faithful He is. Then when difficulties come, you will be able to rest on God's *ability and willingness* to help you.

'Second,' said Müller, 'try to keep your conscience clear. Don't make a habit of doing things which are displeasing to God. Otherwise when your faith is tested, you will have no confidence in God because of your guilty conscience.

'Third, don't try to avoid situations where your faith may be tested. Naturally we don't like trusting in God alone but it is when we do this that our faith is strengthened.

'Finally, remember that God won't test you more than you are able to bear. Be patient, and He will prove to you how willing He is to help and deliver, the moment it is good for you.'

If you have never yet embarked on a life of faith, two brief sentences on the theme of 'Christianity' written by Müller one hundred and sixty years ago bear repeating today: 'There is life,' he wrote, 'and power, and reality in our holy faith. If you have never yet known this, then come and taste for yourself.'

If you seek reassurance that the God of the second decade of the twenty-first century is the God in whom George Müller delighted, you should note his declaration: 'The living God is with us, whose power never fails, whose arm never grows weary, whose wisdom is infinite and whose power is unchanging. Therefore today, tomorrow and the next month, as long as life is continued, He will be our helper and friend. Still more, even as He is through all time, so will He be through all eternity.'

26

NEW FOUNDATION, SAME FOUNDATION

'Why is this place so different and the people so caring?' asked a mother who, after eight months desperately trying to deal with a difficult child, was taken along to a Day Care Centre run by the George Müller Trust in the 1990s. 'God is here and we pray daily for you and your family,' was the quiet reply. 'A few months later', the same mother recalls, 'I met with God and was born again. I felt like a new person. I thank God for these wonderful people, for it was through God's work at the Centre that I was saved.'

From the first Wilson Street orphanage opened by George Müller on the 11th of April 1836, through the imposing orphanages at Ashley Down, to the smaller family-based residential children's homes, the centre-based work of the late twentieth century and onto the work of today, the Trust has continued caring for children in need. Society's needs are very different today compared with those of the 1830s. Children in need of care or who are orphaned today are comparatively a small number in the U.K. However, throughout each generation there has been the continued need for love.

Today in its partnership with churches in local communities, all of them seeking to work more effectively with children and families in need, the Trust is still aware of the basic human need for love. While the work requires a variety of skills, the workers always want to show the love of God to each child and each parent in need. Supporting local churches to help them to become more effective in faith, care and evangelism amongst children, families and young people (especially the neediest), the Trust continues to care because God continues to care.

Underlying the desire to show the love and compassion of the Lord Jesus is the understanding that wholeness comes only through a relationship with Him. Our physical, material and emotional needs can be met in a variety of ways but the Trust believes that our spiritual needs can only be met by God through Jesus. Although the Trust is not and never has been primarily an evangelistic organisation with overt methods and techniques of evangelism, every act of love and compassion is undergirded by an acknowledgement of the need to share the gospel. It is to be 'lived as well as spoken'. Many people have found faith through the unconditional love shown to them and by hearing the good news in a non-threatening and encouraging way. That the work of the Trust is explicitly Christian is undeniable but it is a mix of showing and sharing, acting and speaking the love and salvation of God in word and deed. The key characteristics of the Trust have been faith, care and evangelism and that has been evident from the 1830s to today.

In George Müller's day, the Homes developed along institutional lines, and with the care of more than two thousand children and some two hundred members of staff, this seemed the most appropriate way to meet the need. Indeed, very few alterations were thought necessary until the end of the Second World War. The introduction of the Welfare State brought about many changes in this country, and among these was the method of caring for children.

As a result of the 1948 Children Act the Trustees decided, after much prayer, to sell the five large Homes at Ashley Down. They bought, instead, smaller properties to house family groups of ten to twelve children. It was felt that this would provide the children with a more natural environment in which to grow. Married couples were taken on as house-parents to care for the children, helped by assistants.

It took several years to complete the changeover and eventually the five Ashley Down Homes were all purchased by the local

Education Authority in 1958. They have been used continuously since then as either a Further or Higher Education College. Today two of the buildings have been purchased to be converted into flats but, because the buildings are Grade 2 listed, they will continue to have their distinctive appearance.

The smaller family group homes were located in various parts of Bristol, Clevedon, and Weston-super-Mare, each with its own staff of house-parents (a married couple), two assistants and part-time domestic help. There was also a home in Backwell and a holiday home at Minehead. The emphasis was no longer on formal education; it was more concerned with healthy, emotional and physical development. All the children attended local state schools. Most of the children came from broken homes, many were emotionally deprived in one way or another and a few were quite seriously disturbed. In many ways this new approach had been vital to meet the needs. However, the basis of the Müller Homes remained the same and it was essential for all staff involved to have the same faith in God and obedience to His will. The same basic principle of God meeting every need, through the power of prayer, was still the same.

In the late 1970s and early 1980s, it became apparent to the Trustees of the Homes that even family group care, as had been practiced since the war, was no longer appropriate to meet the ever changing needs of society. Indeed, children were no longer coming into residential care in sufficient numbers; local authorities and other childcare agencies preferring that the children be fostered with private families. After much discussion and prayer it was felt that the way forward was in some way to meet the needs of *whole* families who for one reason or another were finding difficulties and pressures hard to bear.

The Family Group Homes closed in the 1980s and were replaced by a commitment to day care, family care, community based work and schools work. In each of these areas, opportunities to show and share the love of Jesus were evident and many can testify to the quality of that care. As well as having work based in its own premises, the Trust also developed an increasingly close working relationship with local churches who desired to have an impact on their communities amongst children and families, often in considerable need. The Trust's staff therefore started to work with local churches to see them become more effective in encouraging, inspiring, equipping and training local Christians in the God-given command to show God's love.

Part of the work in the Centres was the care for children of 2-5 years of age on a daily basis, many with mental, physical and emotional needs. Helpers created an environment at each Centre where advice and practical help could also be given to parents as well as sharing about Jesus. The Centres provided preventative care, play and learning opportunities. Children in groups of 5-10, looked after by nursery nurses, had the opportunity to try their hand at cooking and painting and all sorts of creative activities. They had the space to play, explore and develop. Parents appreciated the 'breathing space' and the genuine efforts by staff to involve them and help them in their difficulties. Parents and children joined together for special outings in the summer which were always highlights, together with the special Christmastime activities. Many gifts of toys are still received each year at Christmas and distributed to needy families around greater Bristol through the Trust's Local Partnership scheme.

Staff involved in day care had opportunities to share the love of Jesus with both parents and children. Often questions were asked as a result of the things children said to their parents. Many disadvantaged children had the opportunity of a better start to their lives, and parents frequently expressed appreciation of the progress that their children made. Some who were very withdrawn and suffering behavioural difficulties 'came out of themselves' and began to develop as whole children.

Much of the work of the Trust during that time was with whole families. Referrals came from health visitors, social workers and local churches. The Trust worked closely with other caring agencies so that, together, effective help might be offered. Families came for all sorts of reasons, to make new friends or to escape for a while from cramped accommodation, to have space for the children to play or to find help in working through difficulties. The staff sought to provide a welcoming, supportive atmosphere where the parents could build up confidence and receive help for their particular problems, whether debt, marriage problems, learning household management, or how to play with and relate to their children in better ways. Parents became involved in cooking as well as fun activities like keep fit, handicrafts, group work and drama. Some children had specific needs such as difficulties with speech, behavioural problems or poor development and parents would be involved in seeking to help in these areas.

'I have changed gradually', reported one mother, 'By meeting people I have become more self-confident. I have been able to stop taking the anti-depressant tablets I was on. I have got out of the house. I was stuck in for over two years with depression and illness. What's more, I've found a living faith in the Lord Jesus.' The experience helped this mother deal with the resentment that she had been showing towards her daughter and to rebuild their relationship.

The work in Centres took place in Bristol, Clevedon and Weston-super-Mare and sought to give priority to the most needy socially, physically and spiritually. Needs are great, especially in urban priority areas. There are so many pressures on family life to cause it to become dysfunctional. Parents often need help to be better parents; children need to experience good quality family life.

A further development in care among children and a fulfilment of George Müller's original vision for schools was the work of the Educational Care section started in 1987. A small team of full-time schools workers had the opportunity of working with some of the secondary schools in Bristol in educational care. The team sought to convey to young people in schools how the good news of Jesus touches all areas of life. They went into secondary schools taking Assemblies, Social Studies, Religious Education classes and Humanities lessons and Personal and Social Education Groups. They were encouraged to see schools realizing the need and relevance of introducing a Christian perspective to issues faced by young people. Many young people showed a real interest in the Christian gospel and what it had to say in their lives. Joint activities such as camps, evening and fun events were arranged among the schools. School weeks and music events, where young people could identify with what is said and sung, were seen to be very important.

'How do we know God loves us?' a boy called out in the middle of a year 11 lesson. It was the desperate plea of a battered heart. What hope of certainty can anyone give to such a question? Young people today still want something living and real which touches them at their point of need. A demonstration of love in Jesus is the answer they need. The Müller schools team had a vision for sharing that good news.

It has already been mentioned that the Trust has sought to meet the challenges of the day by re-focusing its work without losing the basic values upon which it was founded. By the beginning of the 21st century, another major change was taking place as the Day and Family Care Centres were closed and the schools work gradually changed. More and more churches are reaching out into their own local communities and schools with the hand of care and the message of salvation. Therefore the Trustees felt that the time was right for the Trust to end its own children's work and undertake a new but vitally important supportive role to help underpin that work amongst churches and other organisations. The Trust had gained so much experience as it ran the Centres which needed to be shared with local churches that were, and are, God's chosen vehicle for reaching a needy world.

Today the Trust is working in partnership with an increasing number of churches (and other Christian organisations) locally as they work with children, young people and families, especially the poorest. This is mainly in sharing something of its experience gained over many years of child and family care to ensure that churches offer services to the local community that reflect best practice. So the Trust is vitally involved in networking, training, encouraging, mentoring, supervising, discipling, inspiring, sharing good practice and praying. Every year the Trust trains many young people who may become the leaders of the future. Every year lives are touched through the work of the organisation as it helps churches. Every year other Christian organisations are encouraged and supported through relationship with the Trust. Church leadership teams are challenged concerning the health and vision of the church for which they have responsibility. It is the Trust's vision that there will be 100 churches (and other organisations) networked together in partnership, each seeking to reach out and touch the lives of many children and families in the Greater Bristol area.

The various individual trusts which made up the work were merged into one in 2009 under the new name of The George Müller Charitable Trust, with composite charitable objects which embrace all of their activities. So the work of the Scriptural Knowledge Institution, the original charity founded by George Müller and Henry Craik in 1834, continues under the new name as it sends gifts each month to Christian workers and organisations abroad and at home. This work continues to grow and it is wonderful to see how prayer brings together the needs of Christian workers who are living by faith and of donors seeking to give as God directs. A significant part of the amazing growth has been in support of workers amongst orphans, children and families, especially through child sponsorship schemes. More orphans are cared for through the Trust's financial support in various parts of the world today than were cared for by the orphanages, even at the high point of their operation in George Müller's day. For this reason, the Trust is now pursuing an 'Orphans of the World' initiative, reflecting its roots and prioritising the meeting of needs of orphans and needy children around the world.

Although the Trust has recently withdrawn from direct care of the elderly through residential care home provision, the commitment to provide appropriate support and encouragement to growing numbers of vulnerable and lonely elderly people living at home remains. Tranquil House sheltered accommodation, with eight comfortable flats, is still within the Trust's ownership and is supervised by a warden. There is much need for elderly care in Bristol and beyond from a Christian perspective, including sheltered accommodation and community-based care. Just as George

Müller brought all that he did before the Lord in prayer, so the Trust prays that this next stage may become clear.

So, too, guidance for the next development of the children's work amongst churches. There are many needs and many geographical areas in which such needs are inadequately met. As the Trust seeks God for His guidance in the work amongst the elderly and children (and also amongst Christian workers world-wide), there is great confidence because God has shown himself to be faithful time and time again. Many prayers have been answered over many years. George Müller said that he could prove with evidence that he had received 50,000 answers to prayer in his lifetime, of which 30,000 had been within 24 hours. It is still true today that the Trust has seen many answers to prayer. Whilst the ways in which the Trust seeks to work are very different in these days from the days of George Müller, the basic principles of the work remain.

With an updated museum and newly digitised orphan records, the Trust is well positioned to answer enquiries about the life and work of George Müller and to present the evidence of God's faithfulness from the start of the work until today. Many visitors come, either to trace family histories or to see how the work has progressed and developed through the years. People frequently ask whether the Trust still follows the principles laid down by George Müller when he started the work. Many question whether a simple faith in God is adequate (or appropriate) to provide for the needs of today's complex society. The Trust exists to re-affirm confidence in the biblical principles reflected in George Müller's initial aims expressed in the following terms:

> 'The first and primary object of the Institution is that God might be magnified by the fact that the children under my care are provided with all they need, only by prayer and faith, without anyone being asked by me, or my fellow labourers, whereby it might be seen that God is faithful still, and hears and answers prayer'

The Trust continues to look to God and does not fundraise in any way, nor does it seek to declare its financial needs to anyone other than to God in prayer. This is such a crucial distinctive for the Trust and it knows the truth of God's commitment to us as a faithful God. God still answers prayer today because 'He is the same yesterday, and today and forever'.

Today the Trust is led by a Board of Directors and a Chief Executive, Keith Hagon. You may obtain further information from:

The Chief Executive
The George Müller Charitable Trust
Müller House
7 Cotham Park
Bristol, BS6 6DA
United Kingdom

Website www.mullers.org
E-mail admin@mullers.org
Telephone 0117 924 5001

Please visit the Trust's website for further information and latest news on the work of the Trust; the latest Annual Report can also be downloaded. The museum is open on weekdays from 10 a.m. until 4 p.m. and contains a wealth of material, both written and in photographs, concerning the work of George Müller. Visitors are welcomed without advance notice but are advised to make contact, if possible, for an appointment. Similarly, an almost complete set of records concerning the former boys and girls who stayed in the Homes is available. These can now be made available digitally. Please contact the Trust for details.

Main Events of Müller's Life

1805 (September 27)	Born, Kroppenstaedt, Prussia 1810. The family moved to Heimersleben. His father is appointed collector of taxes
1820	His mother dies
1821	Arrested for debt in Wolfenbüttel. Spends four weeks in prison
1825 (Easter)	Enters Halle University to study theology under Friedrich Tholuck
1825 (November)	Becomes a Christian following a visit to a small house meeting
1828 (March)	Graduates at Halle
1829 (January)	Rejected from army service on grounds of 'a tendency to tuberculosis'
1829 (March)	Arrives in London to train with London Society for Promoting Christianity among the Jews (now the Church Mission to the Jews
1829 (May)	Falls ill. Believes he is dying.
1829 (Summer)	Convalescence in Teignmouth, Devon, Meets Henry Craik and becomes associated with the founders of Brethren movement
1830 (January)	Ends association with London Society for Promoting Christianity among Jews
1830	Becomes pastor of Ebenezer chapel in Teignmouth
1830 (August)	Marries Mary Groves (sister of Anthony Norris Groves) in Exeter
1830 (October)	Pew-rents abandoned at Ebenezer chapel. Müller gives up a regular salary.
1832 (May)	Müller and Henry Craik accept an invitation to become pastors of Gideon chapel in Bristol.
1832 (June)	Müller and Craik begin to work at Bethesda chapel, Bristol
1832 (September)	Lydia Müller (Their only child to survive infancy) is born
1834	Establishes Scriptural Knowledge Institution for Home and Abroad
1836 (April)	Opens first children's home in Wilson Street, Bristol, for thirty children. Subsequently opens three further homes in same street

1837 (June)	Princess Victoria becomes Queen
1841	His father dies
1848	Split between 'Open' and 'Exclusive' Brethren (Followers of J. N. Darby)
1849 (June)	Opens new purpose built home on Ashley Down, Bristol for three hundred children (Now Allen House)
1857	Second Ashley Down home opened (Brunel House)
1862	Third Ashley Down Home open (subsequently named Müller House)
1866 (January)	Henry Craik dies
1866	Dr Barnardo opens children's homes in London
1869	Fourth Ashley Down home open (Davy House)
1870	Final Ashley Down home opened (Cabot House) Müller now cares for two thousand children and employs over two hundred staff
1870 (February)	Mary Müller dies
1870s	Sends £10,000 abroad annually to nearly two hundred missionaries
1871 (November)	Marries Susannah Sangar
1875	Begins preaching tours. Travels two hundred thousand miles to fourty-two countries
1878 (January)	Meets President of the United States and (with Susannah) is conducted round the White House
1881	Church of England's Children's Society opens first home
1890 (January)	Lydia Wright (his daughter) dies.
1892 (May)	Last preaching tour ends
1894 (January)	Susannah Müller dies
1895 (September)	Ninetieth birthday presentation at Bethesda chapel
1897 (June)	Preaches at Bethesda chapel on occasion of Queen Victoria's Diamond Jubilee
1898 (March 9)	Leads evening prayer meeting on Ashley Down
1898 (March 10)	Dies peacefully at 6.00 a.m., aged ninety-two